LIBRARY EFFECTIVENESS:
A Systems Approach

LIBRARY EFFECTIVENESS:
A Systems Approach

Philip M. Morse

THE M.I.T. PRESS
Massachusetts Institute of Technology
Cambridge, Massachusetts, and London, England

6/71

Z
670.5
M6

Preface

This book is an experiment — in several respects. The pressures of rising publication, together with the dazzling potentialities of the electronic computer, are forcing librarians to think more quantitatively about their libraries than most of them ever have before and, simultaneously, have aroused the interest of the computer expert and the systems analyst in information storage and retrieval systems, of which the library is still the most successful exemplar.

And so this book is written in the hope that it will be of use to two quite different sorts of people: the librarians, some of whom are less ashamed that they cannot understand mathematics than that their Latin is rusty; and the systems analyst or operations research expert, who can read the mathematics but has little knowledge of the facts of life in regard to libraries. It is hazardous to try to address both groups in a single book, but the author is convinced the need justifies the attempt. He hopes the librarian will not be stopped by the equations but will use their translations, into words and graphs and tables (which are provided in some profusion) in order to follow the main threads of the argument. To assist those who would like to increase their mathematical literacy, an introductory Chapter 2 is included that sketches the elements of probability theory.

In fact, the plan of the book, with discussion of the theoretical models first then application to a specific library in the second half, was chosen in the hope that some would prefer to get a feel for the methods and point of view of operations research before they see how its methods can be used to learn more about library behavior. Those who are willing to take the author's word for the theory can turn directly to Chapter 6, which begins the applied half. The systems analyst may also wish to start with Chapter 6, to learn what kind of an operation a library is, and return only to those parts of the earlier chapters which deal with the more specialized models. Since the book is an attempt to break new ground, the book does try to be self-contained; a long series of references to unrelated attempts was not considered necessary.

The book is experimental in another sense; it is carrying theory well beyond the point where it can be solidly backed up by presently available data. The systems analyst will be horrified at the lack of data in this field; for example, most large libraries have never been inventoried. There are a number of reasons for the dearth, some of them compelling, which will be discussed in the text. But it has meant that most of the models discussed here, and their application demonstrated, are backed by the flimsiest of corroborative measurements. Operations research experts will appreciate the need for this sort of extrapolation when one is entering a new field; librarians and the more mathematically inclined of the analysts are asked to appreciate that the method exposed here is the important thing, not the details of any particular model. The first approximations sometimes used are bound to be wrong in part, but they at least show what sort of data should be collected to develop a better model. Initially, approximations may be justified that would not be favored later. If more data can be collected, and less approximate mathematics developed, which eventually supersede most of the formulas presented in the following pages, then this book will have achieved its purpose.

Some will complain that this volume neglects many aspects of library operation: book ordering and cataloguing and other activities that consume much of the effort of the library staff. The excuse is that many of these other activities are rather similar in their structure to activities in industry and government, which have been studied by others and reported elsewhere. In essence the library is a store of information, and the unique features of the library operation lie in the interactions between the units of information, the books and periodicals, and the seekers of information, the library users. This volume concentrates on the pattern of book use, on its change with time and on the problem of estimating and evaluating the degree to which the library satisfies or *fails to satisfy* the seeker of information. The writer believes that this aspect of the operation will remain important, even when the library is "computerized," and thus that progress in its analysis is urgently needed now, while the computer is being introduced.

Therefore this book has to do with the service library, not the specialized research library of the historian. The criterion will be the providing of information (in book form) to *all* the faculty and students of a university or all the citizens of a city. There must, of course, be libraries (or parts of libraries) that collect and store unique documents and rare volumes, which may be used, only rarely, by a few scholars. But the major task of most libraries nowadays is to provide the material desired by the majority of its users, and to provide it as quickly and to as many users as is compatible with its budget. These are the problems to which this book is addressed.

Many members of the staff of the M.I.T. library have been of great assistance in the evolution of this book. Vernon Tate, previous Director of Libraries, had a hand in the initiation; Prof. William N. Locke, present Director of Libraries has, by his continued encouragement, helped persuade the author to complete the task. Mr. Joseph Dagnese and Mrs. Irma Johnson, Science Librarians, and Miss Natalie Nicholson, Associate Director of Libraries, have been both patient and most helpful in arranging for the various intrusions into library operation occasioned by data gathering. Appreciation is due the Army Research Office, which helped finance the machine calculations resulting in the tables at the back of the book, and to Miss Caroline Elston, who programmed and ran the calculations. Also to be thanked are the graduate students in the laboratory course 8.75 in Operations Research, given in the fall of 1962, which took as its subject library operation. I hope they will feel the data they gathered and summarized in their reports, referred to in the text, are not slighted or misused.

PHILIP M. MORSE

Cambridge, Mass.
December 1967

Contents

Model. An Alternative Model. Multiple Copies. Balking and Reneging Models for Circulation Interference. Estimation of Penalties for Performance Failure.

LIBRARY EFFECTIVENESS:
A Systems Approach

1 Motivation

Whether or not it ever were so run, the modern library certainly cannot now be operated as though it were a passive repository for printed material. The opposed requirements of storing an increasing collection and of maintaining easy access to the most-used part of it can only be balanced by active and discriminatory planning. Whether the material be stored on shelves, in microfiles, or magnetically, the exponential increase in publication makes it uneconomical, and even undesirable, to have all items equally accessible. In spite of this, however, the library must be operated so that the majority of its users can find their way to the items of information they need, with a minimum of delay and frustration. To achieve a balance between these opposing requirements, the manager of an existing library or the planner of a new one must know in some detail how the user of the library will act, how often he will use a catalogue or other reference material, for example, what books or periodicals he will refer to and how long he will need to use each item. As with any other organization in these rapidly changing times, the librarian should know, as accurately as possible, what now is going on and should be able to predict what probably will be going on in the future.

This is particularly true of science libraries. As D. J. de Solla Price[1] has indicated, most reference material in the sciences has a very short

[1] See References at the back of the book.

1

useful life; about one-third of the citations in the scientific research literature are to material published in the previous 10 years and the references to earlier material are mostly to a relatively small group of "classic papers," with more than half of the earlier papers ignored completely. In physics, for instance, most books published 20 years ago are out of date and a not inconsiderable fraction contain erroneous or misleading material, in the light of later findings. Surely such volumes do not deserve accessibility equal to the most recent publications. Since the first year of the average physics book's life constitutes roughly 20 per cent of its total utility, it certainly is worth staff effort to get these books bought, catalogued, and shelved before half their first year has elapsed and to spot quickly the more popular of them so additional copies or reserve arrangements can ensure multiple access during their most useful period.

Policy Decisions

Administrative decisions, both major and minor, regarding all aspects of library planning and operation, can be wisely reached only in the light of knowledge of present library use and by the help of careful estimates of future use. Here are some typical administrative questions that must be answered, either actively or by default, often or occasionally, by every librarian or library board:

1. What fraction of the yearly budget should be allocated to the purchase of books; to the purchase of periodicals? How should this be allocated among the various fields covered by the collection? How does one decide which books (or periodicals) within a covered field should be purchased? How and when does one decide to buy a duplicate? How can one evaluate alternative decision procedures?

2. How should books (periodicals, etc.) be placed in regard to accessibility? Which items should be put on open shelves, which in stacks, which on reserve shelves, to be used only in the library, and so on? Can the amount of use of a book be predicted, so that one can estimate the fraction of users who will be frustrated or delayed by reducing the book's accessibility? Can this be compared with the relative cost of moving books to a less accessible region individually or collectively? With a popular book, what fraction of prospective users will find the book has been borrowed by another user? How high must this fraction be before a duplicate should be bought or the book be put on the reserve shelves?

3. How much is the usefulness of a book (or periodical) reduced

if its use is restricted to the library reading room? Can the reduction be expressed in dollars and cents or in any other measure allowing comparison with other methods of ensuring multiple access (such as purchase of duplicate books)?

4. What is the relative value of "browsing"? How much easier is it to browse in an open-shelf collection than in a stack library, or than from a card catalogue? Is it better to ensure that a popular book always be on the shelf, available for browsing, or should it be allowed to circulate, thus being unavailable for browsing part of the time? Should different books be treated differently in this respect? Will any of the proposed automated systems for information retrieval, using electronic computers, permit browsing? Can they be modified to do so? How important would this modification be?

5. Can a measure be devised for the loss of utility produced when a book (or periodical) is missing from the collection for a period, either because "it is being rebound" or because it has been mislaid or stolen? How can this measure be compared with the cost of a guard or of more speedy rebinding or of occasional inventories to discover which books are lost so as to forestall the frustration of the next potential user?

6. What should be done when there are more books than accessible shelf space? Are there less accessible but more compact ways of storing some of the less-used books? If so, which books should be relegated to such "cold storage"? Are there ways of estimating how many users would be discommoded by this action?

7. In the case of a university library, which has priority (in service, in book choices, etc.) the student or the faculty? Does the library use by the faculty differ enough from that by the student, so that there should be libraries (or collections or rooms) for each separately?

8. Should there be one central library for the whole university or should there be many branch libraries? What would the difference in cost be? Would this difference be "worth it" in some measurable sense, and how much duplication of books would be required to stock adequately a set of departmental (or school) libraries (in other words, how many physics books does a geologist or a psychologist frequently use, and vice versa)?

Questions of this sort are being answered all the time, either consciously or by implication, by librarians or by their governing boards. Much of the time the operating decisions, which should be based on an explicit analysis of such questions and their answers, are implicitly based on a reluctance to change past practices or a desire to emulate some other library, though it should be apparent that the answers may differ appreciably from library to library and even from time to time in the same library. Occasionally attempts are made to arrive at answers by "market surveys" of a sample of users. Experience is showing the dangers of such opinion surveys, unless they are very carefully worded and unless they are quantitatively checked against the actual behavior of the same users. Too often has the questionee persuaded both himself and the questioner that he would use some proposed new service, only to find that he seldom gets around to using it, once installed.

The Need for Data

For some time to come many of the questions listed above will have to be answered on the basis of the librarian's experience and intuition. Some of them may always have to be so answered. But surely a greater quantitative knowledge about library use can assist in getting answers and will make it easier to determine when conditions have changed enough to warrant changes in operation and wherein procedures in one library should differ from those in another. Data on some or all of the following questions would be of value in this respect:

What services (chance to sit down, chance to look at a book, chance to take a book home, chance to look at the catalogue or to talk to the reference librarian, etc.) does the library attendee use and how often does he use them each visit? How do different attendees differ in their use patterns?

What is the pattern of visits by various attendees (users) of the library? Is there an hourly, weekly, or seasonal periodicity in attendance? How long do they stay; what is the distribution of lengths of stay? Is there a correlation between length of stay and the attendee's use pattern?

What is the pattern of book (periodical, etc.) use? With a freely circulating book, what is the ratio between use in the reading room and borrowing to take home? What fraction of the collection is not used at all during a year? How do these use factors change with the age of the book? Is there a correlation between the use factors for successive years? How do the use factors differ for different classes of books (field of specialty, foreign language, text, periodical, report, and so on)? Is there any correlation between the use factor of a book and the way the library was persuaded to buy the book (request from faculty, decision of librarian, decision based on list of new publications or on book advertisements, etc.)?

Data on all of these items can be obtained. Most of them are not gathered by most libraries. Expense and lack of librarian's time are the usual excuses given for the neglect. Certainly any of the data mentioned costs time and therefore money to gather; to answer all the listed questions in detail each year would overburden any library's budget. It is the thesis of this monograph that librarians must learn, just as managers of industrial, mercantile, and military operations are learning, to gather and use data of this kind. As use patterns change and publication increases, lack of data may lead to wastage and loss of utility; expenditure of time and money in gathering some of the data mentioned could save more than this in improved utility. In the near future, the introduction of data-processing equipment in library operations will make it easier to amass the data; librarians should experiment with such data gathering before mechanizing, comparing the various methods of data gathering and the value of the various kinds of data in assisting policy decisions, so the data-processing equipment can be designed to produce the effective data most efficiently. In the end it will be better to buy fewer books, for the time being, in order to collect the data.

It is also the thesis of this report that the application of modern techniques in the theory of probability makes it possible to reduce greatly the cost and time involved in keeping a running record of much of the data listed earlier. By developing and testing out (at 10- or 20-year intervals) a number of probabilistic models of the operation, the models can be kept current in the intervening years by the gathering of a relatively small amount of data. From the models the other details, which would be more expensive to gather regularly, can be reconstituted with a good degree of expected accuracy. Prediction of next year's operation thus consists of extrapolation of the few items of gathered data; the models then provide the details of the prediction. (The use of experimentally checked theories to predict the behavior of some system is, of course, the usual method of physical science and of engineering.)

The Need for Theory

Thus an effective and efficient procedure for determining how well a library is satisfying the needs of its users involves both data gathering and data analysis. The two aspects are complementary: analysis, particularly the use of probabilistic models, can drastically reduce the amount of data required; on the other hand analysis without enough data may lead to erroneous predictions and decisions. Both aspects deserve more detailed study than they have hitherto received; only an introductory and somewhat fragmentary discussion can be attempted in the present monograph.

Contrary to usual practice, this book will concentrate first on the theoretical or analytic aspect, partly because it is less familiar to librarians and partly because the choice of predictive model determines, to a considerable degree, the nature and amount of the data required. The concept of feedback control must be introduced and illustrated early in the discussion to emphasize that the data are gathered and analyzed, not for historical reasons, but to ensure that the library operation is in fact carrying out the policy determined by management and that these policies do in fact satisfy the needs of the library users.

Another dichotomy, orthogonal to the separation between measurement and theory, involves the concentration on one or another part of the system. One can study, for example, the library user, what he does, what books he uses, and the like; or one can focus on the items in the library's collection, the books, periodicals, and reports, and ask who uses a particular item, how often it is used and the like. Both aspects must be studied to attain an adequate evaluation of library operation.

It will be amply apparent, as the reader progresses, that the examples discussed here will indicate only a few of the ways in which the techniques of operations research can assist the librarian in his operational decisions and his planning for the future. The whole subject of acquisition and cataloguing, the functions of the reference librarian, and other activities of considerable importance in library operations will hardly be touched on. All the author can hope to do, with a subject as undeveloped as this, is to give a few examples of the method in some detail and hope that others, with a more intimate knowledge of library operation, can extend the theoretical models and develop others, to correspond to those aspects which have been perforce omitted in this monograph.

PART I

THEORETICAL MODELS

2 Library Use and Probability Distributions

The use of a library by its clientele, just as any other operation involving many people, is the result of a large number of random occurrences. Each library user differs in his objectives; each book has a different audience. The behavior of an individual user, or the degree of use of a given book, cannot be predicted with any degree of certainty. But, as insurance companies have long since discovered, the average behavior of many individuals *can* be predicted, with a certainty that increases as the number of individuals or the time span considered is increased. What we must do, in analyzing library operations, is to reduce the daily occurrences to a set of probabilities; from these one can predict average behavior, average deviation from average behavior, and other useful criteria, which will be accurate enough on which to base decisions, when they involve hundreds of users or books or time spans of a year or more.

Definition of Probability

Probability is the quantitative means of prediction in the face of uncertainty. Suppose some future event may have a number of different possible outcomes. For example, when a library user visits the library tomorrow he may look at one or more books before leaving, or he may borrow one or more books, or he may use the card catalogue, or he may do none of these things (call them *tasks*). To say that the prob-

9

ability that one of tomorrow's attendees will perform the nth task is equal to the number P_n is equivalent to saying that one expects a fraction P_n of tomorrow's attendees to perform the nth task. The probability P_a, that an event will have the outcome a, represents our prediction that, if the event occurs over and over N times, NP_a of the N are expected to result in outcome a.

This means that probability P_n, being a fraction, must have a value between zero and unity. Absolute certainty is represented only by $P_n = 1$ (we are certain that *all* events will result in outcome n) or by $P_n = 0$ (we are certain that *no* events will result in the nth outcome); all intermediate values of the fraction represent different degrees of uncertainty regarding the outcome. Random events being, by definition, more or less unpredictable, we do not expect that the number N_n of outcomes n which actually occur will be exactly equal to the predicted value NP_n. In fact if there is only one event ($N = 1$), the nth outcome either will occur ($N_n = 1$) or it will not ($N_n = 0$). If our prediction had been $P_n = 0.8$, all we could have said about a single event was that the nth outcome was rather more likely to occur than not. The N_n for a single trial could only be 0 or 1; neither result invalidates the prediction that $P_n = 0.8$. To say that $P_n = 0.8$ is to expect that out of 100 trials the actual number N_n of outcomes of the nth sort will be not far from 80, that the number N_n of nth outcomes in 1000 events will be fairly close to 800, that as the number N of trials is increased, the ratio between the number N_n of actual occurrences of the nth outcome and the number of trials N will approach P_n closer and closer. Thus we can condense the definition of the probability P_n into an equation for the *expected value* of the number N_n of nth outcomes in N events, or trials,

$$Exp(N_n) \equiv E(N_n) = NP_n \qquad \text{or} \qquad P_n = \frac{E(N_n)}{N} \qquad (2.1)$$

which, if you like, is also a definition of the phrase *expected value*.

The foregoing also means that a finite series of observations will not exactly determine the value of P_n. Random events being what they are, just because N trials, already made, have resulted in N_n outcomes of the nth kind, it is not likely that N more trials, even if performed under similar circumstances, will result in exactly the same value of N_n. The ratio N_n/N for a past set of N trials is no more likely to come out exactly equal to P_n than is the ratio N_n/N for the next set. Sometimes a study of the nature of the event is of more help in determining the appropriate value of P_n than is a whole series of observations.

As a simple example, we write down the results of a hundred tosses of a coin, labeling the tosses resulting in a head as H, those in a tail as T,

	No. H	No. T
HTHHT TTHHH HTHHH HTTHT TTटHT	13	12
TTटHT THHTH TTHTT THTHT THHHH	11	14
HHHHT HHHTH THHHT THHHT THTTT	15	10
THHTT THTTH TTHTT TTTHH TTHHH	10	15
	49	51

$$(2.2)$$

If we used the first five tosses to tell us the chance of getting a head, we might assume that $P_H = 0.6$; if we use the whole hundred tosses to determine the probability, we might be inclined to say that $P_H = 0.49$. But we could use the symmetry of the coin (and also the honesty of the tosser!) to persuade ourselves that there should be no difference between heads or tails, that the probability of a head should equal that of a tail, $P_H = P_T = 1/2$. If this is our assumed probability, we see that four tosses do not always result in a number of heads equal to $1/2 \times N = 2$; there are sequences of 4 throws in the sample of 100 that have 0, 1, 2, 3, or 4 heads. However, in the first 25 throws the fraction of heads tossed is 0.52, closer to $P_H = 0.50$ than the result for the first 5 throws, and 0.49 of the 100 throws are heads, even closer to the expected ratio. Presumably if the coin were tossed 1000 times, the fraction of heads would be still closer to 0.50 (though there would be a small chance that it would deviate farther; this chance would decrease as the number N of throws were increased).

Properties of Probabilities

Let us use the coin tossing and library attending examples to illustrate some other properties of probability that will be useful later. In coin tossing the coin *either* comes down with head up *or* with tails up; we say these two events are mutually *exclusive;* if one occurs in a trial, the other cannot occur in the same trial. This is not the case with the outcomes (or tasks) listed for a library attendee; just because he borrowed a book does not exclude him from going to the card catalogue during the same visit. We can list outcomes for a visit in such a way as to make them mutually exclusive, however. We can concentrate on one sort of task, we can for example consider only the number of books borrowed by the attendee during his visit; he can withdraw no book, or one book, or two, or n, and this listing of outcomes is mutually exclusive; if he withdraws only one book during his visit, he cannot at the same time withdraw five. Or else we can list a number of unit tasks which the attendee can perform, such as the borrowing of a book or the reading from a book in the library or each use of the card catalogue, and the mutually exclusive outcomes could be the total number n of unit tasks, of any of the listed sort, performed by the attendee. In this case the borrowing of three books would be considered to be the same outcome, for the purpose of the survey, as three visits to the card catalogue or the use of three books in the library. This would be a perfectly definite way of dividing up the possible outcomes, though the resulting numbers N_n might not give us as much detail as some other way of consolidating the data.

If the possible outcomes of a trial or unit event are listed so they are mutually exclusive, then the probability of *either* of two possible outcomes equals the *sum* of their individual probabilities. That this must be so is apparent when we look at our expectation for N trials. According to Eq. 2.1 the expected number of nth outcomes is NP_n and the expected number of mth outcomes is NP_m; the expected number of either outcome is the sum $N(P_n + P_m)$, *if* the outcomes are exclusive. The probability of either n or m is, by Eq. 2.1, this expected number divided by the number of trials N, *if* n and m are *exclusive*,

$$P(n \text{ or } m) = P_n + P_m \qquad (2.3)$$

Next, if the listing of mutually exclusive outcomes is *exhaustive*, i.e., if all possible outcomes of an event are listed, the sum of the expected number of all the listed outcomes of N trials must equal N. For example, if we toss a coin $N = 10$ times (and if we let the coin land on a surface which excludes its remaining on edge!), the expected number of heads plus the expected number of tails must equal 10, for there are no other possible outcomes. Thus, since E (Heads) + E (Tails), which equals $NP_H + NP_T$, must equal N, we have $P_H + P_T = 1$; the probability that *either* a head *or* a tail will occur in a throw is 1, indicating certainty that one or the other will happen. In general, therefore, if an event has k possible, mutually *exclusive* outcomes ($n = 1$ or 2 or 3 $\cdots$ up to k) and if this listing of outcomes is *exhaustive*, including all possible outcomes, the sum of all the probabilities is unity,

$$P_1 + P_2 + P_3 + \cdots + P_k = 1 \qquad (2.4)$$

for k outcomes exclusive and exhaustive. For example, since $P_H + P_T = 1$ and for a symmetric coin there can be no difference between P_H and P_T, we see that $P_H = P_T = 1/2$, as we intuitively implied earlier. Such a set of probabilities, representing our prediction regarding an exhaustive list of mutually exclusive outcomes of some repetitive event, is called a *probability distribution*.

Subdivision of Outcomes; Conditional Probabilities

In the example of the tasks performed during library attendance, we may be dissatisfied with the suggested enumeration, which does not distinguish between the kinds of tasks but simply counts the number performed during a visit. We may wish to predict the likelihood (i.e., to determine the probability) that an attendee borrows one book and uses the card catalogue twice during the visit, for example. Here the tasks are not mutually exclusive, but we may separate our possible outcomes into sets, mutually exclusive within each set. For example, we may list the number i of times the attendee used the catalogue and also list the number n of books he borrowed during his visit; we might desire the probability that the attendee went to the catalogue i times during his visit and that he left the library with n books borrowed. Various probabilities can be obtained; their interrelation is important. For example, we could first neglect the catalogue task entirely and obtain the probability P_n^b that the attendee borrowed n books during the visit, regardless of his use of the catalogue, or we could obtain the probability P_i^c that the attendee used the catalogue i times during his visit, regardless of the number of books he borrowed (how these probabilities may be obtained will be discussed later in this chapter). In each of these cases Formula 2.4 holds, since both sets of outcomes are exhaustive,

$$P_0^c + P_1^c + P_2^c + P_3^c + \cdots = 1$$
$$P_0^b + P_1^b + P_2^b + P_3^b + \cdots = 1 \tag{2.5}$$

where the sums extend out to the maximum number of borrowed books or of catalogue uses possible in one visit.

However, we might also wish to obtain the probability that an attendee, who has not consulted the catalogue at all ($i = 0$), leaves with $n = 3$ borrowed books. We will write this as $P(n = 3 \mid$ when $i = 0)$. Or we may wish to find the probability that the attendee who borrows $n = 1$ books has used the catalogue $i = 3$ times; which can be written $P(i = 3 \mid$ when $n = 1)$. These are called *conditional probabilities;* the probability that result a occurs when, during the same event, result b has occurred may be written $P(a \mid$ when b occurs).

Now in N trials we expect $NP(b)$ of them to result in b, according to Eq. 2.1. In all of these $NP(b)$ cases b occurs; by applying Eq. 2.1 again, using the conditional probability $P(a \mid$ when b occurs), we see that the expected number of trials for which *both a* and *b* occur is $[NP(b)] \times P(a \mid$ when *b* occurs). Dividing out *N*, we have shown that the *joint probability* that *both a* and *b* occur in a trial is the product of the conditional probability that *a* occurs if *b* occurs times the probability that *b* occurs, regardless of *a*

$$P(a \text{ and } b) = P(a \mid \text{ when } b \text{ occurs}) \times P(b)$$
$$= P(b \mid \text{ when } a \text{ occurs}) \times P(a) \tag{2.6}$$

In the example of library use, the joint probability P^{bc} (*i* and *n*) that an attendee leaves with *n* books, having used the catalogue *i* times, is equal to the product of the conditional probability $P^b(n \mid$ when *i*) that the attendee, who has used the catalogue *i* times, will borrow *n* books times the probability P^c_i that an attendee in general looks at the catalogue *i* times. Likewise P^{bc} (*i* and *n*) equals the product of the conditional probability $P^c(i \mid$ when *n*) that the attendee, who leaves with *n* books, will have used the catalogue *i* times, multiplied by the probability that any attendee, no matter how many times he has looked at the catalogue, borrows *n* books. We should note, that since the sets *n* of borrowed books and *i* of catalogue uses are each exhaustive, then for any allowed value of *i* or *n*,

$$P^b(0 \mid \text{ when } i) + P^b(1 \mid \text{ when } i) + P^b(2 \mid \text{ when } i) + \cdots = 1$$
$$P^c(0 \mid \text{ when } n) + P^c(1 \mid \text{ when } n) + P^c(2 \mid \text{ when } n) + \cdots = 1 \tag{2.7}$$

In some cases $P(a \mid$ when *b* occurs) is equal to $P(a \mid$ when *b* does *not* occur); in other words the probability of occurrence of *a* is independent of the occurrence or nonoccurrence of *b* and thus can be written as $P(a)$. When the occurrence of *a* is independent of that of *b*, then the occurrence of *b* is independent of that of *a* and the joint probability of *both a* and *b* occurring in a trial is simply the product

$$P(a \text{ and } b) = P(a)P(b) \tag{2.8}$$
(when *a* and *b* are independent)

of the two probabilities of occurrence. For example if the library attendee's proclivity for borrowing books has, on the average, no relation to his interest in the card catalogue, so that the value of $P^b(n \mid$ when *i*) was the same no matter what value *i* had, then we could omit the value of *i* from the label and set it equal to the probability P^b_n that an attendee borrows *n* books, regardless of the number of times he uses the catalogue; in this case the probability of an attendee using the catalogue *i* times *and* taking out *n* books is the simple product P^b_n times P^c_i.

As another example of Eqs. 2.6 and 2.8 we return to the tossed coin and ask the probability that heads may come up twice in two throws. Here the trial is *two* throws, not one, and we can make our calculation by first asking for the probability that the first throw is heads; we have already shown that this is $P_H = 1/2$. Next we ask what is the conditional probability $P(H \mid$ when previous throw is H) that the second throw is heads *if* the first one was heads. But if the throw is a fair one, the result of the first throw should have no effect on the result of the second, $P(H \mid$ when previous throw is H) is equal to $P(H \mid$ when previous throw is T) and both are equal to $P_H = 1/2$. Therefore, by Eq. 2.8, the probability that two throws will result in two heads is

$$P(\text{2H in 2 throws}) = P(H \mid \text{when previous throw is H}) \times P_H$$
$$= P_H \times P_H = (\tfrac{1}{2}) \times (\tfrac{1}{2}) = \tfrac{1}{4} \qquad (2.9)$$

Looking back at Eq. 2.2, the record of 100 throws, we can divide it up into 50 pairs of throws, of these 50 pairs, 13 of them are HH, which is reasonably close to one quarter of 50.

Likewise, of course, the probability of getting two tails in two throws is $P_T P_T = 1/4$. In our sample, 15 pairs out of 50 throws had TT, somewhat larger than $1/4$ of the 50, but close enough considering that there were only 50 trials. The chance of one head and one tail is, from Eq. 2.3, the sum of the probability of a head first and a tail second and that for a tail first and a head second,

$$P(\text{H and T in 2 throws}) = P_H P_T + P_T P_H = (\tfrac{1}{4}) + (\tfrac{1}{4}) = \tfrac{1}{2} \quad (2.10)$$

Or we can calculate it by realizing that the set of possibilities for two throws, two heads or two tails or a head and a tail (regardless of order), is exhaustive, so by Eq. 2.4,

$$P(\text{H and T in 2 throws}) = 1 - P(\text{2H in 2 throws}) - P(\text{2T in 2 throws})$$
$$= 1 - (\tfrac{1}{4}) - (\tfrac{1}{4}) = \tfrac{1}{2} \qquad (2.11)$$

Expected Values and Variances

Suppose we have found the values P_n^b of the probabilities that an attendee to the library borrows n books in a visit, for the different possible values of n; we can next ask for a prediction $E(B)$ of the total number B of books borrowed when N persons visit the library. This will be the sum of zero times the expected number $E(N_0)$ of attendees (out of the total N) who borrow no books during their visit, plus one times the expected number $E(N_1)$ who borrow one book, plus two times the number $E(N_2)$ who borrow two, and so on. But from Eq. 2.1, $E(N_n) = NP_n^b$, so the expected number of books borrowed

$$E(B) = N[0(P_0^b) + 1(P_1^b) + 2(P_2^b) + 3(P_3^b) + \cdots]$$

$$E(n_b) = \frac{E(B)}{N} = P_1^b + 2P_2^b + 3P_3^b + \cdots \qquad (2.12)$$

where n_b is the average number of books borrowed *per attendee* and $E(n_b)$ is its expected value.

Of course, the actual number of books borrowed by any specific attendee may deviate from this, since these are random events; it will be of interest to estimate the degree to which the individual cases deviate from the mean. We might wish to find the expected value of the difference between the number of books actually borrowed in each individual case and the expected value $E(n_b)$. This, however, would be zero, since the property of $E(n_b)$ is that there is just as much deviation to be expected above this mean as below. Therefore the measure of the degree of variability of the individual results from the expected value is taken to be the expected value of the *square* of the difference, called the *variance*, which is not zero. A bit of algebraic juggling shows that the variance, the expected value σ_b^2 of the square of the difference between actual n_b and $E(n_b)$, is

$$\sigma_b^2 = [0 - E(n_b)]^2 P_0^b + [1 - E(n_b)]^2 P_1^b + [2 - E(n_b)]^2 P_2^b + \cdots$$
$$= 1^2 P_1^b + 2^2 P_2^b + 3^2 P_3^b + \cdots - [E(n_b)]^2 \qquad (2.13)$$

To make this more concrete, let us investigate a simple coin tossing game. The player tosses a coin. If it comes down tails he pays one penny, the game stops, and he starts a new game. If it shows heads, he is paid a penny, and he has another throw. If the second throw is tails, he pays a penny and the game stops, but if he throws a second head he is paid a cent and has another throw, and so on. In other words the game continues as long as he throws heads, and he is paid a cent for every consecutive head he throws; the game stops, and he pays a cent whenever a tail comes up. To find out what to expect, we calculate the probability of the various possible outcomes. The chance of a tail coming up the first throw is of course $P_T = 1/2$, which is the chance $P(-1)$ that he loses one cent on the game. The chance $P(0)$ of his tossing a head first, then a tail is $P_H P_T = (1/2)^2 = 1/4$, which is a chance of his breaking even (winning a cent, then having to pay it back on the next throw). The chance $P(1)$ of his winning 1 cent is the probability of his throwing two heads in succession, then a tail, which is $P_H P_H P_T = (1/2)(1/2)(1/2) = 1/8$, and so on; for $n = -1, 0, 1, 2, 3, \cdots$,

$$P(n) = (\tfrac{1}{2})^{n+2} \qquad (2.14)$$

First let us check that this set of probabilities satisfies the *completeness* requirement of Eq. 2.4. We have

$$P(-1) + P(0) + P(1) + P(2) \cdots$$
$$= (\tfrac{1}{2}) + (\tfrac{1}{4}) + (\tfrac{1}{8}) + (\tfrac{1}{16}) + \cdots = 1 \qquad (2.15)$$

so this requirement is satisfied. Next we use Eq. 2.12 (or its extension) to calculate the expected return to the player per game. We multiply each possible return by the probability of that return and add,

$$E \text{ (return per game)} = -1[P(-1)] + 0[P(0)] + 1[P(1)] + 2[P(2)] \cdots$$
$$= -(\tfrac{1}{2}) + 0 + (\tfrac{1}{8}) + (\tfrac{2}{16}) + (\tfrac{3}{32}) + \cdots = 0 \quad (2.16)$$

so the game is fair. To estimate the probable variation in return in any specific game we use the sum of Eq. 2.13 to calculate the variance in the return. Since E (return) $= 0$, the sum is simply that of the squares of the returns times the probabilities of the returns,

$$\sigma^2 = 1[P(-1)] + 0[P(0)] + 1[P(1)] + 4[P(2)] + 9[P(3)] + \cdots$$
$$= (\tfrac{1}{2}) + 0 + (\tfrac{1}{8}) + (\tfrac{4}{16}) + (\tfrac{9}{32}) + (\tfrac{16}{64}) + \cdots = 2 \qquad (2.17)$$

The square root of this, the root-mean-square deviation from the mean, $\sigma = 1.41$, is a measure of the variability of return. Roughly half of the time the player will lose one cent, three times out of eight he will either break even or win a cent, the chances are only 1 in 8 for him to win more than a penny; the value 1.4 for the root-mean-square deviation (or *standard deviation*) σ is an indication of this degree of variability of the returns.

To see how this would work out in "real life," we interpret the throws recorded in Eq. 2.2 as if they were part of such a set of games. The first pair of letters HT represents the first game, in which the player wins a cent and then loses a cent, the next trio, HHT, is the next game, in which the net gain is 1 cent. However, next comes two more T's, representing two games, in each of which the player loses a penny; then comes HHHHT, representing a net gain of 3 cents. And so on, for 50 games, ending at the 96th toss, with the following sequence of gains to the player,

$$
\begin{array}{rrrrr rrrrr}
0 & 1 & -1 & -1 & 3 & \quad & 3 & -1 & 0 & -1 & -1 \\
-1 & 0 & -1 & -1 & -1 & & 0 & -1 & 1 & 0 & -1 \\
0 & -1 & -1 & 0 & 0 & & -1 & 7 & 2 & 0 & 2 \quad (2.18) \\
-1 & 2 & -1 & 0 & -1 & & -1 & -1 & 1 & -1 & -1 \\
0 & -1 & 0 & -1 & 0 & & -1 & -1 & -1 & -1 & 1 \\
\end{array}
$$

with a net loss of 4 cents to the player, an average of -0.08 cent per game, a reasonable approximation to the predicted zero loss. We see that most of the games involve gains or losses of a cent, only in three out of the fifty games did the player win 2 cents, two games netted 3 cents, and one game yielded as much as 7 cents. We list the fractions $F(n)$ of the 50 games which yielded n cents and compare them with the predictions, the probabilities $P(n)$ of Eq. 2.14

n	-1	0	1	2	3	4	5	6	7
$F(n)$	0.54	0.26	0.08	0.06	0.04	0	0	0	0.02
$P(n)$	0.50	0.25	0.125	0.062	0.031	0.016	0.008	0.004	0.002

$$(2.19)$$

The check with prediction is best for the most frequent games, those for n smaller than 3; many more games would need to be played before one could expect an accurate correspondence with $P(n)$ for the less frequent results, such as $n = 7$.

Choice of Probability Distribution

To recapitulate, prediction in the face of uncertainty involves first listing the possible outcomes of the event we wish to predict, in a set of mutually exclusive alternatives, that include all possibilities (i.e., are exhaustive). We then attach to the alternative outcomes n the probability P_n and do this for all n of the set. The value of P_n corresponds to our prediction (or expectation) that, out of N typical events (or trials), NP_n of them are expected to result in the nth outcome, and that the ratio between the actual number N_n of nth outcome and the number of trials, N_n/N, will approach P_n closer and closer as N is increased. From this basic formulation we can proceed to make other predictions, as illustrated in the foregoing discussion.

But to use this procedure we need to give numerical values to the P_n for each n. To do this we need to know something about the event we are making predictions about. Presumably our knowledge cannot be complete, or there would be no uncertainty about the outcome. In the case of the tossed coin, if we were able to measure accurately the initial impulse given the coin and knew the elastic properties of the surface it comes to rest upon, we might be able to predict exactly whether heads or tails will show in a given throw. But we choose not to make the measurements and we take care not to regularize the initial impulse, so we cannot tell which side will show. In the case of the library attendee we might be able to predict an attendee's behavior if we subjected him to examination as to his intentions, ahead of time. But we want to make the best prediction we can *without* subjecting each attendee to examination and moreover we are usually interested in the totality of actions of many attendees; usually we can be satisfied with the expected values and estimates of variance.

Another way of finding out about the event is to observe a sequence and to record the outcomes, as we did with the tossed coin of Eq. 2.2. Having observed N events, we can divide the number N_n of times the nth outcome has occurred by N, to obtain the empirical fraction $F_n = (N_n/N)$ of occurrence of outcome n. But, as we saw with the tossed coin, these fractions F_n will not usually be the same for the next N observed events and none of them are exactly equal to the probabilities P_n we would like to obtain. If we make a very large number of observations, the resulting F would not differ much from the P, but we may not be able to make enough observations, and it may be more efficient for us to use reason and some knowledge about the structure of the event to help us. For example, with the coin tossing, we used the symmetry of the coin to persuade us that P_H and P_T should both be $1/2$, in spite of the fact that the empirical fractions, for the hundred throws, came out to be $F_H = 0.49$ and $F_T = 0.51$. We did, of course, use the fact that these empirical fractions seemed to be coming closer to 0.50 as N was increased ($F_H = 0.60$ for $N = 5$; $F_H = 0.52$ for $N = 25$; $F_H = 0.49$ for $N = 100$) to confirm our assumption that the coin used was sufficiently symmetric as to correspond to our idealized model.

This is the procedure we will use throughout the book. We will look at data taken from actual library operation. Rather than blindly extrapolating from these data (taking the P_n to be equal to the empirical F_n) we will try to devise probabilistic models of the operation, combinations of random elements which correspond reasonably well with the observed data and also are not-unreasonable idealizations of the basic structure of the operation. We will find these models imply other properties of the operating system, predict other characteristics which can be checked by taking more data. If the actual system behaves as the theoretical model suggests, it strengthens our trust in its predictive value; if the measured data do not fit, we look for another, more appropriate model.

It should not require much discussion here to persuade one of the great advantage of a probabilistic model, thoroughly checked by observation, over the empirical extrapolation from data. In the first place it saves the amassing of large quantities of data. By using the model we can work out those properties that can be checked with least effort. Even the simple model of coin tossing enabled us to predict the probability of two heads in two throws, an additional characteristic of random coin throwing, which could be checked on *the same data* which has been used to see whether it was reasonable that the probability of a head in a single throw is $1/2$. Many other implications, such as the structure of the game described in Eq. 2.14, can be worked out from the model, and checked with the same data (as was done in Eq. 2.19). Whereas empirical prediction of the game probabilities would have required a data base that is scores or hundreds of times larger. Further arguments in favor of the combined measurement-model procedure will be given throughout the book.

Some of our models regarding human behavior may seem too "mechanical" to be able to correspond to reality; some of them may seem to assume that every person acts in the same sort of random manner. It must be remembered, however, that our models are concerned with the behavior of large numbers of persons, not with the behavior of single individuals. Each person certainly has his own idiosyncrasies, different from the next, but in the mass these differences tend to disappear and the behavior of many often turns out to be the same *as if* the random characteristics of the individual were similar. Of course we should not suppose that, because the idealized "individuals" of the model all have similar random characteristics, this means that we expect actual individuals to have exactly these characteristics. Averages are useful, even though no individual has characteristics all equal to the average values. Just because a model, devised to predict the behavior of many persons, cannot be used to predict the behavior of a single person does not diminish its value as a predictive tool for the many.

In the first part of this book we will devise a number of probabilistic models, to correspond to some of the things that go on in a library. In each case the model will result in a set of probabilities, from which we can predict average behavior in various circumstances, which will enable us to predict how the behavior will change as circumstances change or are changed. In the second half of the book we will combine the models and look more deeply into their implications, to see how they can assist the librarian in planning library operation and expansion.

A Survey of Use

But let us take some specific examples to illustrate these generalities. We start with a simple one, related to the actions of users of the Science Library at M.I.T. In the early spring of 1955 a random sample of attendees of this library were each handed a questionnaire when they entered. They were asked, among other things, to specify what they did while in the library that time.[2] Note that this was *not* an opinion survey, it was a request for facts, namely what positive and easily countable action each user carried out during his visit. Each of the following actions (called here a *task*) was listed:

1. Consult a book in the library
2. Consult a periodical in the library
3. Consult a report in the library
4. Borrow a book to take out of the library
5. Borrow a periodical to take out of the library
6. Borrow a report to take out of the library
7. Consult the card catalogue

Also, the attendee was asked to specify how many times he performed each task during this particular visit to the library. In addition he was asked his status (undergraduate, graduate student, faculty, other) and his specialty (chemistry, mathematics, biology, physics, other). In all 2700 questionnaires were filled out, sufficiently completely, to be of use (these represented a majority of all users during the period of the survey). This list is representative but naturally not exhaustive.

Data on Tasks Performed

Among other users, 265 chemists (faculty or graduate students) filled out the questionnaire, giving details as to the number of "tasks" they performed during their stay. It then was possible to arrange their sheets in order of the total number of tasks performed by each. We list in Table 2.1 the number of persons in the sample who performed a total of k or more tasks, of any of the 7 kinds.

From these raw figures we can calculate the mean number of tasks performed by a chemist during an average visit to the Science Library (in January 1955). The total number of tasks performed by all 265 is the sum of all the numbers of the middle column which is 1107 (196 performed at least one task, 145 of them performed at least two tasks, one of which has been counted in the 196, and so on). This, divided by 265, the number of attendees in the sample, gives 4.2 as the average number of tasks performed by a chemist during a visit.

But Table 2.1 tells us much more than this. As a matter of fact, if we had just been interested in the mean number of tasks we could have obtained it more easily otherwise, and to sufficient accuracy, by questioning fewer chemists (less than 100). The table also shows us the great variation in usage of the attendees, variation from person to

Table 2.1   Number of Chemists in Sample of 265, Who Reported Performing k or More Tasks During Visit*

Tasks, k	Number Reporting, N_k	Theoretical Model, $E(n_k)$
1	196	190
2	145	157
3	120	130
4	101	108
5	84	89
6	72	74
7	60	61
8	53	51
9	47	42
10	29	35
11	26	29
12	23	24
13	22	20
14	16	17
15	14	14
16	14	12
17	13	10
18	13	8
19	10	7
20	8	6
21	8	5
22	6	4
23	6	3
24	5	3
25	4	2
26	4	2
27	3	2
28	3	1
29	1	1
30	1	1
	1107	1107

* No chemist performed more than 30 tasks during his visit, and 69 chemists (265 minus 196) performed no task during their visit. (The figures in the third column will be discussed later.)

person, and also from visit to visit by the same person, since several attendees made several visits and filled out several questionnaires during the survey. From a similar table listing just the task of withdrawing k or more books from the library, we could see, for example, what fraction of attending chemists would have been frustrated if for some reason

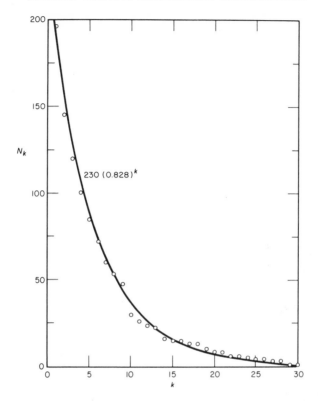

Fig. 2.1.   Dots are the data from Table 2.1. Solid line is the theoretical model of
   Eq. 2.20.

the number of books withdrawn per visit had been limited to 2. As
we continue, further conclusions to be drawn from the table will be
pointed out.

To find the regularity, we first plot the figures in the second column,
Number Reporting, of Table 2.1 against Tasks, k. Figure 2.1 shows
that the usual plot is not very informative; the linear vertical scale
crowds all but the first few points down too close to the axis; we need
to use a vertical scale which will "stretch out" the points near zero.
One such scale is the logarithmic scale, which goes according to powers;
the distance from 1 to 10 is equal to the distance from 10 to 100 as from
100 to 1000, also the distance from 1 to 2 is equal to the distance from
2 to 4 as from 4 to 8, and so on. Thus quantities which go as the kth
power of some number plot as straight lines on a graph that has k for
the horizontal scale and has a logarithmic vertical scale. This is shown

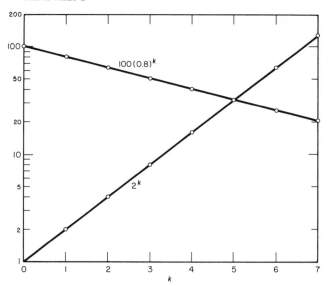

Fig. 2.2.   Geometric progressions on a semilog plot.

in Fig. 2.2, where we have plotted functions 2^k and $100\,(0.8)^k$. Such graphs are said to be on a semilog plot. Thus we try plotting the data in the second column of Table 2.1 on a semilog plot. This is shown in Fig. 2.3.

The Probability Distribution

We notice that, over a range of a factor of over 20, the data points seem to lie on a straight line on the semilog plot of Fig. 2.3. As noted earlier, if the data were exactly on a straight line it would mean that N_k is exactly equal to a constant C times some number γ to the kth power. If γ is greater than unity, the curve will rise with increasing k; our curve falls as k increases, thus γ must be less than 1. Since we cannot expect that data from a sample of finite size would correspond exactly with the numbers we would use for prediction, we are tempted to investigate the hypothesis that the expected values of the N_k form a straight line on a semilog plot. In mathematical form, the probabilistic model we propose to try is

$$E(N_k) = \overline{N}_0 \gamma^k \tag{2.20}$$

which states that the expected number of chemists who perform k or more tasks during their visit, is equal to a constant times the kth power of some quantity γ, smaller than 1. The constant can be written as $\overline{N}_0$, the expected total number of chemists reporting (who all have performed 0 or more tasks) since γ to the zeroth power equals 1 and we want the equation to hold for $k = 0$ as well as for k larger than 0, so that $E(N_0) = \bar{N}_0$.

The solid line corresponds to Eq. 2.20 for $\bar{N}_0 = 230$ and for $\gamma = 0.83$; we will see later how this is determined. The fit with the points representing the data is as good as can be expected from a finite sample. The deviation from the straight line is large only for the less than 5 per cent of attendees who have performed more than 15 tasks, and one may wonder whether these "tail-end" numbers wouldn't fall more closely on the curve if more chemists had been included in the survey.

In other words the proposed model predicts that $\bar{N}_0\gamma$ of the chemists entering the library will perform one or more tasks during their stay, $\bar{N}_0\gamma^2$ of them will perform two or more tasks and so on; the number $E(N_{k+1})$ who are expected to perform at least $k + 1$ tasks is the constant fraction γ times the number $E(N_k)$ who are expected to perform at least k tasks. Of course the formula cannot be carried to absurd extremes; we should ignore the fact that it predicts that a minute fraction of a chemist will perform 500 tasks. Such absurdities can easily be avoided, however, by rounding off figures to the nearest whole number (zero in the case cited).

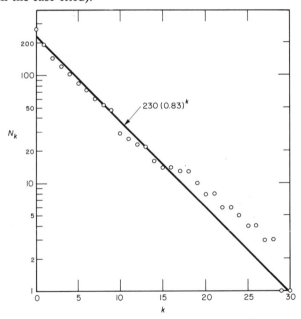

Fig. 2.3. Number of chemists N_k performing k or more tasks during visit to library. Dots are from Table 2.1. Solid line is theoretical prediction.

The temptation to use the formula, with the appropriate values of N_0 and γ, instead of the empirical data, is impelling. In the first place it reduces our calculations to algebraic manipulations, instead of lengthy numerical operations. For example, the expected number of persons in the sample who perform *exactly* k tasks is $E(n_k) = E(N_k) - E(N_{k+1})$. If we use the data, this must be subtracted out for each k; if we use the formula we soon find that

$$E(n_k) = N_0(\gamma^k - \gamma^{k+1}) = (1 - \gamma)N_0\gamma^k = (1 - \gamma)N_k$$

in other words, that $E(n_k)$ also plots as a straight line, on a semilog plot, parallel to $E(N_k)$. In still other words the probability that a chemist, visiting the library, will carry out exactly k tasks during his visit, is (see Eq. 2.4)

$$P_k = \left[\frac{E(n_k)}{N_0}\right] = (1 - \gamma)\gamma^k \qquad (2.21)$$

where $P_0 + P_1 + P_2 + \cdots = 1$. This probability distribution is called a *geometric distribution*. The requirement that the sum of all the P equals unity holds for all probability distributions. It simply means that it is certain (probability = 1) that k will be either 0 or 1 or 2 or any other number up to infinity.

Estimating the Parameter

In the present case the model prescribes the form of the distribution (that it is geometric) but does not provide exact values of the parameter γ. Indeed the model suggests that different classes of library users may be distinguished by having different values of γ, corresponding to different habits of library use. We thus are left with the task of estimating the best value of γ for a given class of user. To do this we of course make use of the data, and so in a sense the model has an empirically determined constant. Note, however, that only a single constant needs to be determined empirically, not the value of each probability P_k. Thus we can obtain useful results from much less data than would be required to estimate each individual P_k. We needed to gather data from several hundred chemists to verify that the model of Eq. 2.21 does represent the statistical situation. Once the model is verified, to obtain a sufficiently accurate value of γ we would need data on less than a hundred visits of a given class of attendee.

The simplest way of estimating the value of γ is to draw a straight line through the points of Fig. 2.3. For example N_0 is about 230 and N_{10} about 35; their ratio (1/6) should equal γ^{10}, so γ should be approximately 0.83, the tenth root of 0.167. A somewhat more accurate method is to use the model to calculate the best value of γ, and then check to see how well it fits. We should depend most on the values of N_k, given in Table 2.1, for k small, since these represent the largest sample and thus are presumably nearer the expected values. We use the expression for the sum of a geometric sequence, demonstrated in books on college algebra,

$$\gamma + \gamma^2 + \gamma^3 + \gamma^4 + \cdots + \gamma^{n-1} + \gamma^n = \left(\frac{1 - \gamma^n}{1 - \gamma}\right)\gamma \quad (2.22)$$

Thus, if N_k of Table 2.1 corresponded to the model of Eq. 2.20, the sum of the first n values of N_k should equal

$$N_1 + N_2 + N_3 + \cdots N_{n-1} + N_n \simeq N_0 \gamma \frac{1 - \gamma^n}{1 - \gamma}$$

the constant N_0 times a simple function of γ, given in Eq. 2.22.

Thus the sum of all 30 N_k would be given by this function for $n = 30$; the sum of the first 3 N_k would (if the model is correct) equal N_0 times the function for $n = 3$. To estimate γ and then to calculate the "best" value of N_0, we use the following equations:

$$\gamma^s \simeq 1 - (1 - \gamma^n)\frac{N_1 + N_2 + \cdots + N_s}{N_1 + N_2 + N_3 + \cdots + N_{n-1} + N_n}$$

$$N_0 \simeq \frac{1 - \gamma}{\gamma(1 - \gamma^n)}(N_1 + N_2 + N_3 + \cdots + N_{n-1} + N_n)$$

$$(2.23)$$

In the case of Table 2.1, there are 30 N_k and their sum $(n = 30)$ is 1107. Thirty is large enough to allow us to make a crude approximation for γ (such as the value 0.83) and still obtain a fairly accurate value of $1 - \gamma^n$ (which equals $1 - 0.0037 = 0.9963$ for $\gamma = 0.83$). If we take only one term $(s = 1)$ in the shorter sum, we then have $\gamma^2 \simeq 1 - 0.996(341/1107) = 0.693$ or $\gamma \simeq 0.832$; for $s = 3$, we get $\gamma \simeq 0.834$; so a reasonable value of γ for chemists is 0.83. Using the second of Eqs. 2.23, we then find that for $\gamma \simeq 0.83$

$$N_0 \simeq \frac{0.17}{(0.83)(0.997)}(1107) \simeq 230$$

which are the values plotted in Fig. 2.3 and used in the last column, $E(N_k)$, of Table 2.1. (Note that we have not used the total observed number of chemists, which should approximately equal N_0, in our calculations of γ and N_0; the reasons for this will become apparent later.)

The Probabilistic Model

But there are other reasons than mere convenience for being attracted to the formula, rather than to the raw data. For the geometric distribution is typical of a class of ideal random events. Imagine the chemist entering the library with a coin or die or some other random device which has a probability γ of coming up heads when tossed (and a corresponding probability $1 - \gamma$ of coming up tails). Every so often he tosses the coin; if it comes up tails he leaves the library, if it comes up heads he performs a task and a little later tosses again and so on. Note the analogy with the game of Eq. 2.14. Such a visitor would have a probability $1 - \gamma$ of having the coin come up tails the first throw, in which case he would leave the library without having performed a task. If he threw a head the first time and a tail the second, he would leave the library having performed only one task; the probability for this would be γ, the probability of the first head, times $(1 - \gamma)$, the probability of the second tail. The probability of his performing two tasks would be γ times γ times $(1 - \gamma)$ and that of performing k tasks before having a tail come up would be $(1 - \gamma)\gamma^k$, which is exactly the formula given for P_k in Eq. 2.21.

We do not imply that any individual chemist's action in the library exactly duplicates this ideally random model, all we say is that the collective behavior of many chemists statistically seems to be remarkably close to the model. The individual chemist may come into the library with his mind made up as to how many tasks he will perform, in contrast to the indetermination of the model. But his determination on one visit may be quite different from that on another visit, and it will differ from the plans of a colleague. Furthermore books may be missing, or other extranea may deflect him from his plan. All we say is that chemists exhibit a great deal of random variability in their use of the library, so it is perhaps not surprising that they behave, statistically, in a manner similar to the ideal, random model.

Uses of the Model

Let us follow this matter to see whether other correspondences will shake or strengthen our preference. The number N_0 should be the total number of chemists entering the library and $N_0(1 - \gamma) = n_0$ should be the number of chemists in the sample who enter the library and leave it without performing any task. According to the model, they entered *intending to use* the library but were either thwarted or distracted and left. The model, in other words, does not include those chemists who entered the library *not intending to use it as a library*.

Now a glance at Fig. 2.3 shows that the straight line, corresponding to the model, strikes the $k = 0$ axis at $N_0 = 230$, whereas the total number of chemists in the sample is 265. If we are to believe in our model, 35 chemists (265 minus 230) should not be included in the model; i.e., we should conclude that these 35 entered the library not intending to use the library facilities other than a chair and a table. As it happens, one of the questions in the questionnaire was whether the attendee was using the library this time as a study hall, using his own books. And, it turns out, 32 of the 265 chemists (graduate students, mostly) *did* admit that they had used the library as a study hall. Thus our model has already predicted an extra fact, which is nicely verified by an independent piece of data, and our faith in the model is thereby strengthened.

The probabilities P_k of Eq. 2.21 can be used to calculate the average behavior of the group or class under study. Suppose P_k is the probability that k events occur. (In the present case the events are the number of tasks carried out by the visitor, but they could be the number of times a book circulates during the year or the number of persons in the library at a given instant.) The mean, or average, or *expected* value K or $E(k)$ of k is, by the definition of P_k, equal to 1 times P_1, the chance that one event occurs, plus 2 times P_2, the chance that 2 occur, plus 3 times P_3, and so on,

$$E(k) \equiv K = P_1 + 2P_2 + 3P_3 + 4P_4 + \cdots$$

In general, if each occurrence of k events brings a result $y(k)$, where $y(k)$ is some function of k, then the expected value Y or $E(y)$ of $y(k)$ is (see Eq. 2.12)

$$E(y) \equiv Y = y(0)P_0 + y(1)P_1 + y(2)P_2 + y(3)P_3 + \cdots \quad (2.24)$$

which is true for any probability distribution. The equation for K is the special case when $y(k) = k$.

We could use the data to give us the quantities $F_k = N_k/N$, where F_k is the fraction of times the event k occurred during the N observations, and then use F_k instead of P_k in Eq. 2.24 to give us an empirical value of Y for the particular set of observations. But, unless the observations are very large in number, another set of observations will yield a different empirical value of Y, because of the random nature of the events. Thus if we find a theoretical formula for P_k (as in Eq. 2.21) which fits the empirical set of F_k in one fairly large set of observations, the mean value of Y calculated (as in Eq. 2.24) from theoretical P_k is no more likely to deviate from the next measured value of Y than is the empirical value calculated from a single, finite set of observations. In many cases it is easier and more conducive of understanding to use P_k; this will be done most of the time in our discussions.

In the case of the geometric distribution of Eq. 2.21 we can use the following formulas to obtain closed forms for average values. Texts on algebra show that, as long as x is greater than -1 and smaller than $+1$,

$$1 + x + x^2 + x^3 + x^4 + \cdots = \frac{1}{1-x}$$

$$1 + 2x + 3x^2 + 4x^3 + 5x^4 + \cdots = \frac{1}{(1-x)^2}$$

(2.25)

The closed forms on the right of these equations are much easier to manipulate mathematically than is an empirical number. For example, with the set of P_k of Eq. 2.21 we can quickly check that the sum of all P_k is unity (as it must be, according to Eq. 2.4). Using the first of Eqs. 2.25, we get

$$P_0 + P_1 + P_2 + P_3 + \cdots = (1-\gamma)(1 + \gamma + \gamma^2 + \cdots)$$

$$= \frac{1-\gamma}{1-\gamma} = 1$$

Other uses of Eqs. 2.24 and 2.25 will be made shortly.

The Experimental Check

We used the rather complex formulas of Eqs. 2.23 to estimate N_0 and γ since we wished to eliminate the 35 study-hall users. Once this is done (or if we estimate that this number is small), we can compute much more easily by adjusting the model so it corresponds to the measured average or expected number of tasks performed per visit $E(k)$. The average is obtained from Eq. 2.24:

$$E(k) \equiv K = 0(P_0) + 1(P_1) + 2(P_2) + \cdots$$

$$= (1-\gamma)\gamma(1 + 2\gamma + 3\gamma^2 + \cdots) = \frac{\gamma(1-\gamma)}{(1-\gamma)^2}$$

$$= \frac{\gamma}{1-\gamma} \quad \text{or} \quad \gamma = \frac{K}{K+1}$$

(2.26)

by using the second of Eqs. 2.25. In other words if the model is valid, then there is a simple relationship between K and γ so that if the value of one is known that of the other can be computed. Since the total number of tasks (1107), divided by N_0 (230, since we exclude the 35 nonparticipants) is 4.81, this should equal K, the mean number of tasks per visit. Substituting this into Formula 2.26 we find $\gamma = 0.828$. Now we can check the accuracy of fit of our model by computing $E(N_k)$ from Eq. 2.22 and rounding off each result to the nearest integer. These are given by the numbers in the third column (Theoretical Model) in Table 2.1 and the straight line shown in Fig. 2.3. The check with the data is as good as can be expected, considering that we have only sampled 230 chemists; another 230 would not have given us exactly the same results as the first set, because of the fluctuating nature of the behavior studied. We would have had to question several thousand chemists' visits to have noticeably improved the accuracy of the data, and this would have been impractical. The data in the "tail," in Fig. 2.3 from $k = 16$ to $k = 28$, all lie somewhat higher than the model, but the discrepancy is small in actual magnitude, and it may be because the numbers involved are small and thus subject to fractionally larger fluctuation. (Another possibility will be discussed later, see page 37.)

Generalization of the Model

Thus accuracy of fit, convenience, and a certain degree of reasonableness all combine to persuade us to use the ideal model of a geometric probability distribution for the use of the library by chemists. We should, of course, see whether other users (physicists or mathematicians, for example) follow the same random use pattern, with perhaps a different value of γ. The survey provided data enough to check this, and indeed the semilog plots of N_k for these other classes of user also were close to straight lines (excluding those using the library as a study hall), with different slopes, indicating different use habits, but all in accord with the general theoretical model.

Furthermore curves drawn for the numbers of chemists (or physicists or mathematicians) who performed k or more task number 1 (i.e., consult a book in the library) during their visit also produced fairly good straight-line semilog plots (the deviations were greater because we were dealing with smaller numbers). Now it is a further characteristic of the geometrical distribution that if the various tasks are performed in a random manner this should be so; both probabilities for individual tasks, as well as probabilities for all tasks combined, should be geometrically distributed. The γ for the individual tasks are related to the expected number of times $E(k_s)$ the task is performed per visit according to Eq. 2.26.

Thus our model works as though each chemist, for example, is carrying the equivalent of a die with sides equal to one more than the number of different tasks, with probability γ_s that the sth side comes up on a throw and a final zero side with probability γ_0 equal to one minus the sum of the other γ. At each toss, if the sth side comes up, the person performs the sth task; if the zero side comes up, he leaves the library. If there are N different tasks, the probability that the person carries out n_1 tasks of class one, n_2 tasks of class two, and so on, irrespective

Table 2.2 Statistical Use Pattern of Four Classes of Users of the Science Library in January, 1955

Task	Biologists		Chemists		Mathematicians		Physicists	
	Average Number of Tasks K	Geometric Parameter γ	Average Number of Tasks K	Geometric Parameter γ	Average Number of Tasks K	Geometric Parameter γ	Average Number of Tasks K	Geometric Parameter γ
Book withdrawn	0.25	0.042	0.11	0.019	0.36	0.082	0.21	0.051
Periodical withdrawn	0.25	0.042	0.03	0.005	0.05	0.011	0.07	0.017
Report withdrawn	—	—	—	—	—	—	0.01	0.002
Book consulted	1.17	0.198	0.88	0.151	1.39	0.315	1.24	0.305
Periodical consulted	2.28	0.385	3.50	0.603	0.57	0.129	0.92	0.225
Report consulted	0.08	0.014	—	—	—	—	0.08	0.020
Catalogue consulted	0.89	0.150	0.29	0.050	1.04	0.236	0.55	0.135
Total K or $1-\gamma_0$	4.92	0.831	4.81	0.828	3.41	0.773	3.08	0.755

of the order in which the tasks are carried out, before leaving the library, is

$$P(n_1, n_2, \cdots) = \frac{(n_1 + n_2 + \cdots + n_N)!}{n_1! n_2! \cdots n_N!} (\gamma_1)^{n_1} (\gamma_2)^{n_2} \cdots (\gamma_N)^{n_N} \gamma_0 \quad (2.27)$$

where K_s is the mean number of times task s is carried out during a single visit. If we concentrate solely on task s, the probability that this task is performed n_s times, irrespective of the other N-1 tasks, is the sum of $P(n_1, n_2, \cdots)$ over all the n's except n_s. This turns out to equal $[\gamma_0/(\gamma_0 + \gamma_s)] [\gamma_s/(\gamma_0 + \gamma_s)]^{n_s}$, which corresponds to Eq. 2.21 if we set the γ of that equation (which dealt with a single task), equal to $\gamma_s/(\gamma_0 + \gamma_s)$. As before we do not propose that each user mentally carries out this die tossing before each action; we are saying that, in a situation where random choice (and random causes of change of plan) prevails, the users behave *as though* they were following this random procedure.

If we trust our model, therefore, we can describe the statistical use pattern of four of the principal users of the Science Library at M.I.T. in January 1955 in terms of the expected number K_s of tasks of the sth sort performed by each class of user (or else by the related probabilities γ_s). The survey produced the values of K_s shown in Table 2.2 and from them can be computed the γ_s, also listed.

We see here the differences in use patterns of these 4 classes of attendees. On the average, the biologists and mathematicians used the catalogue more; they also preferred to withdraw more books, for more prolonged study, than did the chemists or physicists, who presumably could more often get what they wanted by using the book while in the library. The chemists and the biologists preferred the periodical literature, at least for library consultation, in contrast to the mathematicians and physicists, who preferred to read books. The results also will have a bearing on the decisions regarding the placing of books on reserve that are to be used only in the library.

Advantages of the Model

We now can point out that the values of K, the average number of tasks of the various kinds, could have been obtained more easily than by carrying out the elaborate survey that was done. A smaller sample could have been chosen and a simpler questionnaire could have been used; conceivably the data could have been obtained by observation, without the use of a questionnaire. But the average values of K, by themselves, would not answer all the questions we may require from the data, which only the full probability distribution can answer. Only when we are persuaded that this distribution is a geometric one can we answer all questions after a measurement of K alone, otherwise we must make the much more elaborate survey, which was done at M.I.T. Only after the theoretical model is "proved out" can we use it to fill out the whole picture from average K obtained by a simpler survey.

For example, we may wish to know what fraction of chemists (or physicists, etc.) would be disappointed if we imposed the (somewhat improbable) rule that only 2 items (book, periodical, or report) could be withdrawn at a visit. This, the fraction of users, of a given class, who would expect to withdraw 3 or more items, should be equal to (N_3/N_0) for the combination of the first 3 tasks. If we did not use the theoretical model, we would have to calculate N_3 for this combination from the data obtained from a large survey. If we trust the model, we can obtain N_3 by use of Eq. 2.20. Then $(N_3/N_0) = \gamma^3$, and γ can be obtained from the K taken from a simpler survey. They are shown in Table 2.3.

Table 2.3   Powers of γ for Four Homogeneous Populations

	Biologists	Chemists	Mathematicians	Physicists
K	0.50	0.14	0.41	0.28
γ	0.333	0.123	0.300	0.225
γ^2	0.111	0.015	0.090	0.051
γ^3	0.037	0.002	0.027	0.011

Note in Table 2.2 that while the K for any combination of tasks is the sum of the K_s's, the γ for this combination must be obtained by using Eq. 2.26. This can be proved by using Eq. 2.27, after considerable manipulation of the symbols. To find the γ for the 3 first tasks, corresponding to the withdrawal of an item (book, periodical, or report), we add the first three K ($0.25 + 0.25 + 0 = 0.50$ for biologists, for example) and then calculate the corresponding γ from Eq. 2.26 (for example, $0.5/1.5 = 0.333$ for biologists). Thus by use of our model we can go from the average number of tasks K to the probability that a person would wish to take more than two items out per visit. Thus restriction of withdrawal to two items would hurt the biologists and mathematicians hardest, but even here, only about 1 biologist in 27 and 1 mathematician in 37 would be affected. On the other hand, if only 1 item per visit can be withdrawn, the fraction disappointed would be the fraction who withdraw two or more items, which our model says is γ^2. We see that 1 biologist in 9 would be affected, 1 mathematician in 11 but only 1 physicist in 20.

Still more can be deduced from the model, however. For if all those who wish to withdraw any item can only withdraw 1, the number withdrawn will be (instead of the number $N_0K = N_0\gamma/(1 - \gamma)$ of Eq. 2.26)

$$N_0(P_1 + P_2 + P_3 + \cdots) = N_0(1 - P_0) = N_0\gamma \qquad (2.28)$$

and the rate of withdrawal of items will thus be reduced by the fraction

$$1 - \frac{N_0\gamma}{N_0K} = 1 - (1 - \gamma) = \gamma \qquad (2.29)$$

Thus a limitation to 1 withdrawal per visit will affect 1 biologist in 9 but will reduce the number of items borrowed by biologists by one-third. A little further juggling of figures shows that, if the library clientele consists of equal numbers of these four classes, a rule limiting withdrawals to one item per visit would reduce the number of books out of the library, on the average, by about 25 per cent, at the expense of frustrating 1 biologist in 9, 1 chemist in 70, 1 mathematician in 11, and 1 physicist in 20. On the other hand forbidding all withdrawals would disappoint 1 biologist in 3, a similar proportion of mathematicians, 1 physicist in 4, and even 1 chemist in 8. These conclusions, and many others, cannot be obtained from data on average withdrawals K alone; they require either a full, empirical distribution, obtained from an elaborate survey, or else trust in the theoretical distribution, plus data on K alone, obtained from a much less elaborate survey.

Homogeneous Populations

But the argument just elaborated does not mean that all librarians should trust the one survey made at M.I.T. in 1955, nor should they assume that all their clientele obey the geometric distribution and thus that all they need to do is to measure average task rates K for them. In the first place the task-performance distribution for a mixture of chemists and physicists is not a geometric distribution. If equal numbers of chemists, with parameter γ_c and of physicists with parameter γ_p constituted the clientele then, if we do not distinguish between chemist and physicist, the expected number of persons who do k or more tasks will be a combination of *two* geometric distributions,

$$E(N_k) = \tfrac{1}{2}N_0(\gamma_c)^k + \tfrac{1}{2}N_0(\gamma_p)^k \qquad (2.30)$$

which does *not* have a straight-line semilog plot, if γ_c differs much from γ_p. Figure 2.4 shows such a plot for all the data gathered in the survey for all kinds of users, to compare with Fig. 2.3 for chemists. It certainly

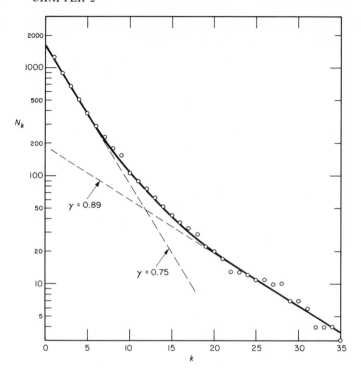

Fig. 2.4. Total task distribution for all library users sampled (dots). Solid line is sum of two geometric distributions.

cannot be represented adequately by a single straight line, as could be the plot of Fig. 2.3.

At the very least, as indicated by the lines drawn, the data can be represented crudely by about 1100 study-hall users (2700 − 1600), plus a group of about 1400 users with a γ roughly equal to 0.75, corresponding to a mean total task rate $K = 3$, plus another group of about 200 users with $\gamma = 0.89$ and thus a $K = 8$. Our analysis of four of the classes of users shows that at least some of the 2700 had a K of 3. None of the classes discussed previously had a K as large as 8, but this very studious group of at most 200 comprises less than 10 per cent of the total. We know already that the curve should be represented by more than 2 straight lines, since, included in the sample, are 230 chemists, with $K = 4.8$, $\gamma = 0.83$. But it is quite impossible to sort out, from the combined curve, all the constituent parts. The curve can separate roughly the study-hall users (the difference between the total number 2700 sampled and the intercept 1600 of the steepest straight line). This checks with the number 1100 of attendees who indicated they were using only their own books. It also can indicate that about 1600 − 1250 = 350 are persons who came to the library intending to use it as a library but who left without performing a task. This checks fairly well with the report, answering another part of the questionnaire, that about 550 items were asked for, which were not available; presumably in about 350 cases the attendees left without doing anything else. But the combined curve cannot efficiently produce the use habits of the different classes of users. Somehow the data must be separated ahead of time into the different classes, in order to get the most from the application of the theoretical model (of course the combined curve can be used directly, calculating the various quantities of interest numerically, but we then would lose the advantages enumerated in the previous pages).

We can define a *homogeneous population*, in regard to the performance of these tasks, as one which has a geometric task distribution, exhibiting a fairly straight semilog plot of N_k, as shown in Fig. 2.3. Chemists are a homogeneous group, or are nearly homogeneous (since the tail of the curve indicates the possibility of a small subgroup of about 70 with a γ of about 0.89 and a K of 8), but the whole sample of users of the Science Library is not a homogeneous population. Physicists are also a homogeneous group (since the plot of their task distribution is also a fairly straight line), but all of the graduate students do not comprise a homogeneous population (since their semilog task plot is as curved as is Fig. 2.4). Further sorting and plotting of data indicate that the graduate students already have use patterns corresponding to their specialties; the plot for chemist graduate students is a straight line, fairly parallel to that for all chemists (faculty and staff) and so on. All undergraduates is not a homogeneous group, but all freshmen and sophomores are (with a $\gamma = 0.71$, $K = 2.5$ for all tasks), and so on.

There is no infallible procedure by which to separate the data into homogeneous groups, in fact the separation is not unique; groups can be split into subgroups and groups with the same K's can be combined into supergroups. Intuition and general observation regarding various users' habits can suggest various possible subdivisions to sort out, to see whether the result is a homogeneous group. If it is, this very fact is a piece of information which may be valuable. For example we have just mentioned that the freshmen and sophomores are a fairly homogeneous group, with use habits rather different from the professional groups discussed in the previous section. Thus it is sensible at least to consider the question as to whether these habits are sufficiently different from the professional ones to warrant having a separate undergraduate library. On the other hand the chemist graduate students are close enough in their work habits, in these tasks, to those of the professional chemists that whatever will satisfy their seniors will also satisfy them.

Need for Further Surveys

The survey analyzed here was for the use of a science library by a predominantly technical clientele. It is possible that the findings are sufficiently complete to persuade librarians of other science libraries that the homogeneous groups found in this survey will also be homogeneous groups with respect to use of their library; in which case they need measure only the average use rates K for a small (50 to 100) sample of chemists, of physicists, etc., for their collection and then apply the theory. But other large surveys (1000 to 2000) must be made for other kinds of libraries and other clientele, to determine what groups are homogeneous in their library use patterns. For example, do historians differ from philologists or may all specialists in the humanities be included in a homogeneous group, with a straight-line, semilog plot of tasks common to all? Are economists the same, in regard to library use, as sociologists, or must they be considered as a separate group? And so on. When these relatively few large surveys are made, to supplement the results of the survey analyzed here, it will then be possible to determine how to separate the clientele of any particular library into homogeneous groups, to obtain expected use rates K for each group by means of much smaller surveys, made in the particular library, and then to use the theoretical model for each group to determine the details of attendee use behavior for guidance in management decisions, as was illustrated in the preceding section.

Length of Stay

A discussion of the distribution of lengths of stay in the library, a rather less interesting statistic, will nevertheless serve to introduce some concepts of use later. Records were taken of the times of arrival and departure of all participants in the M.I.T. survey. The times of arrival showed some periodicity, both daily and weekly, obviously correlated with the scheduling of classes. One might expect that the total length of stay in the library would have similar periodicity; the data, as displayed in Figs. 2.5 and 2.6, show little periodicity; there is a small dip in the curves at 60 minutes and at 120 minutes, but the dips are quite small. Indeed the pattern (for a homogeneous group) turns out to follow

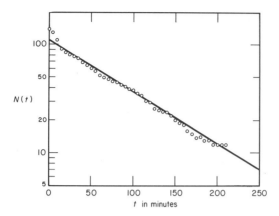

Fig. 2.5. Number $N(t)$ of graduate students staying in library longer than t minutes, from 30 per cent sample of data. Solid line is plot of function $110e^{-t/100}$.

the geometrical distribution characteristic of the use pattern discussed earlier. If we neglect the small hourly dips, the expected number of attendees, of a given homogeneous group, who stay in the library *longer* than t minutes is

$$E[N(t)] = N(0)a^t \qquad (2.31)$$

where a is a fraction, less than unity, characteristic of the group and analogous to the γ of Eq. 2.20. This is graphically illustrated by the semilog plot Fig. 2.5 of the stay interval for all graduate students. Evidently graduate students are a homogeneous group with respect to length of stay. Evidently also the random factors that produced the geometrical distribution of numbers of tasks performed also operates with respect to the "task" of leaving the library.

Since t is continuous, it is more convenient to write $a = e^{-1/\tau}$, where $e = 2.718$ is the base of the natural logarithms so that $(1/\tau) = -\ln a$ ($\ln a$ = natural log of a). Thus, we can write the formula for the expected number of persons staying longer than t minutes as

$$E[N(t)] = N(0)(e^{-1/\tau})^t = N(0)e^{-t/\tau} \qquad (2.32)$$

where τ now turns out to be the mean length of stay of the homogeneous group under consideration. Thus, again, for a group we have verified as being homogeneous (i.e., which we or someone else has shown has a straight-line semilog plot for length of stay), we need determine only the mean length of stay of the group to be able to apply the theoretical distribution (in this form called the *exponential distribution*) to compute other characteristics of the group's occupancy. The quantity

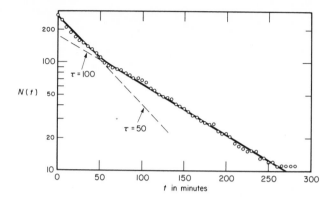

Fig. 2.6.   Number of users of all kinds staying longer than t minutes, from 30 per cent sample of data. Dots are from survey data. Solid line is plot of distribution of Eqs. 2.33.

$[N(t)/N(0)] = e^{-t/\tau}$ is the fraction of this group which stays longer than t minutes. Table 2.4 provides a short table of exponentials for

Table 2.4   Values of the Negative Exponential e^{-x}

x	e^{-x}	x	e^{-x}	x	e^{-x}
0	1.000	1.0	0.368	2.0	0.135
0.2	0.819	1.2	0.301	2.5	0.082
0.4	0.670	1.4	0.247	3.0	0.050
0.5	0.607	1.5	0.223	3.5	0.030
0.6	0.549	1.6	0.202	4.0	0.018
0.8	0.449	1.8	0.165	5.0	0.007

reference. The mean stay of the graduate students' sample, plotted in Fig. 2.5, is about 100 minutes. Thus about two-thirds of the group stay longer than 40 minutes ($x = t/\tau = 0.4$), somewhat less than a third of them stay longer than 2 hours ($x = 1.2$) and 1 in 20 of them stays longer than 5 hours ($x = 3$). We again ignore absurd extremes of the model, which would pretend that a small fraction of 1 student would stay longer than 24 hours.

Of course if we plot a sample consisting of two or more differing homogeneous groups the semilog plot will not be a straight line. For example, Fig. 2.6 shows the plot of a random sample of all users of the library. It is not a straight line, but, as the solid line shows, it can be represented fairly accurately by the combination of two distributions

$$E[N(t)] = 105e^{-t/50} + 170e^{-t/100} \qquad (2.33)$$

which is plotted as the solid line, for a comparison with the dots, obtained from the data. The dips at 60 and 120 minutes are somewhat more pronounced than with Fig. 2.5, but in general the curve can be represented by two straight lines as the formula suggests. This would indicate that the attendees can be divided into two homogeneous groups, in regard to length of stay, one group consisting of about 40 per cent (105/275) of the total having a mean stay of about 50 minutes and the other 60 per cent (170/275) having a mean stay of about 100 minutes (identical with the mean stay of the graduate-student group). Since we have already concluded that about 40 per cent of the attendees of the Science Library at M.I.T. were using it not as a library but as a study hall, we are tempted to say that the group with 50 minutes mean stay (just less than one class period) are the study-hall group and that the homogeneous group with mean stay 100 minutes consists of those who are actually using the facilities of the library. This hypothesis is strengthened by the fact that a plot of other groups which we would expect to be homogeneous (such as the chemists, mathematicians, etc.) also display roughly straight-line plots with mean times clustering around 100 minutes. Thus we conclude that the study-hall users are a homogeneous group with mean stay of about 50 minutes and all the rest, the true library users, are also a homogeneous group with respect to stay (though not with respect to tasks performed, as we have seen), with mean stay of about 100 minutes. This does not mean that all true library users stay 100 minutes, in fact the exponential distribution predicts that 10 per cent of them will stay less than 10 minutes and another 10 per cent will stay longer than 4 hours. In fact the exponential model predicts in some detail the degree of variability of the duration of stay.

One interesting and useful property of the exponential distribution is that if n persons are in the library at any instant and if they constitute a homogeneous population with respect to stay, with mean length of stay τ minutes, then the mean rate of persons *leaving* the library at that instant is (n/τ) people per minute. With any other distribution, one would have to know how long the persons had been in the library before he could compute the rate of leaving. With the exponential distribution some leave quickly, some stay a long time and the leaving is such that the rate does not depend on their previous length of stay (as long as they are still in the library). Thus $(1/\tau)$, which we will occasionally write as μ, can be called the *mean rate of leaving* of members of the group. For actual users of the Science Library this rate was 1 per

100 minutes, so if 100 users were present in the library at some time, 1 user would be leaving each minute on the average. If n_1 persons of Group 1, with mean rate $\mu_1 = (1/\tau_1)$, and n_2 persons of Group 2, with $\mu_2 = (1/\tau_2)$, and so on, are all present in the library at a given time, then the expected total rate of leaving will be, where S is the number leaving per minute,

$$S = n_1\mu_1 + n_2\mu_2 + \cdots \tag{2.34}$$

This formula will be useful later.

3 Arrivals and the Poisson Distribution

The occurrence of clicks in a Geiger counter exposed to radioactivity (or, less accurately, the arrival of 5th Avenue buses at 42nd Street) is an example of events occurring at random in time. There is a certain average rate of occurrence; on the average λ of them, say, will occur per minute. But the time intervals between successive occurrences will vary considerably; some of them will be short, the clicks coming rapidly one after another, then there will be occasionally long pauses. It is an interesting example of the way the theory of probability "hangs together" that the distribution of lengths of these intervals is just the exponential distribution we have been discussing in connection with the distribution of lengths of stay. If we measure the durations of each of N sequential intervals between successive occurrences then, if these occurrences are truly randomly distributed in time, the expected number $E[n(t)]$ of these intervals that are longer than t minutes will be given by

$$E[n(t)] = Ne^{-t/\tau} \tag{3.1}$$

where $\tau = 1/\lambda$, which is just the exponential distribution of Eq. 2.32. Parameter τ is just the mean time between occurrences; its reciprocal λ is called the "mean rate" at which they occur. (Note, however, that λ is *not* the mean value of the reciprocals of the intervals; it is the reciprocal of the mean interval. Thus strictly speaking it should not be called the mean rate.)

43

Random Arrivals

The arrival of attendees to a library very likely is distributed exponentially in time. On the average, during a given hour, λ attendees will arrive per minute; sometimes they will arrive in bunches, sometimes singly, sometimes no one will arrive for a while. Thus there is reasonable expectation that the distribution of interarrival intervals is exponential, in line with Eq. 3.1. Every detailed measurement of arrival distributions, whether of customers coming to a store, of automobiles arriving at a toll booth, or of telephone subscribers dialing a new number, displays an exponential distribution of interarrival intervals, within the degree of accuracy attained by the measured data. More accurate surveys simply result in better correspondence. Thus we can confidently assume that the successive intervals between arrivals at the library are distributed exponentially.

Of course the distribution holds, in its simplest form of Eq. 3.1, only during periods when the "mean arrival rate" λ is constant. To compare periods of time with different arrival rates, we should use the appropriate value of λ (obtained from the appropriate value of τ) for each period separately.

The consequences of these conclusions are manifold. For example, reference to Table 2.4 shows that if, for example, the mean arrival rate λ is equal to 1 per minute over a period of time, nearly a fifth of the arrivals in that period will come sooner than 12 seconds after the previous arrival ($t/\tau = 0.2$; $1 - 0.819 = 0.181 \simeq 1/5$) and, in 1 case out of 20, the interval between arrivals will be 3 minutes or longer ($t/\tau = 3$; $0.050 = 1/20$). Furthermore, because of the likelihood of short, as well as long, interarrival intervals, the mean number of arrivals in a short interval of time (Δt) within the period of constant λ will be $\lambda(\Delta t)$, independent of which interval in the period is measured, in the beginning or anywhere later, as long as the interval length is Δt. This is in contrast to the case of regular arrivals, spaced $\tau = (1/\lambda)$ apart, when, if the interval is short and between the regular arrivals, no arrivals are to be expected. With the exponential distribution there is *no* regularity; arrivals are as likely to occur at one time as at any other.

This, together with the facts of visitors' length of stay, makes it possible to predict the number of persons in the library at any time during the day, given the history of arrivals for the day. First we note that the mean number of attendees entering the library in a time Δt is $\lambda(t)\,\Delta t$, where $\lambda(t)$ is the mean rate of arrival at time t (as noted in the previous paragraph, this is true only when arrivals are random). Next we state that it can be proved by the same arguments that when $N(t)$ persons are in the library at time t and if these belong to a homogeneous population with respect to duration of stay (exponential stay distribution) with mean stay $\tau = (1/\mu)$, then the mean number of persons leaving the library in an interval of time Δt at time t is $\mu N(t) \Delta t$, a quantity proportional to $N(t)$ and also to Δt.

Arrival, Departure, and Number in Library

Thus we can set up an equation relating the rate of change of $N(t)$, the expected number of attendees in the library at time t, of a given homogeneous group, with the rate of arrival λ of members of this group and their "rate of departure" $\mu = (1/\tau)$; (τ is the mean length of stay, $\mu = 1/\tau$ is the mean "rate" at which members of the group terminate their stay). The rate of change of N is

$$\frac{dN}{dt} = \lambda(t) - \mu N(t) \tag{3.2}$$

The solution of this equation, for the number in the library a time t minutes after it has opened its doors, may be written in the shorthand formulation of an integral,

$$N(t) = \int_0^t \lambda(u) \, e^{-(t-u)/\tau} \, du \tag{3.3}$$

which states that the contribution, to the number present at time t after opening, of the entrances and departures that took place at time u after opening (u less than t) is equal to the number $\lambda(u) \, du$ that entered during the instant du, attenuated by the exponential factor $e^{-(t-u)/\tau} = e^{-(t-u)\mu}$ representing the fraction of those, who entered at time u, who still are in the library a time interval ($t - u$) later (see Eq. 2.32). Of course Eq. 3.2 and its solution deal in expected values, and expected values of $N(t)$ can have fractional values instead of being restricted to integers. This formulation is not a bad approximation if $N(t)$ is large; later in this chapter we shall see what happens when we have to consider the random fluctuations of arrival and departure.

This equation can be solved for any specified variation of arrival rate $\lambda(t)$ with t. Figure 3.1 shows an example, for a population with mean stay $\tau = 100$ minutes (the population of users of the M.I.T. Science Library if study-hall users are disbarred). Suppose the library opens at 10 AM, and closes at 8 PM, 10 hours (or 600 minutes) later. Suppose the mean arrival rate $\lambda(t)$ is 1 per minute from 9:00 to 12:30 ($t = 0$ to $t = 150$), is 1 every 2 minutes from 12:30 to 4:40 ($t = 150$ to 400), is again 1 per minute from 4:40 to 6:20 ($t = 400$ to 500), and no

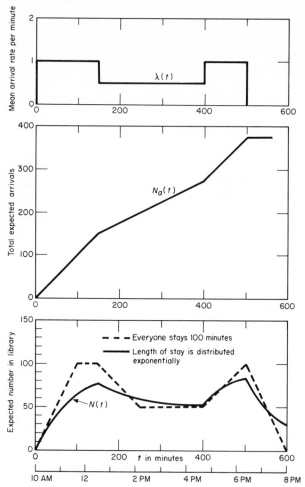

Fig. 3.1. Expected number in library $N(t)$ at time t after opening when length of stay is distributed exponentially.

one arrives from 6:20 to closing time. The rate of arrival $\lambda(t)$ is plotted at the top of Fig. 3.1, reproducing what has just been specified in words. The total number of arrivals, counting from the opening of the library, is shown in the middle plot (the slope of this curve equals λ); a total of 375 users will have gone through the entrance door by the end of the day.

The lower plot, solid line $N(t)$, is the solution, Eq. 3.3, for this case. We have assumed random arrivals and an exponential stay distribution to obtain Eq. 3.3, so these are the assumptions for the solid line to be appropriate. The number in the library rises initially by 1 per minute, since initially few are present and thus few leave. The curve for $N(t)$ begins to flatten out soon, because more and more leave as N increases. If the arrival rate of 1 per minute continued all day the curve for N would reach a horizontal limit of 100 persons in the library (1 entering each minute just equals $n/\tau = 100/100 = 1$ leaving each minute, on the average). In fact the "steady-state" number in the library if λ stays constant for a long time is

$$N_{st} = \frac{\lambda}{\mu} = \lambda\tau \qquad (3.4)$$

But the library population does not reach steady state since $\lambda(t)$ drops to $1/2$ at $t = 150$, before n flattens out completely. It then sinks back to the new steady-state value of $(1/2)\ 100 = 50$, which it nearly reaches by $t = 400$. The population then rises in conformity with the increase in arrival rate and then falls toward zero after $t = 500$, when no more enter. By $t = 600$ about 40 late stayers will have to leave before they are ready to leave. The solid curve is the predicted population at time t; because attendance and stay are random occurrences, the actual population will fluctuate a bit above or below this prediction, but the discrepancy will seldom be more than about 5 persons and rarely more than 10, as will be shown shortly.

We see that the statistical nature of arrivals and departures tends to smooth out the rise and fall of the library population. Each piece of the plot is a part of an exponential curve, approaching the steady-state value. Increases and decreases of arrival rate are not immediately felt inside the library, it takes several hundred minutes (about 3τ) for $N(t)$ to settle down to its steady-state value N_{st}, and if λ changes before that $N(t)$ never does settle down.

To show the effect of the random nature of duration of stay, the dashed line in the lower plot of Fig. 3.1 shows the library population $N(t)$ if every attendee stayed exactly 100 minutes and then left. During the first 100 minutes no one is leaving, so $N(t)$ is equal to $N_a(t)$, the total number of arrivals. From $t = 100$ to $t = 150$ as many leave as enter, so $N(t)$ is constant at the steady-state value (Eq. 3.4 holds whether arrivals or departures are random or regular). After $t = 150$ the arrival rate decreases but the departure rate does not, so $N(t)$ decreases until it reaches the new steady-state value 100 minutes later, and so on. Since no one enters during the last 100 minutes, by 8 PM all attendees have just left and none curtailed their visit. This dashed curve seems less likely to fit the actual situation than the solid curve.

Solutions for a population comprised of several different, homogeneous groups can be worked out by dealing with each separately, with their different arrival rates and durations of stay, and then adding the results together.

The Poisson Distribution

It often is easier to measure the number of arrivals occurring in a specified interval of time Δt than it is to measure the time spans between successive interarrivals. A most useful consequence of the exponential distribution of random arrivals can be demonstrated by mathematical manipulation of Eq. 3.1. The results are as follows. We have just stated that if arrivals are at random with a mean arrival rate λ, the mean or *expected* number of arrivals in a time interval Δt is $\lambda(\Delta t) = N$, independent of the exact time when the interval starts. But an actual series of measurements of the number of arrivals in Δt would not always result in the value N; in fact N is not usually an integer, whereas the number actually recorded during each interval Δt would be an integer, sometimes smaller and sometimes larger than N. All we can say is that if we repeat the measurement enough times, and if the arrivals are truly random, with constant mean rate λ, then the *average* value of our individual measurements should approach the value N as we increase the number of measurements. Furthermore, we can predict the frequency of occurrence of different numbers of arrivals in time Δt. Using Eq. 3.1, we can show that the probability that n arrivals actually occur in a time interval, for which the expected number of arrivals is N, is

$$P_n(N) = \frac{N^n}{n!} \, e^{-N} \qquad (3.5)$$
$$P_0 + P_1 + P_2 + \cdots = 1$$

where $n! = 1 \times 2 \times 3 \cdots (n - 1) \times n$ is called *n factorial*. This probability distribution is called the *Poisson distribution*. It has many applications.

Let us tabulate a few such distributions for different values of the expected number N in Table 3.1. Note the wide spread of these frequencies of occurrence. For an interval in which the arrivals will average to 2, 2 arrivals would actually occur only about a quarter of the time, no arrivals will occur in one-seventh of the intervals measured, and 4 arrivals will occur 1 in 11 times. The probabilities are largest for n near the mean value N, but the peak is pretty broad.

The expected value of n for the distribution is of course (see Eq. 2.12)

$$0(P_0) + 1(P_1) + 2(P_2) + 3(P_3) + \cdots = N \equiv E(n) \qquad (3.6)$$

Table 3.1 Poisson Probability $P_n(N)$ that n Events Occur When the Expected Number of Random Occurrences is N

n	$N = 0.5$	1.0	1.5	2.0	3.0	4.0
0	0.61	0.37	0.22	0.14	0.05	0.02
1	0.30	0.37	0.34	0.27	0.15	0.07
2	0.08	0.19	0.25	0.27	0.23	0.14
3	0.01	0.06	0.13	0.18	0.22	0.20
4		0.01	0.05	0.09	0.17	0.20
5			0.01	0.04	0.10	0.16
6				0.01	0.05	0.10
7					0.02	0.06
8					0.01	0.03
9						0.01
10						0.01

A measure of the "spread" of the distribution is the mean-square deviation of the individual measurement from the mean value (see Eq. 2.13)

$$\sigma^2 = (0 - N)^2 P_0 + (1 - N)^2 P_1 + (2 - N)^2 P_2 + (3 - N)^2 P_3 + \cdots$$
$$= 0(P_0) + 1(P_1) + 4(P_2) + 9(P_3) + 16(P_4) + \cdots - N^2 \qquad (3.7)$$

which is called the *variance* of the distribution. For the Poisson distribution the *variance equals the mean*,

$$\sigma^2 = N \qquad (3.8)$$

uniquely for this distribution. The square root of the variance, σ itself, is called the *standard deviation* of the distribution. Roughly two-thirds of the time the individual measurement falls within the limits $N \pm \sigma$ and roughly one-third of the measurements are either larger than $N + \sigma$ or smaller than $N - \sigma$. For the Poisson distribution, the standard deviation is the square root of the mean value, $\sigma = \sqrt{N}$. The value of σ for any distribution is the number which often is added, with a plus or minus sign, after the mean value, to indicate the degree of variation that can be expected in the individual measurements. The mean value for the Poisson distribution could thus be written $N \pm \sqrt{N}$. The *fractional deviation*, (σ/N), is thus $1/\sqrt{N}$ for the Poisson distribution, a quantity that diminishes, but slowly, as N increases.

Thus if the interval of time Δt is small, so the mean number of arrivals in each Δt is only about 1, the occurrence of 0 or 2 arrivals per interval is nearly as likely as the occurrence of 1 (see Table 3.1). But if the mean number is 4, for example, the occurrence of 0 or 8 is much less likely, the "spread" is ±2, only half the mean value. Thus, for $N = 3$, 62 per cent $(0.23 + 0.27 + 0.22)$ of the measurements result in 2, 3, or 4; 38 per cent of the time the measurement will either be larger than $3 + 1.7$ or smaller than $3 - 1.7$. When $N = 1$, the standard deviation is also 1, so half of the 0 should be considered to be "outside" the limit 1 ± 1 and half inside; similarly with the 2. Thus, from Table 3.1, $37 + (1/2)(37 + 19) = 65$ per cent of the measurements can be considered to be "within" the range 1 ± 1.

When N is larger than 15 or 20, an approximate formula for $P_n(N)$ is, for $N > 15$,

$$P_n(N) \simeq \frac{1}{\sqrt{2\pi N}} \exp\left[\frac{-(n - N^2)}{2N}\right] \tag{3.9}$$

which is fairly accurate over a range of n from about $N - 2\sigma$ to $N + 2\sigma$, with $\sigma = \sqrt{N}$ as required by Eq. 3.8. From this we can calculate that, for large expected numbers of arrivals, the probability that n is larger than $N + \sigma$ is roughly $1/6$, that it is less than $N - \sigma$ is equally about $1/6$, and the chance that the actual number of arrivals in the interval Δt between $N - \sigma$ and $N + \sigma$ is about $2/3$. To the degree of approximation of Eq. 3.9, there is an even chance that n is larger than N or that it is smaller than N.

An Example

But an actual example, worked out in detail, will best illustrate these generalities. A radioactive source and Geiger counter were set up so the mean count was exactly 3 per minute. The radioactive source was used because it is known to produce a perfect Poisson distribution, but the clicks could just as well represent purely random arrivals to a library, with an expected rate of 3 per minute. Counts were made of the number of "arrivals" in each of 50 consecutive minutes, and the results are tabulated here

Counts for Individual Minutes	N	σ^2	
2, 1, 4, 4, 4, 8, 5, 3, 0, 3	3.4	4.4	for first row
2, 3, 0, 4, 3, 2, 2, 2, 1, 3	2.8	3.2	for first 2 rows (3.10)
6, 2, 7, 2, 1, 2, 1, 6, 5, 2			
3, 2, 4, 5, 4, 2, 3, 0, 6, 4			
2, 1, 1, 4, 3, 0, 4, 4, 3, 4	2.98	3.26	for all 5 rows

Because of the wide variability of the results, a quick glance gives no good estimate as to the mean number of arrivals per minute, or even as to the most likely number; zero occurs nearly as often as 1 or as 6, and 3 occurs a little less often than 2 or 4. The mean value of the first row of figures is 3.4, of the first two rows is 2.8, of all 5 rows is 2.98, approaching the expected value $N = 3.0$ closer as the number of measurements increases.

Let us see whether we can decide whether this distribution of arrivals per minute is really Poisson. We count the frequency of occurrence of the different integers in the sample and divide by the number in the sample, to obtain a relative frequency F_n to compare with the ideal probabilities $P_n(3)$ of Table 3.1. This is tabulated, for the first row, for the first 2 rows and finally for all 50 measurements.

$n =$	0	1	2	3	4	5	6	7	8	
F_n	0.10	0.10	0.10	0.20	0.30	0.10	0	0	0.10	first row
F_n	0.10	0.10	0.25	0.20	0.20	0.05	0	0	0.05	first 2 rows (3.11)
F_n	0.08	0.12	0.24	0.18	0.22	0.06	0.06	0.02	0.02	all 5 rows
$P_n(3)$	0.05	0.15	0.23	0.22	0.17	0.10	0.05	0.02	0.01	theoretical

The correspondence with P_n for the ten numbers in the first row is not too good, there are more 4's than there are 3's and there are as many 0's as 2's or 8's. But the correspondence gets better as the number of measurements is increased, from the first 2 rows to all 5 rows.

A rough-and-ready test as to whether the distribution is Poisson or not is whether the variance is equal to the mean. Let us compute the variance of the results. Taking the first row only, the sum of the squares of the figures is 160, so the mean square of these 10 n is 16. Since the formula for σ^2 indicates it is equal to the mean square minus the square of the mean (which for the first row is $3.4^2 = 11.6$), the variance for the first row is $16.0 - 11.6 = 4.4$, as indicated to the right of the row in Eq. 3.10. This is not equal to 3.4, but 10 measurements are not enough for accuracy. As indicated in Table 3.2, the variance 3.2 for the first 2 rows is closer to the mean 2.8 and the variance 3.26 for all 5 rows is still closer to the mean value 2.98. We thus are justified in deciding that the distribution is Poisson and that the "arrivals" are random. Thereafter we need measure only average rates of arrival λ; we can produce the corresponding distribution from Eqs. 3.5 and 3.8 and Table 3.1.

General Properties of the Poisson Distribution

The Poisson distribution can be generalized in several ways. In the first place if two different groups (say faculty and students) each arrive at random, with mean arrival rates λ_f for the faculty and λ_s for the students, the expected number of students arriving in an interval of time Δt and the probability that n arrive in time Δt are given by the Poisson distribution $P_n(\lambda_s \Delta t)$; similarly for the faculty, using λ_f instead of λ_s. But in addition, if we make no distinction between student or faculty, the mean rate of arrival of either is the sum $N = (\lambda_s + \lambda_f)\,\Delta t$ and these arrivals *have a Poisson distribution* given by $P_n(N)$, where N is the sum of the expected arrivals of the two classes. A sum of two Poisson distributions equals a Poisson distribution.

In addition, if the rate of arrival varies with time during the interval Δt over which the arrivals are measured, the Poisson distribution still holds when we use for N the product of Δt and the *mean* rate of arrival λ, averaged over the interval. For example, in the middle plot of Fig. 3.1, the expected number of arrivals between $t = 390$ and $t = 410$ is 20 which is Δt, times the average value of λ, $\frac{1}{2}(\frac{1}{2} + 1) = \frac{3}{4}$, or 15 arrivals expected in the 20-minute interval; thus the probability that n persons actually will enter in that interval is P_n (15). From the plot one can see that N also can be read as the difference between N_a (410) and N_a (390), which is $(285 - 270 = 15)$.

Furthermore the Poisson distribution also determines the fluctuations in the number in the library in the lower plot of Fig. 3.1. The solid line for $N(t)$ on the lower plot of Fig. 3.1 actually represents a mean or *expected* value for the number in the room. Because both arrivals and departures are random events the actual number in the room will fluctuate about this mean value; it can be proved that the actual figures will vary in accord with the Poisson distribution. Thus some estimate can be made regarding the chance of deviation from the plot for $N(t)$ of Fig. 3.1, or for similar curves for other similar situations.

For example, suppose the library considered in Fig. 3.1 has 75 chairs for attendees. At $t = 110$, $t = 190$, $t = 430$, and at $t = 520$ the expected number $N(t)$ in the library is approximately 67. For the Poisson distribution the standard deviation σ of this number (the square root of its variance) is equal to the square root of the mean, the expected number $N(t)$. Since $\sqrt{67}$ is approximately 8, our earlier discussion leads us to predict that in about 1 time out of 6 when the expected number is 67, the actual number present would be larger than $67 + 8 = 75$. Thus on 1 day out of 6 at 11:50, at 1:10, 5:10, and at 6:40 there would be more than 75 persons present in the library and some would have to stand. At $t = 150$, 450, and 510 the expected number $N(t)$ is 75; we would expect that in half of the days at this time the actual number would be less than 75 (everyone could sit) and in the other half there would be more people than chairs. At $t = 500$, when $N(t)$ is 84, the standard deviation is $\sqrt{84} \simeq 9$, in only 1 case out of 6 would the actual number present be less than $84 - 9 = 75$, 5 days out of 6 there would not be enough chairs at that time.

Thus, except for the interval between 5:30 PM and 6:30 PM, when $N(t)$ is greater than 75, there is always a better than even chance that there will be chairs for everyone in the library. On the other hand, if there were only 50 chairs in the library, the only times when the chance of unoccupied chairs would be better than even is during the first 70 minutes and the last 50 minutes of the day; around noon and around 6:00 PM the chance of there being more chairs than people would be very small.

The following conclusion might seem paradoxical, at first sight. In Fig. 3.1, at 10:30 AM, N_a is shown equal to 30 and $N(t)$ is approximately 25. According to our discussion, there is 1 chance in 6 that the actual number present in the library at 10:30 is more than $25 + \sqrt{25} = 30$. However, the N_a curve shows that only 30 are expected to have entered the library by then (and, on the average, 5 of them have already left). How then could there be more than 30 present that early in the day? Of course the answer is that N_a also is an expected value, on some days more than 30 will have entered by 10:30, in fact in $1/6$ of the days more than $30 + \sqrt{30} \simeq 35$ would have come in by 10:30. On some of *these* days, less than 5 would have left by 10:30, but on some other days less than 35 will have entered, fewer than 5 would have left. The result of all these possible fluctuations is the probability $1/6$ that the actual number in the library at 10:30 is more than 30.

4 Queues and Book Circulation Interference

In many situations, some of them connected with library operations, people have to line up, either in person or by proxy, to wait to have some service performed. People have to queue up to buy tickets, automobiles queue up to pay bridge tolls, airplanes "stack up" to land in bad weather, and customers sometimes have to wait until a store inventory is replenished. There are queues, actual or potential, in the library. Users sometimes have to wait in line to have their books checked out or to speak to the reference librarian; if a popular book is out on loan, several prospective readers may be waiting its return. Queuing theory, the probabilistic analysis of such situations, has become a powerful tool in the study of many industrial and merchandising operations; it can also be useful in the study of library operations and can provide criteria for evaluating some library procedures. It can even help us estimate the number of persons who tried to use a book but could not because someone else was using it, an important quantity that measures the degree to which the library is failing to serve its public.

Description of a Queuing Situation

The parameters of major importance in determining the characteristics of a queuing situation are λ, the expected arrival rate of the persons desiring service, and μ, the expected service rate, where $1/\mu = \tau$ is the mean time per service of one person when the service facility is working continuously. Of course when the arrival rate λ is greater than μ the service rate, for any appreciable length of time, the situation is unstable; the queue builds up continually, and arrivals either must be turned away or the service rate must somehow be made greater than λ. But even if λ is less than μ, a queue will occasionally form if arrivals and/or service are randomly distributed. If arrivals are Poisson distributed, they tend to arrive in bunches, sometimes arriving momentarily faster than the service facility can accommodate, when a queue will form, and sometimes with a long gap between, when the service facility can rest. Thus the service facility has *busy* periods when one or more persons are served sequentially (as soon as service is completed for one person, service is started on the next one if one is waiting), separated by *idle* periods. The fraction of the total time during which the service facility is busy is called the *utilization factor* for the queuing system.

Other determining characteristics of such systems are, of course, the statistical properties of the arrivals and of the service times. We have already discussed the statistics of arrival; it is usually that of the Poisson distribution discussed in the previous chapter, the interarrival times being distributed exponentially, as are the lengths of stay shown in Fig. 2.5 and specified in Eq. 2.32. The service time distribution, measuring the variability of the length of time taken to service one person, can be expressed in terms of the probability $P_s(t)$ that a service time takes longer than time t to complete. This probability would be unity for $t = 0$ (all service times are longer than zero time) and would diminish as t increases, going to zero for t larger than some upper limit (no service times would be longer than this limit). In a large number of cases this distribution also is exponential; $P_s(t)$ turns out to be equal to $e^{-\mu t} = e^{-t/\tau}$ (as in Eq. 2.32). Some service times are short, some long; their average length is $\tau = 1/\mu$ and their standard deviation σ_s (see Eqs. 2.13 and 3.7) would be equal to this average length $1/\mu$ *if* the service time is exponential.

Another characteristic of the queuing situation is called the *queue discipline*, whether people are served in the order they arrived (first come, first served) or whether they are served at random or otherwise makes a difference in the variance of the time persons spend waiting in queue, but it seldom makes any difference in the average length of wait. If instability is threatened, the service rate of the single facility may be increased or else another, separate facility may be opened (a second ticket window, or another runway at the airport, for instance). The separate facilities, each carrying out the same service function, in parallel with the others, are called *service channels*. Separate queues can form in front of each channel or, what is more efficient, each channel can draw from one master queue as soon as it finishes with the previous service. Note that the sequential stations in a cafeteria are *not* parallel service channels, since everyone must pass every station and each station serves a different item; they are an example of service facilities *in tandem*, a different and more difficult problem of little interest to us.

Finally the arrivals, desiring service, may either be compelled to go through a service channel before leaving (as would be the case with an inspection station in a library or a toll booth at the end of a bridge) or else they may be free to refuse to queue up if they have to wait or if the queue is too long (this is called *balking*). Or they may be somewhat less impatient, leaving after waiting a while, if the wait seems to be too long (this is called *reneging*). In addition the queue order may be manipulated by giving some persons *priority* over others in getting service. Some of these situations will not result in queues, and for this reason it has been proposed to call the subject the theory of systems with variable supply and demand. But this title is too long, and the general theory is customarily called queuing theory, even though some of the "queuing systems" have no queues.

We have already considered one such queuing system, the library as a whole. Users arrive at a mean rate λ, they stay in the library (and are thus served) for a variable length of time and then leave at a mean rate μ per person. Since every person entering is being served, the library as a whole behaves as though it had an unlimited number of parallel service channels, no queue ever forms (unless there is a guard). Nevertheless because of the random nature of the arrivals and of the length of stay (the service time), the number of persons in the library at any time may vary in a random manner, and we must express our predictions in terms of mean values, variances (or standard deviations), and probability distributions. This we have done in Eqs. 3.3, 3.4, and 3.5 and Fig. 3.1.

But inside the library there are other queuing situations. Obvious ones are those at the inspection station and at the book-withdrawal desk. Less obvious but more important ones have to do with the fact that users may wish to borrow a book already borrowed by someone else, or have to do with the queue of new books waiting to be catalogued, or with the queue of requests for new books waiting to be processed into orders. The general characteristics of many of these can be described in terms of a single, simple, ideal model. The behavior of a few will require more complex models.

The quantities of interest to the administrator are the average length of queue, the mean time a person spends in the system, first in queue then in service, the relative advantages of having one fast, single-service channel versus having m channels, each $1/m$th as fast, the utilization factor for the service channels and, for cases when the arrival rate changes with time, the *relaxation time*, the time required for the system to return to steady state.

The Simplest Queuing System

The simplest model of a queuing system that is applicable to many library situations is the one of a single service channel, with exponentially distributed service times (analogous to Eq. 2.32) with mean service time τ and service rate $\mu = (1/\tau)$ for all arrivals. The arrivals are random, with a Poisson distribution corresponding to a mean arrival rate, λ, and every arrival must stay in queue until serviced (no balking or reneging). The queue discipline of first come, first served is usually assumed but, as mentioned earlier, this detail matters little. Such a model corresponds fairly well with the line that forms at the outgoing circulation desk and the inspection station, and also with the book-cataloguing and book-ordering operations. In the first two cases the service times are sufficiently variable so that an exponential service distribution is not a bad approximation; we will see that greater uniformity in service times does not change the essential characteristics of the operation, as long as arrivals are random.

If the mean arrival rate λ is greater than the mean service rate μ, the system is unstable, as was pointed out earlier; the queue will continually lengthen until steps are taken to speed up service or reduce arrivals. Even if λ is smaller than μ, a queue will occasionally form because of the variability of service and arrivals, but there will also be times when the service facility is idle. In fact, if all arrivals must eventually be serviced (i.e., if there is no balking or reneging) the fraction of time the service facility is busy, the utilization factor ρ is equal to the ratio λ/μ between the arrival and the service rates, as long as λ is less than μ. To demonstrate this, we note that there will be, on the average, λT arrivals in a time interval T; to serve each arrival requires a time $1/\mu = \tau$, on the average; to serve all of them will keep the service channel busy an aggregate length of time λT times $1/\mu = T(\lambda/\mu)$; the rest of the time interval T the channel is idle, on the average. In other words, the expected fraction of the time the service channel is busy is $\rho = \lambda/\mu$.

Parenthetically, we should point out that some of the service channels in the library may not be truly idle during the so-called idle period; they may have alternative tasks. For example, the service provided to the library user by the circulation desk is the check-out of the borrower's books and the collection of the book cards, but when they are not serving the user the circulation staff may be filing book cards and making out overdue notices. We can analyze this multiple-duty activity in detail if need be. However in the present discussion, we are concerned with just one activity and will neglect other possible duties. From this point of view, the service performed by the circulation desk, for instance, is the checking out of books; when the desk is not doing this it is idle. This simplification is justifiable if the other duties do not interfere with book check-out.

The mean length of each idle period is $1/\lambda$, the mean interval of time between arrivals; if the service channel finishes service on a person when no one else is waiting in queue, it will wait, on the average, a time $1/\lambda$ before a new arrival turns up to be serviced. Between these *idle* periods are the *busy* periods, when the service channel is serving one or more persons consecutively until it again runs out of customers. The fraction of time the facility is busy, the ratio $\lambda/\mu = \rho$, which is the ratio between mean service time $1/\mu$ and mean interarrival time $1/\lambda$, must equal the ratio between the mean length τ_b of a busy period and the mean length of a busy-idle cycle, the sum $\tau_b + (1/\lambda)$. Therefore the mean length of a busy period can be computed in terms of λ and μ, when $\lambda < \mu$,

$$\tau_b = \left(\frac{\lambda}{\mu}\right)\left(\tau_b + \frac{1}{\lambda}\right) \quad \text{or} \quad \tau_b = \frac{1}{\mu - \lambda} \tag{4.1}$$

Since the mean length of a *service* period (the time taken to serve *one* person) is $1/\mu$, there are $[\mu/(\mu - \lambda)] = [1/(1 - \rho)]$ persons served during an average busy period.

We see that the duration of busy periods and the mean number served during one such period, before the temporary oversupply of arrivals runs out and the service facility has a chance to rest again, increase without limit as the mean arrival rate λ approaches in value the mean service rate μ. The rest or idle period lasts only until the next arrival, its mean length is just $1/\lambda$.

If mean arrival and service rates do not change with time, we can express most of the properties of this queuing system in terms of probabilities and expected values, all of them independent of time. The quantities of greatest interest are the mean length L_q of the queue (i.e., the time average of the number of persons waiting to be served), the average interval of time T_q a person remains in queue before his service starts, the mean number in the system L (i.e., the time average of the number in queue, if any, plus the one being served, if there is one), and the average time in the system T (i.e., the time spent both waiting in queue and being served). In addition there is the probability P_n that exactly n persons are in the system (in service or in queue) as well as the probability $G(t)$ that the total time spent (queue plus service) by a person joining the queue is greater than t. It is not difficult to show[3] that these quantities can be expressed as follows in terms of the constants λ and μ and their ratio ρ, the utilization factor,

$$P_n = (1 - \rho)\rho^n \qquad \rho = \frac{\lambda}{\mu} \qquad G(t) = e^{-(\mu-\lambda)t}$$

$$L = \lambda T = \frac{\rho}{1 - \rho} \qquad L_q = \lambda T_q = L - \rho = \frac{\rho^2}{1 - \rho}$$

$$\sigma_L = \frac{\sqrt{\rho}}{1 - \rho} \qquad\qquad \sigma_{L_q} = \frac{\rho}{1 - \rho}\sqrt{1 + \rho - \rho^2} \qquad (4.2)$$

where σ_L and σ_{L_q} are the standard deviations of L and of L_q, respectively. (See the discussion of Eqs. 2.13 and 3.7.)

These quantities are constant as long as λ and μ are constant, but this does not mean that the actual number of persons in the system or in the queue is constant with time; only their average values L and L_q are constant. Figure 4.1 shows typical plots of the change of these numbers with time. The top plot is for $\rho = 0.5$ when, on the average, the service facility is busy only half the time. The predicted average number L in the system is 1 ± 1.4. As with any random fluctuation, a finite sample does not exactly correspond with the predicted average, which is the limiting value for a sample of size approaching infinity. This is particularly true here, for the standard deviation of L is 1.4, larger than L. In the sample shown the facility is busy somewhat more than half the time, and the mean value of L in the interval shown is somewhat more than 1; other samples would show longer idle periods and mean values of L somewhat less than 1 so that, in the long run, the average number would approach unity. There is 1 chance in 4 that the number in the system is greater than 2.

The curve for $\rho = 0.9$ also deviates from the predicted, long-term average, which is $L = 9 \pm 9.5$. In the sample shown in the lower plot the average value is somewhat less than 9 and no idle period is shown, though in the long run, the service facility is idle (with the number in the system equaling zero) 10 per cent of the time. There is about 1 chance in 4, in the long run, that the number present is greater than 13.

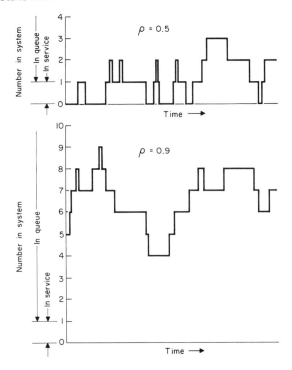

Fig. 4.1.   Typical examples of the fluctuations of queue length with time. Upper plot is for $\rho = \lambda/\mu = 0.5$; lower plot is for $\rho = \lambda/\mu = 0.9$. Upward jumps represent arrivals; downward jumps represent completion of a service.

Utilization Versus Queuing Delays

The formulas of Eq. 4.2 illustrate the major dilemma posed by most queuing situations. The utilization factor $\rho = \lambda/\mu$ is a measure of how efficiently the service facility is being used; it is, as we have said, the fraction of time the facility is busy. If we look *only* at the facility, we would feel impelled to adjust things so that it would be idle as seldom as possible, so that the service rate μ is only a little larger than the arrival rate λ. But a glance at Fig. 4.2 shows what such a "suboptimization" (optimizing one part of a system at the expense of another part) policy will do to the persons desiring service. If $\rho = 2/3$, the service facility being idle $1/3$ of the time, the mean number in the queue will only be $4/3$ and the average total wait of a person, in queue and during service, will be only 3 times the mean service time. On the other hand, if ρ is increased to $4/5$, with the service facility idle only $1/5$ of the time, the mean length of the queue jumps to over 3 and the mean total time spent by a person is also more than 5 times the mean service time. For $\rho = 0.9$ the curves are off the plot, but we can easily verify that $L_q = 8.1$ and the mean stay in the system is 10 times the mean service time.

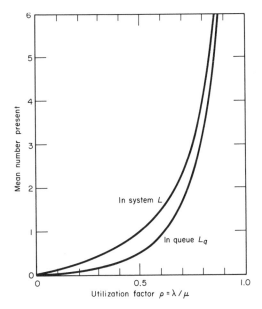

Fig. 4.2.   Mean numbers L and L_q for the simple queuing model of Eq. 4.2, for different values of the ratio ρ between arrival rate λ and mean service rate μ.

Thus *decreasing* the fraction of time the service facility is idle to less than 1/3 *rapidly increases* the time wasted by the customer. If customer irritation is to be avoided the service facility should never be busy more than about 2/3 of the time, on the average. This is typical of a situation often encountered in the study of operations, where a portion of the system must be operated "inefficiently" in order that the system as a whole operate "efficiently." As indicated a few pages earlier, the personnel in a service channel may be busy at some alternative task during idle periods, in which case efficiency may have a different meaning. Nevertheless, the foregoing analysis will still be of value, for it will indicate the limitations on the continuity and relative importance of the alternative task, beyond which it will markedly increase delays in queue. For example, if the elements of the other task take longer, on the average, than the mean time between arrivals of customers to the queue, then the mean wait in queue will be appreciably increased and the efficiency of the operation *as a customer-servicing system* will be impaired. For some library circulation desks, at least half of the wait in queue is because the clerk prefers to finish filing a book card or making out an overdue notice before checking out the customer's book.

One might ask how dependent these results are on the degree of "randomness" of arrivals and/or service times. The answer would be that the results *are* dependent, but that it is usually difficult in practice to reduce this randomness sufficiently to achieve any appreciable improvement. For example, if both arrivals and service times were perfectly regular, each next arrival occurring exactly a time $1/\lambda$ after the previous arrival and each service taking exactly $1/\mu$ units of time to complete, then (if λ is less than μ), there is never a queue and the mean number in the system L equals the fraction of time the service facility is busy, $\rho = \lambda/\mu$. But as we have said before, it usually is out of the question to obtain this sort of regularity of both service and arrivals. If the service facility is the circulation desk it is practically impossible to have each book check-out take exactly the same time but, even if this were possible, regularizing service while leaving arrivals purely random turns out to reduce the formula for L_q, given in Eq. 4.2, only by a factor of $1/2$. Also, L, being equal to $L_q + \rho$, is even less affected.

Measurement of service times at the check-out desk indicate that the actual service-time distribution is much closer to random (exponential distribution) than it is to complete regularity. Thus the formulas of Eq. 4.2 probably represent the situation at the circulation desk and at the inspection station (if there is one) to within an error of less than 10 per cent. Certainly the conclusion to be drawn, that a serious queuing bottleneck will arise unless the service facility is idle more than about $1/3$ of the time, holds for these library locations.

Multiple Service Channels

If the service rate μ is not sufficiently greater than the arrival rate λ (or is actually less than λ), it is necessary to increase the service rate. This can be done either by speeding up the single service channel or else by having two or more channels to spread the load. For example we could double the speed μ of the single channel, or we could add another channel of the same speed as the first. Doubling the speed of the single channel halves the value of ρ the utilization constant, and thus more than halves L and L_q, as can be seen from Fig. 4.2. But doubling the speed of a channel may be more difficult to achieve than doubling the number of channels, though in either case the total service rate has been doubled.

The effect of increasing the number of service channels depends on the queue discipline (we are again assuming Poisson arrivals and exponential service, i.e., both being random). If each arrival chooses a channel at random and is then not allowed to change queues later, the situation with regard to L and L_q for each channel is the same as for the single channel with doubled rate. Instead of μ being doubled, the mean arrival rate for each of the pair of channels is halved, so the λ for each channel is halved, with the corresponding reduction in L and L_q for each. But the mean waiting times $T = L/\lambda$ and $T_q = L_q/\lambda$ are not the same in the two cases. For the single channel with doubled service rate, the reduction in T and T_q is exactly proportional to the reduction in L and L_q. But for the two channels, each with the undoubled service rate, the mean arrival rate for each channel is halved, so the waiting times T and T_q for the 2 channels are twice the waiting times for the single channel with doubled rate. Doubling the channels but keeping separate queues for each channel reduces the length of the queues but reduces very little the length of time spent in queue. The reason for this is that for separate queues, 1 channel can frequently be idle when a queue exists in front of the other channel, thus leading to loss of efficiency.

However if the queues in front of the 2 channels are not kept separate, if anyone waiting for service in front of either channel is allowed to enter whichever service channel becomes idle first, the multiple-channel service facility becomes more efficient. In this case (the nonseparated queue) the total number in queue *and* the mean wait in queue are reduced by the doubling of channels. But the total time spent in the system (in queue *and* in service) is not similarly reduced, because the mean time spent in service is still $1/\mu$ and not $1/2\mu$ as it would be for the single channel with doubled service rate.

The curves of Fig. 4.3 show this effect. They are curves for L and L_q (and, when multiplied by $1/\lambda$, curves for waits T and T_q) for different systems, each with the same arrival rate λ and with equal *total* service rate μ, differing only in the number of channels M over which the service rate is spread (so that, for the case of M channels, the service rate of a single channel is μ/M). We see that, as M is increased and $\rho = (\lambda/\mu)$ is kept constant, the total number of persons L_q waiting for service is reduced (and their average wait T_q to be serviced is likewise reduced). But we also see that as the service is distributed over more channels (and thus the service rate for each channel is slowed) the total number present, in queue and in service, is *increased* (though not quite proportionally to *M*) and the corresponding mean time for an arrival to get through both queue and service is similarly increased. Thus if our operating policy is just to reduce queue length and delay in queue, we multiply the number of channels; if our policy is to reduce the total

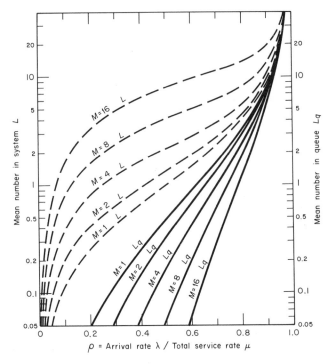

Fig. 4.3.   Mean numbers waiting as functions of utilization factor ρ, for different numbers of service channels *M*.

time spent and the total number present, we multiply the speed of the single channel (if this is possible). The implications of this result in regard to the planning of circulation desks and of new-book cataloguing should be obvious.

Circulation Interference

An important application of queuing theory to library operations is in connection with the circulation of books (or periodicals or other material that are allowed to be taken from the library). Each book is a separate channel, the "service" is the withdrawing of the book from the library, the service time is the interval before the book is returned and made available for another borrower, and the "queue" consists of those persons who desire to borrow the book but cannot yet do so because someone else has borrowed it. Since the circulation of the book interferes with its use by others, we can call this situation one of *circulation interference*.

The queuing model to fit this situation must differ from the simple model discussed earlier in several important respects. In the first place there is a great deal of "balking" or "reneging"; many persons, looking for the book and finding it out on loan, will give up and not wait for the book to be returned. They may give up immediately (balking) or they may get discouraged after a time (reneging); probably there is some of both. In the second place the length of time the book is off the shelves because of a single withdrawal (i.e., the "service time") is not exponentially distributed, but neither is it completely regular. If the standard loan period is 2 weeks (roughly 1/25 of a year) the book may be returned in a week or less or (if the library is lenient with faculty members) it may occasionally be out more than a month. In some cases notices are sent to the borrower only when it is known that someone else wants the book, in which case the mean service time may depend on the length of queue in some rather complex way.

The theory of queues is sufficiently developed so that any of these complications could be included in the model, but the resulting formulas would be complicated and would depend on additional parameters that would be hard to evaluate. In such situations it is well to "creep up" on the problem by starting with simple models that represent upper and lower limits of possible behavior, to see how much difference this makes. If the difference is too great, we can then add further complications, one by one, until sufficient accuracy is obtained.

With book circulation, we assume that λ persons a year (magnitudes are such that the unit of time in regard to circulation is most conveniently set to be a year) desire to borrow a given book (or periodical, etc.). This quantity cannot be measured directly; its magnitude must be inferred from the data on circulation, i.e., on the fraction of these "arrivals" who are successful in borrowing the book. We can assume that the λ arrivals are randomly distributed throughout the year, unless we have reason to think otherwise (in which case we would divide the year into high and low activity periods, with random distribution within each).

We also assume that the mean length of time $1/\mu$, between the instant the book is taken from the shelf to be borrowed by 1 person until the time the book is replaced on the shelf, ready to be used by the next person, has been measured or is known accurately enough for the present purpose. For some formulas the probability distribution of these times is necessary, for others it is not. Data taken at M.I.T. indicate that this distribution is approximately exponential, as illustrated in Eq. 2.32, that the probability of a book staying out longer than time t is $e^{-\mu t} = e^{-t/\tau}$, with $\tau = 1/\mu$ being the mean length of time the book is off the shelf per individual circulation (which we can call the *mean loan period*). In any case we can describe the distribution in terms of the probability $P_t(t)$ that an individual loan period is longer than t, resulting in a mean loan period $\tau = 1/\mu$ and a standard deviation σ (which would equal τ if the distribution were exponential).

Another circulation characteristic of importance is the *expected circulation rate R* of a book, the number of times per year we expect the book to be borrowed. This, of course, varies greatly from book to book (and we shall have much to say later about its distribution), but even the average circulation rate $\overline{R}$ of a whole class of books is of importance in planning. For example, if we can assume that the mean loan period $1/\mu$ of a book is statistically independent of its circulation rate R, then we can devise a fairly simple way to calculate $1/\mu$, knowing the mean circulation rate $\overline{R}$ and the fraction of books in the collection which are out on loan at any given time.

If $1/\mu = \tau$, the mean loan period for a class of borrowable books is expressed in terms of fractions of a year (2 weeks, for example, is $1/25$ of a year) then $1/\mu$ is the average fraction of the year the book will be off the shelf for each circulation. This, times the mean circulation rate $\overline{R}$ for all borrowable books of some homogeneous class (i.e., $\overline{R}/\mu$) must be equal to the average of the fraction of the year each book of the class is off the shelf, borrowed by its $\overline{R}$ borrowers. When a book is out on loan, its card is kept in a circulation file until it is returned; therefore $\overline{R}/\mu$ is the mean fraction of the year a book's card is in the circulation file. *If* the demand for books is more or less constant throughout the year (and if book withdrawals are random), then $\overline{R}/\mu$ must also equal the fraction of books, of the class, which have cards in the circulation file at any given time. (If on the average, each book is out a tenth of the time then, because of the random nature of borrowing, a tenth of the collection will be out at any given time.) Thus this fraction $\overline{R}/\mu$ times the total number N of books in the borrowable class must equal the number J of cards of this class on hand in the circulation file at any time.

Of course the actual number of cards of the class on hand at any time will fluctuate throughout the year, partly because of the random nature of borrowing and partly because book demand may vary seasonally. But the mean value J of the circulation file count, averaged throughout the year, still must equal the quantity $N(\overline{R}/\mu)$. And if we are dealing with a collection of several thousand books, the number of cards in the circulation file will not change rapidly, so an average of 4 quarterly counts should be equal to $N\overline{R}/\mu$ to within a few per cent. Knowing the number N in the collection, the mean circulation rate $\overline{R}$, and the average circulation-file count J, we can calculate the mean loan period $1/\mu$ for the class of books. This will be done in later chapters.

A Simple Circulation Model

In regard to the arrival's behavior when he finds the book out on loan, we make two limiting assumptions, to begin with. In the first case we assume that every arrival, if he does not find the book on the shelf, gives up and does not try again (in other words we assume complete balking, and thus no queue). As we mentioned earlier, the book is not on the shelf a fraction R/μ of the year, where R is the circulation rate per year and $1/\mu$ is the mean circulation time (the *loan period*), which can be measured by counting cards in the circulation file. (We neglect renewals and the presence of duplicate books just now; these complications can be added later if it proves to be necessary.) During this time, $\lambda(R/\mu)$ persons have come looking for the book and, having found it missing from the shelves, give up and leave; by definition, λ is the arrival rate, the number of persons per year who would like to borrow the book. Conversely, the number of persons per year who have found the book on the shelf and who thus have borrowed it is $\lambda - \lambda(R/\mu)$. But this, by definition, is equal to R, the number of times the book is borrowed per year. Thus we have $\lambda[1 - (R/\mu)] = R$, or $R = \lambda\mu/(\lambda + \mu)$, giving the expected circulation rate in terms of the demand rate and the "return rate" μ (the reciprocal of the mean loan period $1/\mu$ in fractions of a year per loan). It should be noted that R is an *expected value*, the mean circulation of a number of books which happen to have the same demand rate λ. For any given book of the group, the actual circulation could be larger than this mean (because, for example, a number of actual loan periods happened to be shorter than average) or it could be less than R (because, for example, fewer than average of the prospective borrowers happened to come when the book was on the shelf). All we can say definitely is that the probability a prospective borrower will find the book on the shelf is P_1, the probability he will come by when it is out is P_0, the expected circulation rate of a number of such books is $R_1 = \lambda P_1$ and the mean unsatisfied demand per book, the average number of prospective borrowers who do not get the book (and, according to our model, give up) is $U_1 = \lambda P_0 = \lambda - R_1$, where

$$P_0 = \frac{\lambda}{\lambda + \mu} \qquad P_1 = \frac{\mu}{\lambda + \mu} \tag{4.3}$$

$$R_1 = \frac{\lambda\mu}{\lambda + \mu} \qquad U_1 = \frac{\lambda^2}{\lambda + \mu} = \frac{(R_1)^2}{\mu - R_1} \tag{4.4}$$

Note that as long as the demand rate λ is smaller than the return rate μ, the unsatisfied demand U_1 is smaller than the mean circulation rate R_1, but when λ becomes larger than μ, then U_1 overshadows R_1; as λ tends to infinity, U_1 also tends to infinity, whereas R_1 approaches the finite value μ. On the average, the most a popular book can circulate is μ, the number of mean loan periods in a year; any larger demand than this usually goes unsatisfied. This is shown in Table 4.1 for R_1 and

Table 4.1   Circulation Interference for $\mu = 20$*

If the demand per year is	0	1	2	5	10	20	40	60
Then expected circulation per copy R_1 is	0	0.95	1.82	4.00	6.67	10.0	13.3	15.0
Expected unsatisfied demand per copy U_1 is	0	0.05	0.18	1.00	3.33	10.0	26.7	45.0
Expected circulation for 2 copies R_2 is	0	0.999	1.991	4.88	9.23	16.0	24.0	28.2
Expected unsatisfied demand if 2 copies circulate U_2 is	0	0.001	0.009	0.12	0.77	4.0	16.0	31.8
Expected circulation if 3 copies circulate R_3 is	0	1.000	2.000	4.99	9.87	18.8	31.5	39.3
Expected unsatisfied demand if 3 copies circulate U_3 is	0	0.000	0.000	0.01	0.13	1.2	8.5	20.7

* See Eqs. 4.4 through 4.8.

U_1 (and other quantities discussed later) for books with mean loan period 2.6 weeks, i.e., for $\mu = 20$. We note that, as R_1 becomes larger than 5 (i.e., when R_1/μ becomes larger than about $1/4$), the unsatisfied demand rises rapidly, and when R_1 is greater than 10 (when R_1/μ is greater than $1/2$), more people miss getting the book than take it out. The meaning of the quantities U_2 and R_2 in Table 4.1 will be discussed later.

We shall later present some evidence to the effect that when U_1 becomes larger than 3 or 4, a duplicate volume should be bought. According to this criterion, every book with a demand rate λ greater than 12 to 15 a year should be duplicated if $\mu = 20$.

An Alternative Model

The less realistic, limiting case is to assume that each one of the λ arrivals, everyone who desires the book during the year, either hands in a reservation card or otherwise pesters the librarian until he eventually gets the book. In this case the model is that of the simple queuing system of Eq. 4.2: All arrivals are eventually served, but on the average L_q of them are waiting to get the book; and the mean length of time from when an arrival first tries to borrow the book until he returns it, having finally borrowed it himself, is (L/λ). This model is probably not a good approximation for the case of popular books, but it does represent one limiting case and should be investigated.

For this model the actual rate of circulation R per year is equal to the arrival rate, because all arrivals eventually are able to borrow the book. Therefore, from Eq. 4.2 the average number of persons, at any time, waiting to borrow the book and the mean length of time a would-be borrower has to wait until he can borrow it himself are

$$L_q = \frac{R^2/\mu}{\mu - R} \qquad \frac{L_q}{R} = \frac{R/\mu}{\mu - R} = T_q \qquad U = \mu L_q \qquad (4.5)$$

Also the fraction of time the book is in the library $= P_0 = 1 - (R/\mu)$. In each period $1/\mu$, there are L_q unsatisfied persons waiting, so the measure of unsatisfaction per year is $U = \mu L_q$. This results in the same formula for U as with the other model, given in Eq. 4.4, only the definition of U is now different. For a 2-week book ($\mu = 25$) if the circulation is 10 per year, L_q is approximately $1/4$, and T_q is approximately 10 days. On the other hand if the circulation rises to 20 per year there will, on the average, be about 3 persons waiting to borrow the book and their mean length of wait, before they can borrow it, will be about 8 weeks. In this latter case the book will be on the shelf only 20 per cent of the time.

In both limiting cases of Eq. 4.4 or 4.5 the measure of dissatisfaction is the same, proportional to U. Therefore it may not be worthwhile working out all the intermediate cases, where some would-be borrowers give up, some turn in reserve cards, and some try later to see whether the book is back on the shelf. In any of these cases the measure of unsatisfied demand will turn out to be roughly proportional to the U of Eq. 4.4, though the exact definition of U, and the exact value, above which a duplicate book should be bought, may differ somewhat from model to model. In general, however, this value of U will be between 2 and 4. Both limiting models bring us to the same conclusion: namely, that whenever the yearly circulation rate R shows signs of being greater than about $1/3$ of μ too many would-be borrowers are either waiting too long to borrow the book or else are giving up entirely; in either case the library is not serving them adequately. For books to be returned in 2 weeks $\mu \simeq 20$, in which case this upper limit for R would be about 7 circulations per year.

We should note that these formulas assume random arrival of demand and therefore the results are expected, or average, values. Individual samples may be larger or smaller than the formula predicts.

Multiple Copies

Of course we should ask what happens when a second copy of a popular book is made available for circulation. Since arrivals of prospective borrowers are at random and since the two copies circulate independently of each other, there will still be times when both copies are out of the library and some potential borrowers will still be disappointed. Taking the somewhat more realistic limit discussed earlier, assuming that all prospective borrowers give up when they cannot find the book on the shelf, we can work out the probability P_n that n copies ($n = 0, 1, 2$) are present on the shelf:

$$P_0 = \left(\frac{\lambda^2}{2B}\right) \qquad P_1 = \frac{\lambda\mu}{B} \qquad P_2 = \frac{\mu^2}{B} \tag{4.6}$$

where $\qquad B = \mu^2 + \lambda\mu + \frac{1}{2}\lambda^2$ and $P_0 + P_1 + P_2 = 1$.

Quantity P_0 is, of course, the fraction of time neither of the copies is on the shelf. This is quite small when λ/μ is less than $1/2$, but as λ/μ increases it approaches 1; two copies are not sufficient if the demand is very large. Nevertheless when demand is fairly large, the second copy will reduce the number of unsatisfied users substantially. The number U_2 per year who are still unsatisfied is, of course, the mean arrival rate λ times the fraction of time P_0 both copies are out and the expected circulation for both copies is R_2, where

$$U_2 = \frac{\lambda^3}{2\mu^2 + 2\lambda\mu + \lambda^2}$$

$$R_2 = \lambda - U_2 = \frac{2\mu^2\lambda + 2\lambda^2\mu}{2\mu^2 + 2\lambda\mu + \lambda^2}$$

(4.7)

A similar set of equations can be worked out when there are 3 copies of the book that can circulate. The relationship to Eq. 4.6 is fairly obvious. The probability P_n that n copies are on the shelf ($n = 0, 1, 2,$ or 3), the mean circulation R_3 per year for all 3 copies, and the expected number U_3 of persons who come in when no books are on the shelf and thus do not get the book they desire, are

$$P_0 = \frac{\lambda^3}{6E} \qquad P_1 = \frac{\lambda^2\mu}{2E} \qquad P_2 = \frac{\lambda\mu^2}{E} \qquad P_3 = \frac{\mu^3}{E}$$

$$U_3 = \lambda P_0 = \frac{\lambda^4}{6E}$$

(4.8)

$$R_3 = \lambda - U_3 = \lambda \frac{\mu^3 + \mu^2\lambda + \frac{1}{2}\mu\lambda^2}{E}$$

where $\qquad E = \mu^3 + \mu^2\lambda + \frac{1}{2}\mu\lambda^2 + \frac{1}{6}\lambda^3$

Table 4.1 gives values of R and U for different demand rates λ, for $\mu = 20$.

Table 4.1 is straightforward to use, but it of course is based on the assumption that books on loan are returned, on the average, in 2.6 weeks ($\mu = 20$). As we shall see in Chapter 6, book borrowers often are more dilatory than this, and the mean loan period is often larger than 3 weeks, particularly if renewals are allowed. In these cases Fig. 4.4 may be used to make the calculations. As an example of its use, suppose that in a given library the average loan period is 3.25 weeks ($\mu = 16$) and that 16 persons wished to borrow a given book in the year; therefore $\lambda/\mu = 16/16 = 1$. If only 1 copy is available, we see that $R_1/\mu = 0.5$ for this book and thus that $R_1 = 16/2 = 8$. The un-satisfied demand $U_1 = \lambda - R_1 = 16 - 8 = 8$, which also may be read off the lower set of curves, the right-hand scale; for $\lambda/\mu = 1$, $U_1/\mu = 0.5$ and $U_1 = 16/2 = 8$. If, instead of 1 copy, we had 2 copies of this fairly popular book, the total circulation of both (assuming that the total demand λ and return rate μ are unchanged by adding a second copy, a reasonable supposition) would have been R_2 and the resulting unsatisfied demand would have been $U_2 = \lambda - R_2$. The value of R_2/μ for $\lambda/\mu = 1/2$ is 0.8. So the circulation of the two books would have been $0.8 \times 16 \simeq 13$, an average of 6.4 per book, leaving only 3 prospective borrowers still unsatisfied.

One more example. Suppose we have predicted, by models we will discuss later, that the demand for a single-copy, popular book will be 30 next year, and we have found that the mean loan period for this class of book is 3.5 weeks ($\mu = 15$). In this case $\lambda/\mu = 30/15 = 2.0$,

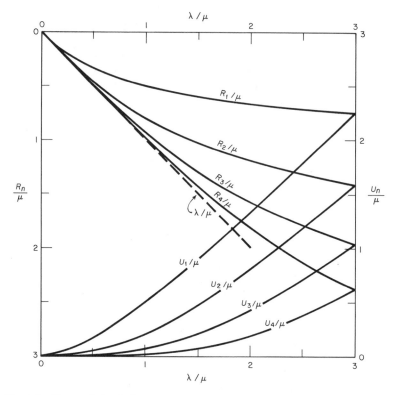

Fig. 4.4.   Expected circulation R_n and expected number U_n of unsatisfied borrowers versus total demand λ during a mean circulation time $1/\mu$ when n copies of the book are available for circulation.

which the chart says corresponds to $R_1/\mu = 0.67$, an expected circulation R_1 equal to 10, only a third of the demand. If we add one more copy, the chart shows that R_2/μ for $\lambda/\mu = 2$ is 1.2, corresponding to a circulation of both copies of $1.2 \times 15 = 18$, or 9 circulations per copy; but there will be $30 - 18 = 12$ customers still unsatisfied. If we had bought 2 extra copies, the total expected circulation would have been $R_3 = 24$ ($R_3/\mu = 1.6$, and this times 15) a circulation of about 8 per copy, leaving only 5 unsatisfied customers (adding a fourth copy would satisfy only about 3 of these 5).

Instead of buying 2 extra copies and satisfying 25 out of the 30 customers predicted for next year, we could buy one extra copy and make both copies 7-day books. Assuming that 7-day books are policed more strictly than 14-day books, so that their mean loan period really is 1/50 of a year, we now have $\lambda/\mu = 30/50 = 0.6$ and the chart predicts R_2 to be 26 (i.e., $R_2/\mu = 0.52$ for $\lambda/\mu = 0.6$, this times $\mu = 50$ is 26). Thus all but 4 of the 30 expected borrowers would be satisfied, at some cost to both library and borrowers. A single copy, designated a 7-day book, would satisfy only 19 of the 30, as further use of the chart will show.

Several items of interest may be noted from Fig. 4.4 that are unavoidable consequences of the random nature of book borrowing. In the first place no matter how many of the copies of a book are put on the shelf, there will be times (perhaps only once in a century, but it will occur!) when all the copies are out on loan. During these times a prospective borrower may appear. Consequently, we never can be *sure* we can satisfy all the demand. For the case of $\lambda = 30$ and $\mu = 15$, just discussed, 3 copies would more than satisfy the demand if the arrival of users could be scheduled to come just after a book is returned. With this regimented borrowing each copy could be circulated 15 times a year and 3 times 15 is greater than 30. Nevertheless, since borrowers do not come in on schedule, some of the time all of the copies will be in the library (not satisfying anyone) and some of the time all will be out (disappointing customers who come in then). As a result only 25 of the 30 will succeed in borrowing a copy, and the other 5 will not get a copy. Unless, of course they elect to turn in a reserve card, but we are not considering this for the moment.

A second item, related to the first, is that the expected circulation of 2 copies is not twice that of 1 copy. In the example, 2 copies are expected to circulate 18 times in the year, whereas a single copy would circulate 10 times. Again the random nature of the demand results in this degradation of effectiveness of extra copies.

Finally we should point out again that the figures of Table 4.1 and the curves of Fig. 4.4 are *expected* values and that actual results may be larger or smaller than those shown. With $\mu = 25$, for example, there will be an occasional book that circulates more than 25 times a year. Likewise there may be cases for $\mu = 15$ and $\lambda = 30$ when the addition of a duplicate will lead to a circulation of only 15 instead of the 18 predicted. All we can say is that if a number of single-copy books each had 30 prospective borrowers during the year then their average circulation per book would be 10 and, if each of them were duplicated, then the average circulation of each pair would be fairly close to 18, as predicted from the chart. In the face of such variability we can only be sure when we deal with many cases and bet on the average. But librarians do deal with many books; the more often the rules are applied, the more likely the outcome will be as predicted.

Note that the model can be of use in making decisions regarding extra copies only if we can predict next year's demand, so something can be done before it is too late. If we cannot predict the demand for a book, then the model will tell us only what might have happened. On the other hand if we can predict next year's demand, even though it be with uncertainty and on the average, we can use the model to help tell us what is likely to happen if we buy (or do not buy) a duplicate or if we change the loan period of certain classes of books. We thus can begin to investigate the possible effects of applying general rules, which can be applied mechanically (perhaps by the computer, when it is at hand) instead of requiring separate decisions to be made for each book.

Note also that the formulas predict values of circulation R and of unsatisfied demand U *if* we can predict the *demand* λ for the book. The formulas should not be read backward. One cannot predict demand, given values for the probable circulation. To put it in other words, if we know that a number of books all have demand λ, the formulas give their average circulation $\overline{R}$; but if we pick out a number of books which have the same circulation R, we cannot say that the mean demand for these books is the λ that would be obtained by working Eq. 4.4 backward. We can see this if we try to work backward (using Eq. 4.4) to obtain an expected value of λ for a book which happens to have a value of R greater than μ (which is possible, though not common). We will return to this problem of statistical inference in Chapter 7.

But before we discuss this further, we should look at more complex models of circulation interference, ones that include such things as reserve cards, for example, to see how much these complexities alter the general characteristics exhibited by the simple model we have just discussed.

Balking and Reneging Models for Circulation Interference

Since the 2 models bound the 2 extremes of potential borrowers' actions, the foregoing conclusions, which are practically identical for the two models, can be deemed sufficient for many management decisions. For purposes of further exploration of users' habits, however, we shall exhibit 2 more complicated queuing models. The first assumes that arrivals (coming at random with a mean rate λ) have a "discouragement time," within which they keep trying to get the book and beyond which they give up. We assume that this discouragement time is exponentially (i.e., randomly) distributed, with a mean value $1/\eta$ so that η is a mean "discouragement rate." In terms of the earlier discussion of queues, we assume that arrivals renege, with a mean renegal rate η. The additional parameter of importance here is the ratio between discouragement rate and service rate $\chi = (\eta/\mu)$, so that the ratio between mean discouragement time $1/\eta$ and mean circulation time $1/\mu$ is $1/\chi$. If people are willing to wait a month on the average for a 2-week book, χ is $1/2$; if they will only wait a week, χ is 2.

This queuing model can be worked out. The probability P_n that n persons are "in the system" (either having the book on loan or waiting for a chance to borrow it) is

$$
P_n = \frac{P_0 \rho^n}{(1 + \chi)(1 + 2\chi) \cdots [1 + (n - 1)\chi]}
$$

$$
P_0 = \left[1 + \rho + \frac{\rho^2}{1 + \chi} + \frac{\rho^3}{(1 + \chi)(1 + 2\chi)} + \cdots \right]^{-1}
$$

(4.9)

where $\rho = (\lambda/\mu)$. Carrying the calculations through we obtain a set of curves, shown in Fig. 4.5, for mean number L_q waiting for the book (not yet discouraged) and number N_f per year of disappointed persons, who wanted the book but became discouraged and gave up before they had a chance to borrow it. Both quantities are plotted against actual number R of circulations per year (or, rather, in terms of the *circulation factor* R/μ). They can also be plotted as functions of λ, since $\lambda = R + N_f$.

For a 2-week book ($\mu = 25$), if the arrivals are willing on the average to wait two weeks to get the book ($\chi = 1$), then if the expected circulation is 10 times a year ($R/\mu = 0.4$), the average number of persons waiting L_q is only 0.1, and the probable number N_f of persons who gave up before they had a chance to borrow it is about 3 (so about 13 persons "arrived" that year, looking for the book). For the same model if the arrival rate λ of would-be borrowers is 40, then the expected circulation is 20 per year ($R/\mu = 0.8$), the mean number in queue is about 0.8, and the expected number per year disappointed has risen to 20 per year. In other words if 40 persons have actually wanted the book, on the average 20 of them were lucky enough to find the book on the shelf or else were persistent enough to wait until they did find it in, the other 20 gave up. Again we see that when the circulation factor (R/μ)

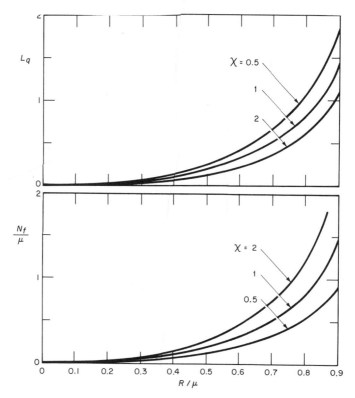

Fig. 4.5. Mean number in queue and mean number N_q of lost customers per year for system with arrivals who become discouraged and leave the queue after a mean time $1/\chi\mu$ with $1/\mu$ as the mean loan period in units of a year.

gets larger than about 1/3, the fraction of disappointed borrowers and the delays involved become large enough so that a second copy should be bought.

A model that perhaps is still more realistic is one in which, if the book is out, arrivals (again random, with mean rate λ) either give up immediately or else wait until the book is available. This would be the case with a library that issues reserve cards for a book which is out, in which case the mean number of reserve cards on hand at any time will be equal to L_q, the number of people who have decided to wait for a chance to borrow the book. Suppose a fraction δ, of those arriving when the book is not on the shelf, fill out reserve cards and "wait in queue."

Then if the mean service time is $1/\mu$, as before, R is the mean circulation rate and W is the mean number of reserve cards per book at any time. We wish to compute N_b the number of users per year who find the book on the shelf, N_w the number of persons per year who turn in reserve cards, N_f the number of would-be borrowers per year who do not get their book, and W_q the mean wait in queue. Then the equations for the model are, where $n > 0$ and $\rho = \lambda/\mu$,

$$P_0 = \frac{1 - \delta\rho}{1 + \rho(1 - \delta)} \qquad P_n = \delta^{n-1}\rho^n P_0$$

$$R = \frac{\mu\rho}{1 + \rho(1 - \delta)} \qquad \text{therefore } \lambda = \frac{R\mu}{\mu - R(1 - \delta)}$$

$$W = \frac{\delta\rho^2}{(1 - \delta\rho)[1 + \rho(1 - \delta)]} = \frac{\delta(R/\mu)^2}{1 - (R/\mu)}$$

$$N_b = \lambda P_0 = R\,\frac{\mu - R}{\mu - R(1 - \delta)} \qquad\qquad (4.10)$$

$$N_w = \lambda\delta(1 - P_0) = \frac{\delta R^2}{\mu - R(1 - \delta)}$$

$$N_f = \lambda(1 - \delta)(1 - P_0) = \frac{R^2(1 - \delta)}{\mu - R(1 - \delta)}$$

$$W_q = (W/\delta\lambda) = \frac{R}{\mu^2}\,\frac{\mu - R(1 - \delta)}{\mu - R}$$

Curves for W and N_f are plotted in Fig. 4.6 as functions of the circulation factor R/μ for several values of δ. They can be used to determine the quantities in Eqs. 4.10, once R, μ and either δ or L_q are known. For example, suppose the circulation for a 2-week book ($\mu = 25$) is 20 during the year (i.e., $R/\mu = 0.8$), and it has turned out that on the average about 1 reserve card for the book is on hand at any time (sometimes there may be none, sometimes 2, but the average over the year is 1). Then, reading between the top set of curves, *if* we assume this model represents what goes on, δ will equal about 0.3; in which case the total number of persons who tried to get the book during the year was 45. Of these 45, about 9 found the book on the shelf and borrowed it without waiting, 11 turned in reserve cards and eventually borrowed the book (having waited, on the average, about 25 days), and 25 left disappointed. As another example suppose R is 10 (and $R/\mu = 0.4$) and a reserve card is on hand about 1 day in 5 (and $W = 0.2$). Then, if the model is assumed to be statistically representative of what is going on, δ was about 3/4, and the probable number λ of persons desiring the book during the year was about 11. Of these 11, about 7 of them found the book on the shelf and borrowed it immediately, 3 found the book was out but decided to turn in reserve cards and eventually borrowed the book after waiting about 8 days, on the average, and only 1 person gave up when he found the book was not in.

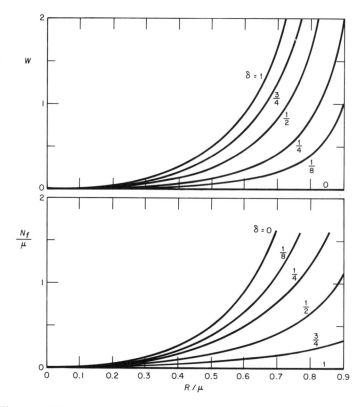

Fig. 4.6. Mean number in queue and mean number of lost customers for system in which $1 - \delta$ of the arrivals, if they have to wait, give up immediately and δ of them turn in reserve cards and wait for book.

It is unlikely that the librarian can determine exactly what is happening in regard to the various users wishing to borrow a particular book, unless he carries out a rather intensive survey aimed at getting these data. But, in spite of this lack of detailed knowledge, if he keeps track of the circulation factor of each book (the ratio R/μ between the number of circulations R of the book in the past year and the maximum possible circulations μ, he will be able to estimate closely enough the degree of circulation interference to be able to decide when to order a duplicate. In fact, with any of the models discussed, the interference begins to be important when the circulation factor is about 1/3 and is quite serious by the time this factor becomes 1/2. If the administrative question is primarily to determine when to order extra copies of a popular book, the curves of Fig. 4.4 will usually be adequate, with U_n some measure of unsatisfied demand when n copies of a book are available for borrowing.

If, in addition, the librarian keeps track of the time average of the number of reserve cards on hand for a popular book, he can use this datum, plus the circulation factor, to distinguish between those who never borrowed the book and those who were delayed in borrowing it, and to estimate how long this last group had to wait before their reserve cards procured for them the book they wanted. Quite evidently, without the model of Eqs. 4.10, these two data could not have enabled the librarian to tell very much about what was going on.

Estimation of Penalties for Performance Failure

From the economist's point of view, operational decisions, such as the decision to buy a duplicate book to satisfy more users, should be based on a balance between the cost of providing the extra book and some sort of monetary penalty that should be charged the library for failure of service. From this point of view a second book should be bought whenever the total penalties, to be assessed because of these failures of service, become equal to the cost of buying another book.

The difficulty in using this purely monetary basis for decision is the difficulty of determining the magnitudes of the penalties that should be charged against the library for various failures of service. The point of this section is to show that any decision to remedy failure of service is equivalent to an implicit evaluation of these penalties, and to indicate how such implicit penalties can be made explicit.

One very crude way of assessing a penalty for failure to loan a book, when wanted, is to ask what is the average circulation rate R_{av} of the whole collection of books that do circulate. One could argue that if the library finds it "profitable" to maintain a collection, each of which, on the average, circulate R_{av} times a year, then it would be profitable to buy an additional copy of a book, if this copy would satisfy the demands of R_{av} more persons a year, who otherwise would not have been able to borrow the book. In other words the penalty to be charged for each prospective borrower who is unable to borrow a given book should be $1/R_{av}$ times the cost of a second copy of the book. In still other words, if the model of Fig. 4.4 indicates that an additional copy would satisfy at least R_{av} more prospective borrowers per year, then that additional copy should be bought.

In this respect it should be noted that the circulation of most books tends to diminish with time, fairly rapidly at first. Thus it is important to learn which books are popular, and to buy additional copies, while the demand is still high. To learn that the first year's circulation of a given book is 10, after the book has been on the shelf for 15 months, and then to spend the next 9 months getting a second copy on the shelf, will be to supply the duplicate at the end of the second year of demand, when the total demand λ may well have dropped from 17 per year to 8 per year and a duplicate copy is no longer justifiable. In this respect the mechanization of library operation will improve response time; these matters will be discussed later.

However the librarian may not prefer to use so crude an evaluation of the "worth" of a potential user's desire to borrow a book. He may have already set, or had set for him, some other operating rule with regard to buying duplicates. For example, the rule may be to buy a duplicate copy whenever the circulation factor R/μ of a book is larger than some fraction ϕ, which the previous discussion suggests should be about $1/3$. If we take the simple model of Eq. 4.4 where every would-be borrower gives up if the book is not in the library, the expected number of failures per year to supply this book to someone wishing to borrow it is $\mu(R/\mu)^2/[1 - (R/\mu)]$. As will be shown later (see Chapter 5) book circulation, at least for science books, falls off rapidly enough so that the total future failures of service, if a duplicate book is not bought, would be about twice this quantity. Therefore a decision to buy a duplicate, which would cost C dollars, whenever R/μ is greater than ϕ, *is equivalent to saying* that the expected number of failures of service $[2\mu\phi^2/(1 - \phi)]$ times the penalty which should be assessed for each failure would just equal C. In other words whenever R/μ is greater than ϕ, the total penalties add up to more than C and it "pays" to buy a duplicate; whenever R/μ is less than ϕ, it does not pay.

Thus the decision to buy a duplicate whenever R/μ is larger than ϕ *is equivalent to setting* the penalty for each failure to supply the book as

$$\frac{C}{2\mu\phi^2} (1 - \phi) \tag{4.11}$$

dollars per failure for the simple model of Eq. 4.4. For $\phi = 1/3$ and for a 2-week book this penalty would be $1/8$ of the cost of the book per failure. For the more realistic model of Eqs. 4.10, wherein N_f would-be borrowers per year give up when they find the book out and $N_w =$

$[\delta/(1 - \delta)]N_f$ of them turn in reserve cards and eventually get the book, but have to wait for it, the corresponding penalties would be

$(C/2\mu\phi^2)(1 - \phi)$ dollars per would-be borrower who never gets the book (corresponding to N_q)

$(C/2\mu\phi^2)(2 - \phi)$ dollars per person who turns in a reserve card and is delayed in getting the book (corresponding to N_w)   (4.12)

corresponding to $\frac{1}{8} C$ per "lost" borrower and $\frac{1}{3} C$ per reserve card for $\phi = 1/3$ and a 2-week book.

This indicates a larger penalty to be assessed for each person who persists, by filling out a reserve card, than to be assessed for those who give up and never get the book. Perhaps this is a correct estimation of relative penalties; the delay imposed upon someone who *really* wants the book perhaps should count more in total cost to the user community than the frustration caused by someone who finds the book out and gives up, because it is not worth the trouble to fill out a reserve card. At any rate these penalties are implicitly equivalent to a decision to buy a duplicate if R/μ is larger than ϕ.

The sorts of calculations we have just gone through, making explicit the decisions regarding penalties for failure, have a number of advantages. For one thing the order of magnitude of the computed penalty can serve as a check on the rationality of the original decision. In the present case ($\phi = 1/3$) a penalty of about $1/8$ of the cost of a new book per failure would appear to be a reasonable amount. In contrast, setting $\phi = 1/7$ would correspond to a penalty of about one C per failure, undoubtedly too large a penalty and thus too small a ϕ to be realistic; setting $\phi = 0.9$ corresponds to a penalty of about $C/400$ per failure, entirely too niggardly a valuation of the users' time and reference needs.

Another advantage is that various operational decisions can be made consistent with each other. Take, as an example, the problem of lost books and the question as to how many books lost per year will "justify" the addition of a guard at the library entrance. In practice at present it takes about a year to replace a fairly popular book after it has disappeared from the library, counting the time required for the library to learn that the book is lost. From the simple model of Eq. 4.4, if the circulation factor R/μ of a lost book is estimated to be about $1/2$ for this year, the number λ of persons who would come in, during the year to borrow the book would be equal to μ, 25 for a 2-week book. Thus the total cost to the library of the loss of this book would be 4 times the cost of the book, i.e., cost C to buy a replacement plus 25 times

$C/8$ as penalty for the denial of its use to a year's worth of would-be borrowers. If the estimated penalties of all the books lost per year are added up to obtain a total cost this would come to an amount larger than the simple sum of all the book replacement costs C. This augmented amount is the one to be compared with the cost of a guard, to see whether the guard is worth installing, if one is to be consistent in one's operating criteria. This problem will be approached from another angle in Chapter 9.

Of course, to be realistic, one should also add a penalty for the frustration of these users who would have used the book in the library. As is pointed out later, there are not sufficient data at present to be able to estimate these penalties. However the present discussion shows how they can be computed and used, once the data are gathered.

5 Book Use and the Markov Process

The models discussed heretofore have been related in some form or other to the user of the library, what services he takes advantage of or how often he is blocked from availing himself of one. Library use can be studied from another point of view, of course, by analyzing the degree of performance of the services. The degree of use of a given book or periodical, or report, for example, can be measured, and models can be devised to predict the variation of its use with its age and with its subject matter. Data of this sort, particularly if it can be distilled into probabilistic models, can be as important in library planning and operation as are data on user behavior.

Every library is experiencing an overcrowding of its shelves; every librarian is caught between the flood of new books and the rising cost of adding new shelves to make the books available to the user. Several expedients have been tried and have been suggested for solving the dilemma: the traumatic one of destroying or otherwise getting rid of some of the less useful books, or the less drastic one of retiring some books to stacks or to deposit libraries, where they can be stored more compactly or more cheaply but where the book is less accessible to the user. Compared to the few minutes it takes for the user to get a book from open shelves, it may take 20 minutes to make out a card and get a book from stacks, and it may take several days to retrieve the book from a deposit library. These delays may be acceptable if they occur only seldom; therefore it is important to be able to predict the future circulation of a book, if only in a probabilistic manner. If one could retire only those books that had a chance of less than 1 in 6 or 1 in 10 of being asked for in the next year, the fraction of disadvantaged borrowers might be small enough to be endurable.

Data on Book Use

Data on the rate of borrowing of a book are automatically supplied to the library. If all circulation cards are kept, the library has, in fairly compact form, a circulation history of each part of its collection, which can be analyzed and from which probabilistic models can be devised. With the advent of computer aids in library operation, more detail can be recorded without additional effort, and subsequent analysis of the data becomes very much easier to accomplish. But even now there is no excuse for a librarian not having, each year, figures on mean circulation rates (R = circulation per book per year) of each class of book in his collection and, more frequently, individual circulation rates for the few, most popular books. These measures of library effectiveness can be of great assistance in determining when to buy duplicates and in deciding budget allocations for next year's acquisitions. With increasing computerization, other data can be prepared, such as the circulation rates for different classes of books and periodicals, rates of circulation by classes of users, and the like.

Of course data on circulation is not a complete measure of the use or utility of a portion of the library's collection. Some books are frequently used in the library, and the circulation of some is restricted or even forbidden. Data on in-library use are not automatically recorded in most libraries, particularly in those with open shelves. Until computerized operation is nearly complete the data on in-library use will often have to be obtained by sample surveys carefully planned and periodically carried out.

A listing of all books or journals left on the library tables, to be reshelved by the library staff, is a fairly efficient way of measuring in-library use. Of course such a list would not include those books removed from the shelves, glanced at, and immediately returned to the shelf, nor would it include those books taken to the table for study but subsequently reshelved by the user. However even though it does not include all books removed, at least momentarily, from the shelves by a user, the count of books reshelved by the staff is usually a good measure of in-library use, particularly for those libraries that discourage reshelving by the user. In the Science Library at M.I.T., for example, it has been[4] found that the books left on the library tables, to be reshelved by the staff, constitute roughly half of the books used at the tables in the library; the other half were reshelved by the users. Thus an occasional listing of books as they are reshelved (for a day chosen at random each month, for example) will provide a measure of the rate of in-library use to compare with circulation rates.

Books on reserve require special treatment if they are supposed to be returned to the reserve-book desk after in-library use. The use of sign-out cards similar to circulation cards, which are to be signed by each in-library user of a reserved book, and the storage of all such completed cards (instead of throwing them away) will provide a complete record of the use of books on reserve. Use records of books on reserve are particularly important, because these books are usually the most used parts of the collection.

Queuing effects similar to the circulation-interference processes, discussed in Chapter 4, will occur with reserve books; persons, wishing to consult a book on reserve, will occasionally find that someone else is already using the book in the library. In fact the probabilistic models, discussed in the preceding chapter, can be used here, with R defined as the number of in-library withdrawals per hour instead of the circulation per year, and $1/\mu$ defined as the average time (in hours or weeks) an individual user spends in consulting the book before returning it to the reserve desk, and λ defined as the average number of persons per hour (or week) who come into the library and wish to consult the book. These matters will be discussed more fully in Chapter 9.

Some corroborative figures on in-library use can be obtained from the use patterns discussed in Chapter 2. For example,[2] except for the chemists, the users of the Science Library at M.I.T. consulted about 4 books in the library for 1 they borrowed; similar ratios for periodicals are misleading, because the circulation of many periodicals is forbidden. But these figures do not provide many details of value to management, such as the relative amounts of in-library use to which various specific books, and various classes of books, are subjected, or whether a book which circulates often is also one which is used often in the library. Data of this sort are needed before models for in-library use of material can be constructed and before penalties for in-library service failures can be evaluated adequately. We will return to this question again in Chapter 9.

Analysis of Circulation Histories

Returning to the study of circulation, for which adequate data is available in those libraries that keep all their circulation cards, let us look at a few typical records in Table 5.1, taken from the Science Library at M.I.T. Each of the digits in each row is the number of circu-

Table 5.1   Yearly Circulation Histories of Four Books

Book A	8 5 3 3 1	2 0 2 2 2	1 1 0 1 1	3 2 3 0 1	2 0 1 1 0
Book B	4 1 0 1 1	1 2 4 0 3	2 2 2 1 0	0 1 0 0 2	1 1 0 0 0
Book C	2 1 0 0 0	0 1 3 4 3	3 4 5 3 0	0 3 1 2 0	1 0 1 0 0
Book D	1 0 1 0 0	1 0 0 0 0	1 1 1 0 1	0 1 0 0 0	0 0 0 0 0

lations per year for 25 successive years, starting from first shelving, of four representative books in the Science Library at M.I.T. The first two horizontal rows represent the histories of Books A and B which were initially fairly popular and which became less read as they got older, as occurs with most books. Of course the yearly circulation figures fluctuate considerably, but the general picture is a gradual decrease in circulation rate. This is also true of the last row, Book D, a typical history of many of the books in the library. Though there was a small surge in popularity in the tenth to seventeenth year of the book's shelf life, there were 3 times as many circulations in its first 10 years as in its latest 10 years.

The third row, Book C, shows a history that is occasionally found: There was a surge of popularity after the book had been on the shelf for 8 years. Presumably the subject matter of the book had become popular among the users of the library; perhaps a new course had been instituted and the instructor had referred to the book. The circulation rate had then died out again, in a manner similar to Books A and B of the first 2 rows. These occasional spurts of popularity are useful guides in our search for a probabilistic model to use in describing, and eventually predicting, book circulation.

If all circulation histories showed a steady tendency toward reduction, with some random yearly fluctuation, as is displayed by the first 15 years of Book A in Table 5.1, the last 20 years of Book B, or the first 25 years of Book D's life, then we might hope that a fairly simple model would fit the data. For example, we might try writing the expected circulation rate of the sth book in its tth year as $C_s f(t)$, where $f(t)$ is a monotonically decreasing function of t, perhaps the same function for a whole class of books, with $f(0) = 1$, and where C_s, the first year's circulation, is characteristic of the sth book. The actual circulation of the sth book in its tth year is, of course, a random variable, with its mean value given by $C_s f(t)$. The distribution about the mean of the actual circulation might be in accord with the Poisson distribution of Eq. 3.5 and Table 3.1, and the probability that the actual circulation rate in the tth year would be $P_n[C_\delta f(t)]$.

But this sort of model, though it allows for fluctuations in circulation, does not automatically take into account the surge of interest illustrated by the third row Book C of Table 5.1. A probability distribution around an expected value does allow for an occasional large value of circulation, but this upsurge would be momentary, just as likely to be followed by an exceptionally small value as another large one, whereas the sample histories of Table 5.1 show a tendency toward continuity in time. When the circulation in a given year is small, it seems more likely to be followed by a small circulation than a large one; alternatively, a large circulation is usually followed by another large one. Even in the less likely case, when the circulation suddenly increases, it seems usually to stay large for a while, rather than dropping immediately back to a low value. A kind of inertia seems to be manifested, a correlation in time. The model mentioned in the previous paragraph is incapable of including such correlation; it has no built-in "memory" of the previous year's circulation.

The Simple Markov Process

The simplest probabilistic model exhibiting a time correlation, or "memory," is the set of equations defining what is known as a *Markov process*. This model describes the behavior of a system that can be in any of a number of different *states*, which are distinguished by means of an index number; the state of the book, in the case under discussion, is the book's circulation R in a given year. In the Markov process the state of the system at the end of a given period of time is determined by its state at the beginning of the period. If, for example, a given book circulated m times last year, its circulation possibilities for the next year would be expressible as a probability distribution, depending on m but only indirectly on the previous circulation history of the book. If a given class of books obeys a Markov process in regard to circulation then the probability that a book, which circulated m times in the year just ended, will circulate n times in the year just commencing is T_{mn}, where T_{mn} depends on m and n but only depends on the book's previous history through the value of m.

Thus the Markov process exhibits the simplest of time correlations, from one time period to the next, and so on, sequentially; dependence on previous states is solely by way of this stepwise connection. It is of course perhaps too great a simplification to expect that a book's circulation, even in a probabilistic sense, should be determined solely by its previous year's circulation without regard to its earlier history (except *via* its previous year's circulation). Nevertheless the model does introduce the time correlation, and it merits investigation in order to see how well it can be brought into correspondence with the data. As will be demonstrated later, embellishments can be added if required.

According to such a model, however, all the books of a class, which circulate m times in a given year, should have an average circulation $N(m)$ the next year, where the value of $N(m)$ depends solely on m. The individual circulations should be clustered around the average value $N(m)$; the conditional probability that an individual book of the class (with circulation m this year) having circulation n the next year is $T_{mn} = P(n \mid \text{if } m)$ where

$$T_{m0} + T_{m1} + T_{m2} + T_{m3} + \cdots = 1$$
$$N(m) = 0(T_{m0}) + 1(T_{m1}) + 2(T_{m2}) + 3(T_{m3}) + \cdots \tag{5.1}$$

as in Eqs. 2.7 and 2.12. This is the definition of the mean value $N(m)$ in terms of the probabilities T_{mn}. The "spread" of the actual values of the next year's circulation away from the mean value $N(m)$ is measured by the variance (see Eq. 2.13)

$$[\sigma(m)]^2$$
$$= [0 - N(m)]^2 T_{m0} + [1 - N(m)]^2 T_{m1} + [2 - N(m)]^2 T_{m2} + \cdots$$
$$= 1(T_{m1}) + 4(T_{m2}) + 9(T_{m3}) + \cdots - [N(m)]^2 \tag{5.2}$$

which is the mean value of the square of the difference between the actual circulation n and the mean N.

For most books $N(m)$ is smaller than m, because *on the average* the circulation for a given year (call it year 1) tends to be less than the circulation of the previous year (call it year 0). But if $\sigma(m)$ is large (of the same size as $N(m)$ for example), some books will have a greater circulation during year 1 than during year 0 (n will be greater than m), and conversely a few books of the class will have zero circulation ($n = 0$) during year 1. The year 1 circulation will be distributed so that the average value of n for year 1 is $N(m)$, somewhat smaller than m. During the next year (year 2), the circulation will depend on the book's circulation in year 1; those having circulation n large will have an average circulation $N(n)$ in year 2, larger than those books which had zero circulation in year 1, which will have an average circulation $N(0)$ in year 2. Thus the Markov model allows the possibility of an occasional increase of popularity, of the sort displayed by Book C of Table 5.1.

An Example

To see more clearly the implications of this circulation model, we need to discuss a specific example; this one[5] is a tabulation of the circulation histories of about 300 books from the Science Library at M.I.T. An attempt was made to choose the books at random from those that had been available for circulation during their life, but the choice had to be limited to those having complete circulation histories from accession. Thus the fraction of older popular books in the sample is somewhat less than that in the library as a whole. The sample size is sufficient to illustrate our model, however.

The data can be displayed in many ways, the most comprehensive being the listing of circulations per year for each book, from its accession, as in Table 5.2. From this mass of figures we can, of course, cal-

Table 5.2   Examples of Book Circulation Histories*

	$t = 1$	2	3	4	5	6	7	8	9	10
Book A	6	0	2	1	—					
Book B	9	3	1	5	—					
Book C	3	2	3	—						
Book D	5	0	0	0	—					
Book E	0	1	0	0	—					
Book F	4	2	1	2	0	—				
Book G	14	5	7	6	0	2	4	0	—	
Book H	1	0	0	0	0	2	2	0	2	—
Book I	10	5	6	4	2	4	0	1	0	—
Book J	3	0	2	1	3	0	0	0	0	1

Average Circulation History of Sample of 300										
t =	1	2	3	4	5	6	7	8	9	10
$R(t)$ =	4.3	2.1	1.6	1.1	0.8	0.8	0.8	0.6	0.4	0.6
Theoretical =	4.3	2.4	1.5	1.1	0.9	0.7	0.6	0.6	0.5	0.5

* Where t is the year after accession of each book and the dash indicates the current year (which may be beyond the end of the table for an old book).

culate the mean yearly circulation $R(t)$ of the books in the sample, as a function of t, the year after accession. The result is given by the next to last row of Table 5.2. The last row will be discussed later.

The result shows that, on the average, book circulation diminishes as the book ages, rapidly at first, then leveling out to a rate of about one circulation in 2 years, which seems to extend out to an age of at least 20 years. During the first 5 years of the life of an average book in this library, its average circulation rate is about 2 per year, for the next 5 years its mean circulation is about 2/3 per year, and for the rest of its life (at least out to about 20 years) its average circulation is about 1/2 per year. If a collection of books had this circulation behavior, with about 3/10 of them having been in the library less than 5 years, another 3/10 with an age between 5 and 10 years, and the other 4/10 were more than 10 years old, the mean circulation of the whole collection would be about 1 per year. Since this is about the age distribution of all the books in the Science Library at M.I.T. and since the mean circulation of all the borrowable books in its collection is about 1 per year, it appears that the sample of about 300, from which we are deriving our figures, is reasonably typical of the whole collection.

Analysis of the Data

But this tabulation of average circulation gives us little real insight. From the average circulations of Table 5.2 we cannot predict the chances of a sudden spurt of popularity of an individual book, of the sort illustrated by Book C of Table 5.1 or by Book H of Table 5.2, for example. In particular, we could not predict the chance of a book's being borrowed after it had not circulated for a year or more, a prediction that would be of use in deciding which book to send to a less accessible "cold storage." We will have to go to the individual histories of Table 5.2, to see whether high circulation follows high circulation, and low follows low, on the average.

To see whether the previously mentioned Markov model could adequately represent the data, we first ask what is the mean circulation $N(m)$, in the second year, of all those books that had circulation m in their first year of service in the library — in other words we calculate $N(m)$, as defined in Eq. 5.1 for different m, for all first-year books (there were 305 of them in the sample). See Table 5.3. The third row of figures will be taken up later.

The value of $N(2)$ is computed, for example, by collecting the circula-

Table 5.3   Mean Second-Year Circulation $N(m)$ for Those Books That in Their First Year Had Circulation m

m	= 0	1	2	3	4	5	6	7	8	9	13
$N(m)$	= 0.4	0.7	1.2	1.3	2.2	2.4	2.5	3.7	3.8	4.5	5.1
Theoretical	= 0.4	0.8	1.3	1.8	2.3	2.8	3.2	3.7	4.2	4.7	6.6

tion histories of all the books that had 2 circulations during their first year. There were 32 of them in the sample. Some of these did not circulate in their second year, some had circulation 1, 2, 3, etc., and 1 circulated 6 times in its second year. The average second-year circulation of these 32 books was 1.2. The other values of $N(m)$ were calculated similarly. However, the entry for $m = 13$ represents 33 books with an average first-year circulation of 13 (some with 10, some up to 15 circulations), which had a mean second-year circulation of 5.1 as shown.

The mean second-year circulations $N(m)$ of this sample seem to be regularly arranged, increasing more or less linearly with m, from a low value of 0.4 for $m = 0$ to 4.5 for $m = 9$. Evidently the books that were more popular in their first year were also more popular in their second year, though the popularity had diminished somewhat. Note that $N(m)$ is smaller than m, except for $m = 0$. Evidently there is a strong correlation between a book's circulation during its first year and its circulation during its second year of presence in the library, a correlation that could not be included in the simpler model dealing only with mean circulations per year, as in Table 5.2.

To see whether this same correlation holds for later years, we tabulate $N(m)$ against m for the fourth and eighth years of book life in Table 5.4.

Table 5.4 Circulation Correlation for Later Years

Mean Fourth-Year Circulation $N(m)$ for Those Books That Have Third-Year Circulation m:

m =	0	1	2	3	4	5	6	7	8	9
$N(m)$ =	0.4	0.8	1.1	2.4	2.8	3.0	3.0	5.0	3.7	3.8
Theoretical =	0.4	0.8	1.3	1.8	2.3	2.8	3.2	3.7	4.2	4.7

Mean Eighth-Year Circulation $N(m)$ for Those Books That Have Seventh-Year Circulation m:

m =	0	1	2	3	4	5	6	7	8	9
$N(m)$ =	0.2	0.5	0.6	4.0	1.0	3.0	—	—	—	—
Theoretical =	0.3	0.7	1.2	1.7	2.2	2.7				

No books in the last sample had seventh-year circulation greater than 5. There were only 60 books in the sample with age greater than 8 years; the mean values of $N(m)$ for so small a sample can be expected to fluctuate rather widely from the value obtained from a larger sample. Nevertheless the general characteristics of behavior of $N(m)$ are quite similar to those for the first 2 years of a book's life. In fact when we plot $N(m)$ against m, as we have in Fig. 5.1 the three cases seem to indicate, within the uncertainties inevitable for these small samples, a common dependence of $N(m)$ on m.

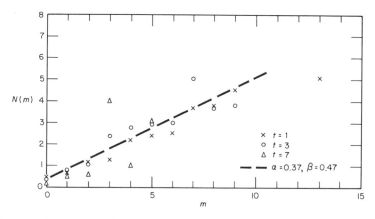

Fig. 5.1.   Mean circulation $N(m)$ for year $t + 1$ as a function of circulation. m for previous year t.

Plots of $N(m)$ against m for year pairs 2-3, 4-5, 6-7, and 8-9, strengthen this conclusion and indicate that the simple linear formula

$$N(m) = \alpha + \beta m \tag{5.3}$$

is a reasonable relationship for all the year pairs. In fact, in view of the small-sample fluctuations, it seems reasonable to use the same values of α and β for all year pairs. In other words, within the accuracy of the data, the mean circulation $N(m)$ of a book during its $t + 1$ year is given in terms of its circulation m during its t year by Eq. 5.3, where the parameters α and β are independent of t. (We will show later that α diminishes slightly with book age after about 5 years.)

Thus to find α and β we combine the data for all year pairs; we segregate, for each book year t, all those that have circulated m times, record the total number of these $M(m)$, and then list the numbers N_{mn} of these that had circulation n in year $t + 1$. From this we obtain the mean circulation

$$N(m) = \frac{1}{M(m)} (N_{m1} + 2N_{m2} + 3N_{m3} + \cdots) \tag{5.4}$$

since $N_{m0} + N_{m1} + N_{m2} + \cdots = M(m)$. The result is given in Table 5.5.

At present we will look at the next-to-last column $N(m)$, which gives the mean circulation in year $t + 1$ of those books that had circulation m in year t. There are 1216 examples $(M = M(0) + M(1) + M(2) + \cdots = 1216)$ in this tabulation, since a 10-year-old book

Table 5.5 Values of $M(m)$, N_{mn}, and $N(m)$ for Different Values of m and n

		N_{mn}											Theo-
m	$M(m)$	$n = 0$	1	2	3	4	5	6	7	8	9	$N(m)$	retical
0	484	373	74	20	6	1	1	0	0	0	0	0.33	0.37
1	240	117	69	31	14	5	3	0	0	0	1	0.90	0.85
2	158	52	35	34	17	15	3	1	1	0	1	1.58	1.33
3	94	20	27	21	16	3	5	1	1	0	1	1.79	1.81
4	72	10	12	18	12	7	8	3	0	1	1	2.60	2.29
5	56	7	14	11	7	6	4	4	2	0	0	2.66	2.77
6	49	7	5	12	9	6	3	2	4	1	1	2.96	3.25
7	25	1	1	4	3	3	3	5	1	2	1	4.68	3.73
8	16	1	3	2	3	1	1	3	1	0	0	3.75	4.21
9	22	0	1	2	4	5	1	3	2	0	2	4.36	4.69

contributes 9 year-pair entries to the table and even a 3-year-old book contributes 2 entries, the 1-2 pair and the 2-3 pair. Thus the conclusion that our year-by-year analysis led us, that the circulation behavior of a book depends (on the average) on its previous-year's circulation and not explicitly on its age or still earlier circulation, enables us to combine the data and improve the accuracy of the results. We can now manipulate the next-to-last column, either graphically or by least squares, to obtain the most probable values of the parameters α and β for Formula 5.3. The resulting values for the sample of Table 5.5 are $\alpha = 0.37$ and $\beta = 0.48$. Therefore, on the average, for these books,

$$N(m) = 0.37 + 0.48m \qquad (5.5)$$

The expected circulation next year of a book from this library appears to be roughly 0.4 plus about a half of its last-year's circulation, independent of the age of the book (at least out to an age of 5 years). Thus, on the average, book circulation decreases as book age increases. But if, occasionally, a book becomes popular again, the circulation history thenceforward is as though it had been popular all along. Likewise, if a book happens suddenly to lose popularity, its future circulation history is as though it had always been neglected. This behavior corresponds more realistically to the ups and downs of book popularity than do other models, based explicitly on book age.

Verifying the Model

This Markovian model for book circulation, represented by Eq. 5.3, is of course only an approximate representation of the actual behavior. In the first place the choice of number of circulations per year, as a measure, is arbitrary; we could have chosen circulations per 2 years or circulations per quarter year as our base, and the model would have come out with somewhat different numbers. Moreover, a more detailed study of the basic data indicate that, although parameter β seems to stay constant throughout the life of the book, α diminishes slightly with age. As accurately as the data permit, α is roughly 0.40 for the first 5 years of the life of the book and then drops slowly to less than 0.2 for t greater than about 10 (see Table 5.12, later in this chapter).

However the purpose of a model is to represent the operation as accurately as is needed and in just sufficient detail to account for the important aspects of its behavior. A more intricate model would produce no better predictions on which to base administrative decisions, would considerably increase the computations required to make the predictions, and would require more data to obtain the appropriate parameters. The same application of Occam's razor, which led us to use the simple circulation-interference model of Eqs. 4.3 and 4.6, rather than the more elegant models of Eqs. 4.9 or 4.10, leads us here to use the model of Eq. 5.3, with a reduction in the value of α for books older than 5 or 6 years.

To check the model, we can apply the Formula 5.3 for $N(m)$ for years 1-2, 3-4, and 7-8, with $\alpha = 0.37$, $\beta = 0.48$ for the first 2 pairs and $\alpha = 0.25$, $\beta = 0.5$ for the last. The resulting values for different values of m are tabulated in the rows marked Theoretical in Tables 5.3 and 5.4. Comparison with the data indicates satisfactory check of the model in considerable detail, as is also the case with the right-hand column of Table 5.5.

The model of Eq. 5.3 has many computational advantages. Since it is linear in α, β, and m, average values yield average equations of the same form. For example, if M_1 books of 1 class have parameter values α_1 and β_1, and M_2 books of a second class have values α_2 and β_2, then a combination of both classes will have parameters α and β that are weighted averages of the α's and the β's.

$$\alpha = \frac{M_1\alpha_1 + M_2\alpha_2}{M_1 + M_2}$$

$$\beta = \frac{M_1\beta_1 + M_2\beta_2}{M_1 + M_2}$$

$$(5.6)$$

The collection of borrowable books in the Science Library of M.I.T. had, in 1962 (see Table 6.2), the following numbers N_s of books of class s; circulation histories[6] of less than 100 books of each class were analyzed to obtain approximate values of α and β, as tabulated in Table 5.6. By multiplying each α_s by N_s, summing and dividing by N,

Table 5.6 Circulation Parameters for Various Classes of Books

Class s	N_s	α_s	β_s	$N_s\alpha_s$	$N_s\beta_s$
General Science and Engineering	1400	0.30	0.70	420	980
Mathematics	4900	0.30	0.60	1470	2940
Physics	3700	0.50	0.60	1850	2220
Chemistry	2800	0.60	0.50	1680	1400
Geology	6700	0.45	0.20	3020	1340
Biology	5000	0.40	0.45	2000	2250
Metallurgy, Food Technology	3500	0.20	0.70	700	2450
$M = 28000$				11140	13580

the total number of books in the collection, we find that average values of α and β are $\alpha = 0.40$ and $\beta = 0.49$ for the whole collection. This checks quite well with the more detailed calculations made on the sample collection[5] of Table 5.5 and indicates again that the sample is fairly typical of the whole collection.

Moreover, if the *average* circulation of a collection of books with collective parameters α and β is $\overline{m}$ during year t, the average circulation of these books during the next year $t + 1$ will be $\alpha + \beta\overline{m}$. Thus we can start with a collection of books having different circulations during their first year but having an average first-year circulation $R(1)$. During the second year, their average circulation will be $R(2) = \alpha + R(1)\beta$. During their third year, their average circulation will be

$$R(3) = \alpha + R(2)\beta = \alpha + \beta[\alpha + R(1)\beta] = \alpha(1 + \beta) + R(1)\beta^2$$

During their fourth year, their mean circulation will be

$$R(4) = \alpha + R(3)\beta = \alpha(1 + \beta + \beta^2) + R(1)\beta^3$$

and during their $t + 1$ year, their average circulation will be

$$R(t + 1) = \alpha(1 + \beta + \beta^2 + \cdots + \beta^{t-1}) + R(1)\beta^t$$

$$= \alpha\frac{1 - \beta^t}{1 - \beta} + R(1)\beta^t \tag{5.7}$$

$$= 0.71 + 3.63(0.48)^t$$

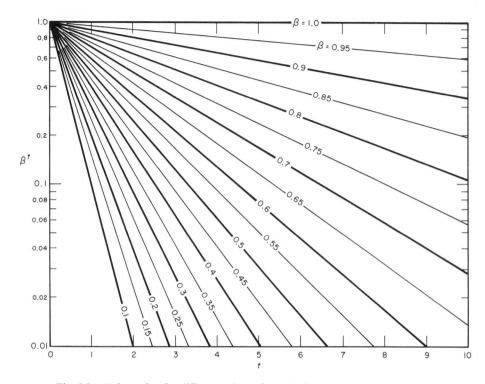

Fig. 5.2. Values of β^t for different values of β and of t.

for the sample of Table 5.5 for the first 5 years. If, after year T, the value of α changes to α', the mean circulation for year t, greater than T, is

$$R(t + 1) = \frac{\alpha' + (\alpha - \alpha')\beta^{t-T+1} - \alpha\beta^t}{1 - \beta} + R(1)\beta^t \qquad (5.8)$$

$$\simeq 0.5 + 0.4(0.48)^{t-5}$$

for the sample of Table 5.5 for which $T > 5$. The bottom row of Table 5.2 labeled Theoretical, corresponds to these formulas. The check with the data on average circulation history of books in the collection is quite satisfactory. Calculations of expected circulation from Eqs. 5.7 or 5.8 can be quickly made by taking values of β^t from Fig. 5.2.

Implications of the Model

Formulas 5.7 and 5.8 show that $\alpha'/(1 - \beta)$ is the final mean circulation rate to which the whole collection will subside, whereas β measures the rapidity with which the circulation rate approaches $\alpha/(1 - \beta)$ or $\alpha'/1 - \beta$; the smaller β is, the more rapidly will the asymptotic value of $R(t)$ be reached. From Table 5.6, if we assume that α'_s is proportional to α_s, we see that geology books lose popularity in a couple of years (β small) after which they are borrowed about once in 2 years ($\alpha \simeq 0.45$, $1 - \beta \simeq 0.8$, $0.45/0.8 \simeq 0.56$). Whereas on the average, mathematics books lose initial popularity slowly ($\beta = 0.6$), but they are eventually taken out less than once a year, since $\alpha = 0.3$ and $\alpha/(1 - \beta) \simeq 0.7$. Chemistry and physics books stay popular fairly long ($\beta \geq 0.5$), and their eventual circulation rate is fairly high as well, since $\alpha/(1 - \beta) > 1$.

Some of these behavior patterns of various classes of books should perhaps be taken into account in allotting budgets for book purchases. Certainly they should be considered when ordering duplicate copies of the more popular books. Table 5.6 indicates that, on the average, a geology book will remain popular less than 2 years, whereas a mathematics book will stay popular, on the average, more than twice as long. To put this in quantitative form, suppose a mathematics and a geology book each had circulation 12 per year the first year. Table 5.7 shows

Table 5.7   Expected Unsatisfied Demand for Two Typical Books

Year of Circulation t	1	2	3	4	5	Cumulative
Math. book expected circulation $R(t)$	12	7.5	4.8	3.2	2.2	29.7
Math. book unsatisfied demand, 1 copy, U_1	11.1	3.5	1.1	0.5	0.2	16.4
Math. book unsatisfied demand, 2 copies, U_2	4.2	0.6	0.1	—	—	4.9
Geol. book expected circulation $R(t)$	12	2.9	1.0	0.7	0.6	17.2
Geol. book unsatisfied demand, 1 copy, U_1	11.1	0.7	—	—	—	11.8
Geol. book unsatisfied demand, 2 copies, U_2	4.2	—	—	—	—	4.2

the subsequent expected yearly circulation of each book (using Eq. 5.7 with the α and β of Table 5.6) together with the unsatisfied demand if 1 and if 2 copies were on hand (obtained from Table 4.1). If it took a year to get a duplicate into service, then 4.6 additional users would be satisfied if the book were a mathematics book and only 0.7 additional users would be expected if the duplicated book were in geology.

Of course the values of $R(t)$ are expected values: Because random events play a part, the actual circulation may be larger or smaller than

$R(t)$; the actual circulation of the geology book in its third year may surpass that of the mathematics book, though this would be unlikely. If however, a number of high-circulation mathematics books were compared with a number of initially popular geology books, their average behavior would come closer and closer to the tabulated results the larger the number of books considered. If duplication decisions are made dozens of times a year on the basis of this model, the fluctuations will tend to even out and the rule of thumb based on the expected circulation formula of Eq. 5.7 will be as good a guide as can be devised, considering the element of chance involved. This rule of thumb, based on working out a number of expected histories such as in Table 5.7, can be stated as in Table 5.8. The decision as to whether the predicted

Table 5.8   Guides for Decisions on Book Duplication

	estimate the total unsatisfied demand as		times the U_1 of	To help, a duplicate should be in use before		years after 1st copy arrived
If $\beta = 0.8$,	demand as	2.5	Table 4.1	before	2	arrived
If $\beta = 0.7$	"	1.7	"	"	1	"
If $\beta = 0.5$	"	1.2	"	"	2/3	"
If $\beta = 0.3$	"	1.0	"	"	1/2	"

total unsatisfied demand is large enough to warrant ordering a duplicate depends on the criterion determined by the librarian, as indicated at the end of Chapter 4.

The Transition Probabilities

But our analysis of the data on the M.I.T. Science Library has not yet gone deep enough. We still need to know the probabilities T_{mn} of Eq. 5.1, the conditional probability, that, if the circulation in year t is m, the circulation in year $t + 1$ is n. This requires still further sorting of the data and strains the capacity of the sample; it would be better if we could take the time to analyze data from 6000 books, rather than 300. We are saved, however, by the indications that these probabilities T_{mn} are the same for the first 5 years, at least, of a book's life, since the mean circulation $N(m)$, defined in terms of the T in Eq. 5.1 is $\alpha + \beta m$, with α and β independent of t, at least for the first 5 years.

Since the process of book circulation is a random one, we might presume that the distribution of circulations in a year would be the Poisson distribution, defined in Eq. 3.5. If the expected number of circulations in year $t + 1$ is $N(m) = \alpha + \beta m$ and if the circulation in year t is m, a Poisson distribution that would predict the chance of actually getting circulation n in year $t + 1$ would be

$$T_{mn} = P_n(\alpha + \beta m) = \frac{(\alpha + \beta m)^n}{n!} \exp(-\alpha - \beta m) \qquad (5.9)$$

This can be compared with the data given in Table 5.5. If $M(m)$ books of the sample had circulation m in year t, then the expected number of books of the sample having circulation n in year $t + 1$ would be $M(m)$ times T_{mn}. Using tables of the Poisson distribution P_n for mean values $\alpha + \beta m = N(m)$, as indicated at the right of Table 5.5, for different values of n, and multiplying this by $M(m)$, we obtain Table 5.9, the

Table 5.9   Computed Values of $M(m)T_{mn}$, to Compare with N_{mn} of Table 5.5

	$M(m)$	$n = 0$	1	2	3	4	5	6	7	8	9	$\alpha + \beta m$
0	484	324	130	26	3	1	—	—	—	—	—	0.4
1	240	108	86	35	9	2	—	—	—	—	—	0.8
2	158	43	56	36	16	5	1	—	—	—	—	1.3
3	94	16	28	25	15	7	2	1	—	—	—	1.8
4	72	7	17	19	15	8	4	2	—	—	—	2.3
5	56	4	10	13	12	9	5	2	1	—	—	2.8
6	49	2	6	10	10	9	6	3	2	1	—	3.3
7	25	1	2	4	6	5	4	2	1	—	—	3.7
8	16	—	1	2	3	3	3	2	1	1	—	4.2
9	22	—	1	2	3	4	4	3	2	2	1	4.7

expected values of N_{mn}, which are to be compared with the data given in Table 5.5. Considering the smallness of the sample, the correspondence is satisfactory.

Having verified the circulation model, we can proceed to work out some of its implications, to be used either to provide additional, indirect verification of its adequacy, or to predict future circulation behavior. For example, for those books that had circulation m in a given year, the probability they will have circulation n the next year is T_{mn} as given in Eq. 5.9 and the probability that one of them will have circulation n in the second year later is

$$(T^2)_{mn} = T_{m0}T_{0n} + T_{m1}T_{1n} + T_{m2}T_{2n} + \cdots$$

$$= e^{-2\alpha}\left[\frac{\alpha^n}{n!}\,e^{-\beta m} + \frac{(\alpha + \beta m)(\alpha + \beta)^n}{1!\,n!}\,e^{-(m+1)\beta}\right.$$

$$\left. + \frac{(\alpha + \beta m)^2(\alpha + 2\beta)^n}{2!\,n!}\,e^{-(m+2)\beta}\cdots\right]$$

Going further, as long as the values of α and β, for a given collection of books, do not change over a period of t years, the probability that one of them has a circulation n in year $T + t$, if it had circulation m in year T is

$$(T^t)_{mn} = (T^{t-s})_{m0}(T^s)_{0n} + (T^{t-s})_{m1}(T^s)_{1n} + (T^{t-s})_{m2}(T^s)_{2n} + \cdots \qquad (5.10)$$

where s can be any integer greater than 0 and less than t. In this notation, the Markov transition matrix T_{mn} would be labeled $(T^1)_{mn}$. Some of these tables of conditional probabilities for different values of α, β, and t are given in the Appendix.

One of the properties of the Markov process we are discussing is that, as time goes on, the collection of books "tends to forget what its initial circulation was." One can see, from the tables in the Appendix that, as t increases, the rows of the matrix tend to become more and more alike, in other words $(T^t)_{mn}$ tends to become less and less dependent on the initial circulation m as t increases. Eventually, as $t \to \infty$, every row is alike; every book in the antiquated collection has the same probability distribution of circulation, no matter what its initial circulation. As $t \to \infty$,

$$(T^t)_{mn} \to P_n^\infty \qquad (5.11)$$

The book collection has settled down to a statistical *steady state*. This is not to say that every book in the collection will have the same *circulation;* it is to say that every book has the same *probability distribution,* irrespective of its initial circulation. The tables in the Appendix give values of the P_n^∞ for a variety of values of α and β. They represent the final circulation distributions of old collections; by the end of t years, where t is large enough so that β^t is small (smaller than 0.05, for example), any collection with parameters α and β will settle down to this distribution.

As an example of how this model can be used, let us imagine a group of books, all having the same values of the parameters α and β and all bought during one year. The first year's circulation distribution will depend on how well the accessions budget has been spent for books of this class. If popular books were bought, there will be a large fraction of high, first-year circulation. Suppose the choice has been good and that the first-year circulation distribution is geometrical, with parameter γ. (In Chapter 8 it will be shown that this is not unusual.) In other words the fraction $P_1(\geq m)$ of the accessions that circulates m or more times in their first year and the fraction $P_1(m)$ that circulates exactly m times are

$$P_1(\geq m) = \gamma^m$$
$$P_1(m) = P_1(\geq m) - P_1(\geq m + 1) = (1 - \gamma)\gamma^m \qquad (5.12)$$

The dots on the curve marked "1st year" in Fig. 5.3 give values of γ^m for $\gamma = 0.8$. They represent the range of popularity of the accessions of this assumed class. One sees that 10 per cent of these books circulate 10 or more times in the first year. However, although the first-year circulation behavior depends on the judgment of the purchaser, the circulation behavior in later years depends more and more on the use habits of the borrowers of books of this class, which is represented by the values of α and β.

According to Eq. 5.9, the chance that one of these books will circulate n times in its *second* year is the sum of the probability $P_1(m)$, that the book circulated m times in its first year times the conditional probability T_{mn} that the book will circulate n times next year *if* it circulated m times the previous year, summed over all possible values of m; the same is true for the third-year circulation in terms of the possible second-year circulations, and so on.

$$P_2(n) = P_1(0)T_{0n} + P_1(1)T_{1n} + P_1(2)T_{2n} + \cdots$$
$$= (1 - \gamma)(T_{0n} + \gamma T_{1n} + \gamma^2 T_{2n} + \gamma^3 T_{3n} + \cdots) \qquad (5.13)$$
$$P_3(n) = P_2(0)T_{0n} + P_2(1)T_{1n} + P_2(2)T_{2n} + \cdots$$

Then the probability that the circulation in the tth year is m or greater is the sum

$$P_t(\geq m) = P_t(m) + P_t(m + 1) + P_t(m + 2) + \cdots$$

The probability that a book of the class under consideration will circulate exactly n times in its tth year after accession is $P_t(n)$, which is built up by successive multiplications by the T_{mn} of Eq. 5.9. The cumulative probability $P_t(\geq m)$ that one of the books circulates m or more times during its tth year on the shelf is then obtained by summing the $P_t(n)$ as shown.

The dots on the different lines shown in Fig. 5.3 are values of $P_t(\geq m)$ for different values of t and m and for $\gamma = 0.8$, $\alpha = 0.4$, and $\beta = 0.5$. They show how the circulation drops off as the books age. In their first year, as we have already pointed out, 10 per cent circulate 10 or more times. Already in the second year these high circulations have dropped off drastically; only 2 per cent of these books circulate 10 or more times in their second year. In the third year only about 1 book

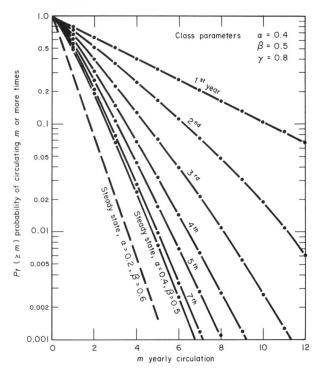

Fig. 5.3.   Example of the Markov model. Expected fraction $P_t \, (\geq m)$ of books of a class, t years old, that circulate m or more times in the year.

in 400 circulates 10 or more times. As the books age, the high circulations decrease drastically and more and more books circulate only a few times a year. Though, as explained earlier, there is always a chance for a few books to regain popularity; this chance also diminishes as the books get older.

The drop in popularity eventually ceases, however, as long as both α and β remain constant. We see that the curves for successive years get closer together, approaching the limiting distribution, marked "steady state" in Fig. 5.3. After some 10 years, the circulation distribution remains the same for books with $\alpha = 0.4$ and $\beta = 0.6$; only 1 in 5 of the steady-state group circulates 2 or more times a year, 1 in 50 circulates 4 or more times, and only half of them circulate at all during the year. Different books in the collection make up these fractions in different years: A book that had not circulated for some years may circulate twice, but others will drop out of circulation; so the average remains the same.

The steady state would be the same, no matter what the first-year distribution had been, as long as the parameters α and β are constant. For example Fig. 5.4 shows the circulation distribution for a collection of books with $\alpha = 0.4$ and $\beta = 0.6$, all of which circulated exactly four times during their first year. In this case the "1st year" curve is the clifflike one shown in Fig. 5.4; all books of the group circulate more than 1, or more than 2, or more than 3 times, and all circulate 4 or more times, but none circulates 5 or more times in the first year. Already in their second year this distribution is beginning to spread out, some circulating more than four times and some not circulating at all. By the end of their fifth year, their circulation distribution begins to be

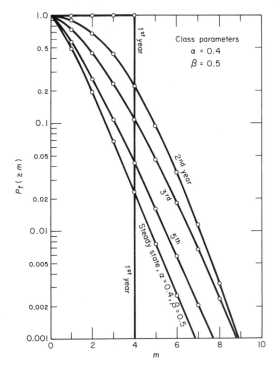

Fig. 5.4. Circulation histories of books, all of which circulated four times in their first year.

very close to that for the books of Fig. 5.3, with the geometric first-year distribution; evidently for books with $\alpha = 0.4$ and $\beta = 0.5$, by the time they are 5 years old, they have nearly forgotten how they started out. And, of course, the limiting steady-state curve of Fig. 5.4 is exactly the same as that of Fig. 5.3.

Unfortunately, in the case of the books in the Science Library at M.I.T., just about the time the books reach their steady-state distribution, their value of α begins to diminish, so that, after about 5 years, the curve continues to drop down to about the dashed curve of Fig. 5.3 at the end of 10 years, and probably continues to drop, though more slowly, thereafter. Also unfortunately, until more detailed circulation records are kept over longer periods, we cannot fit our model to the actual behavior of older books in any degree of detail.

Circulation of Older Books

We can gain some insight as to change of parameters with book age from rather scanty data collected in the Science Library. That α and β remain reasonably constant for the first 5 years can be demonstrated. We saw earlier that, for the first 5 or 6 years the books in the total collection corresponded to the parameters $\alpha = 0.4$ and $\beta = 0.5$. Since $0.5^5 \simeq 0.03$, which may be sufficiently small, we would expect that the circulation of 5-year-old books would be distributed roughly according to P_n^∞. There were 141 books of the sample tabulated which were 5 or 6 years old; the fraction of them having yearly circulation n is shown in Table 5.10 and compared with the calculated P_n^∞ for $\alpha = 0.4$ and

Table 5.10   Fraction F_n of Books Having Circulation n in Their 5th or 6th Year, Compared with the Steady-State Distribution P_n^∞ for $\alpha = 0.4$, $\beta = 0.5$

n	0	1	2	3	4	5
F_n	0.54	0.23	0.16	0.05	0.02	—
P_n^∞	0.50	0.30	0.13	0.05	0.02	—

$\beta = 0.5$. Both the data and the model show less than one percent of the books circulated 5 or more times. The check between data and theoretical model is quite good, considering the smallness of the sample. The books more than 6 years old were not included in the sample; we have already noted that, between $t = 6$ and $t = 10$, the value of α decreases from 0.4 to less than 0.2. Another indirect test will serve to estimate the value of α for $t > 10$.

We start by considering the collection of all books of a class. This is a mixture of ages and of popularities, with a distribution of circulations given by the probabilities $P_c(m)$ that a book in the collection circulates m times during the year, for different values of m. New books are added each year, enough to replenish the high-circulation books and to keep the probabilities $P_c(m)$ more or less the same from year to year. (This will be discussed further in Chapter 6.) Thus the probability that a book, already in the collection, circulated at least once last year is $P_c(1) + P_c(2) + \cdots$, which sum we will designate by the symbol X_0. The probability it circulated last year but did not circulate this year we can call B. (The sum $B + X_0$ is not unity, because the alternative outcomes are neither exclusive nor exhaustive; we have left out for example the possibility that a book did not circulate either year.) The probability that this book, which did not circulate this year, also does not circulate next year is given by the conditional probability of Eq. 5.9 for m and n both zero, $T_{00} = e^{-\alpha}$.

Thus the expected fraction of books in the collection that circulated last year, did not circulate this year, and will not circulate next year is the product $Be^{-\alpha}$. Since the circulation distribution of the whole collection is more or less the same from year to year, we can shift time back a year and say the $Be^{-\alpha}$ is the probability that a book, picked at random today, did not circulate last year or the year previous but did circulate in the year before that, i.e., that its last circulation was between 2 and 3 years ago. It is not difficult to extend this and show that the probability that a book of the collection had its last circulation between 3 and 4 years ago is $Be^{-\alpha}(e^{-\alpha}) = Be^{-2\alpha}$, and, in general, that the probability that a book's last circulation is $t + 1$ years ago is $Be^{-(t-1)\alpha}$.

To find the relation between B and X_0, we note that the sum (see Eq. 2.25)

$$B + Be^{-\alpha} + Be^{-2\alpha} + Be^{-3\alpha} + \cdots = \frac{B}{1 - e^{-\alpha}}$$

is equal to the probability that a book did not circulate last year, regardless of whether it did or did not circulate in previous years. But this does constitute an exhaustive set with X_0, the probability that the book *did* circulate last year (regardless of its circulation in previous years). Therefore, $X_0 + [B/(1 - e^{-\alpha})] = 1$, which determines B in terms of X_0, the probability that a book in the collection circulated at least once last year.

Thus we can write down the probability X_t that a book has not circulated for the past t years (but did circulate $t + 1$ years ago) as

$$X_t = \begin{cases} X_0 & \text{when } t = 0 \\ (1 - X_0)(1 - e^{-\alpha})e^{-(t-1)\alpha} & \text{when } t > 0 \end{cases}$$

where X_0 is the probability that the book *did* circulate during the past year and the coefficient of the term for $t > 0$, which is the B just discussed, is of a magnitude such that $X_0 + X_1 + X_2 + \cdots = 1$. Of course t cannot be larger than the age of the book, but if we deal with the older books, the formula should hold for a reasonably wide range of t. Another way of writing the formula is to give the probability that a book in the collection has not circulated for *at least* t years,

$$X(\geq t) = X_t + X_{t+1} + X_{t+2} + \cdots$$

$$= \begin{cases} 1 & \text{when } t = 0 \\ (1 - X_0)e^{-\alpha(t-1)} & \text{when } t > 0 \end{cases} \tag{5.14}$$

A random sample of 711 books older than 5 years was examined to check this formula. Most of the books in this sample were considerably older than 5 years, and those that had not circulated for several years were mainly the older volumes. Thus the value of α which is obtained should be more nearly equal the value for books 10 years old or older than the value 0.4, appropriate for the younger books. The data are given in the second row of Table 5.11. The third row is computed from

Table 5.11   Fraction $F(\geq t)$ of Older Books That Have Not Circulated for t Years or More, Compared to the $X(\geq t)$ of Eq. 5.14

t	0	1	2	3	4	5	7	10
$F(\geq t)$	1	0.64	0.55	0.48	0.42	0.36	0.32	0.23
$X(\geq t)$	1	0.64	0.56	0.49	0.44	0.38	0.29	0.19

Eq. 5.14 with $X_0 = 0.36$ and $\alpha = 0.15$. The fit is satisfactory, though the "tail" of the curve ($t \geq 7$) would fit better with $\alpha = 0.12$. Thus for the collection of loanable books in the Science Library, the limiting value of α for books 10 or more years old lies between 0.12 and 0.2; we noted earlier that $\alpha \sim 0.4$ for books less than 5 years of age. The relationship between our model and the fact that 36 per cent of the older books circulated the previous year will be discussed in a later chapter.

Once the validity of Formulas 5.14 (which are based on the Markov model) has been verified, a simpler means can be developed of obtaining the limiting value of α for the older books. A random sample is made,

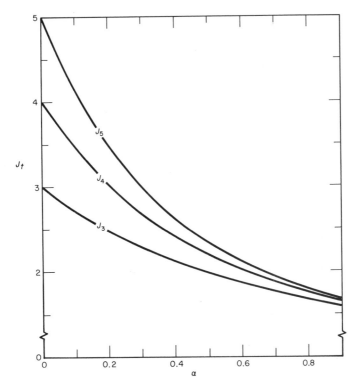

Fig. 5.5. Values of J_t defined in Eq. 5.15 plotted as a function of α for $t = 3, 4,$ and 5 years.

Table 5.12 Markov Parameters for Different Book Classes

Class of Book	β All Years	α First 4 Years	α About 8th Year	α About 12th Year
Biology	0.45	0.4	0.3	0.2
Chemistry	0.5	0.6	0.5	0.3
Engineering	0.7	0.3	0.2	0.1
Geology	0.2	0.4	0.2	0.1
Mathematics	0.6	0.3	0.25	0.2
Metallurgy	0.7	0.3	0.25	0.2
Physics	0.6	0.5	0.4	0.3
All Classes	0.5	0.4	0.25	0.15

from the class of books under study, of those that have not circulated for more than a year and which are more than 10 years old, for example. Suppose there are N_1 books in this sample. By sorting, we count the number N_2 of this sample that have not circulated for more than two years, N_3 those with last circulation three or more years ago, and so on to N_5, the number in the sample with last circulation date 5 or more years ago. The sum of the 5 N's, divided by N_1 is approximately equal to the mean time since last circulation of the sample, which will serve to determine the limiting value of α.

To see this, we note that, if Eq. 5.14 applies, N_1 should be proportional to $(1 - X_0)$, and N_2 should equal $N_1 e^{-\alpha}$, and N_3 should equal $N_1 e^{-2\alpha}$, and so on. Then the ratio defined above, using Eq. 2.22, is in general,

$$\frac{1}{N_1}(N_1 + N_2 + N_3 + N_4 + N_5)$$

$$\simeq \frac{X(\geq 1) + X(\geq 2) + X(\geq 3) + X(\geq 4) + X(\geq 5)}{1 - X_0}$$

$$= 1 + e^{-\alpha} + e^{-2\alpha} + e^{-3\alpha} + e^{-4\alpha} = \frac{1 - e^{-5\alpha}}{1 - e^{-\alpha}} = J_5(\alpha)$$

or, in general

$$\frac{1}{N_1}(N_1 + N_2 + \cdots + N_t) \simeq \frac{1 - e^{-t\alpha}}{1 - e^{-\alpha}} = J_t \qquad (5.15)$$

The quantity J_t is plotted in Fig. 5.5. It tends to the value t years as α goes to zero and it approaches 1 year for α very large. The value of J_5, calculated from the data of Table 5.11, is 3.82, which yields a value $\alpha \simeq 0.15$, checking with the earlier calculations.

Separating the data on time since last circulation according to book class and using the curves of Fig. 5.5, we can arrive at crude estimates of the change of parameter α with book age for the books in the Science Library. This is summarized in Table 5.12. The implication of these results will be discussed in Chapter 8.

Circulation Histories of Book Collections

In many cases we wish to follow the circulation histories of all the books received by the library during a particular year, rather than that of all books having a given circulation during a given year. In this case the first-year circulation distribution must be measured and expressed in terms of the fraction C_m of the collection having circulation m during the first year of accession. If the parameters of this collection, with respect to the Markov model of the chapter, are α and β, we would expect that the probability that, during the tth year after accession, a book in the collection would have the probability $C_m(t)$ of circulating m times, would be (see Eq. 5.11)

$$C_m(1) = C_m \quad \text{when } t = 1$$
$$C_m(t) = C_0(T^{t-1})_{0m} + C_1(T^{t-1})_{1m} + C_2(T^{t-1})_{2m} + \cdots \qquad (5.16)$$
$$\text{when } t > 1$$

Knowing the conditional probabilities $(T^t)_{mn}$, given in the Appendix, and having measured the initial circulation distribution C_m, we can calculate the circulation distribution $C_m(t)$, during the tth year after accession once we know α and β. If α changes for these books during time t, this can be taken into account, as will be shown later.

The mean circulation, each year, of these books can be computed more easily. From Formula 5.7, if the mean circulation of the whole collection the first year after accession is

$$R(1) = C_1 + 2C_2 + 3C_3 + \cdots$$

then the mean circulation of the same collection during the tth year after accession is

$$R(t) = C_1(t) + 2C_2(t) + 3C_3(t) + \cdots$$
$$= \alpha \frac{1 - \beta^{t-1}}{1 - \beta} + R(1)\beta^{t-1} \qquad (5.17)$$

as long as α and β are unchanged. If α, for example, changes value during the t years, Formula 5.8 may be used. We note again the eventual appearance of a steady state. When β^{t-1} has become negligibly small the mean circulation becomes $\alpha/(1 - \beta)$, independent of the value of the initial circulation $R(1)$ of the collection.

Thus our model provides a simple connection between the average behavior of a whole collection and the probable future behavior of individual members of the collection. Curves for the mean circulation histories of several collections have been obtained,[7] all of which have the general form of Formulas 5.7 or 5.8. From these one might attempt to obtain values of α and β, by various curve-fitting techniques, though if α changes as the book gets older, fitting to this single, aggregated curve would not produce a unique pair of values. By contrast, resorting the same data to correspond to Tables 5.3 and 5.4 would produce unequivocal values for α and β and would quickly indicate the extent of variation of α.

Likewise, just measuring the number of books in the collection that have not circulated in the previous t years (or m months or n 5-year periods) will generate a curve of $X(\geq t)$ of the character of Eq. 5.14, from which* one can deduce X_0 and α. As will be seen later, unless all the books in the collection are of the same age, the relationship between X_0 and β is a complex one, so an aggregation of data resulting in a curve for $X(\geq t)$ alone will not allow a prediction of $R(t)$ or of other characteristics of the collection. On the other hand, if both α and β are determined, together with circulation distributions of accessions and of the collection as a whole, then *both* the curves for $R(t)$ *and* for $X(\geq t)$ can be generated, as well as many other probabilistic predictions of interest. This will be demonstrated in a later chapter.

---

* For example, the curve given in R. W. Trueswell,[8] "Determining the Optimum Number of Volumes for a Library's Core Collection," *Libri*, Vol. 16, 1966, p. 54, indicates that for the Deering Library 820's, $\alpha \simeq 0.35$ and $\beta \simeq 0.75$.

PART II

APPLICATION OF THE THEORY

6 A Sample Library

We have outlined a few mathematical models that can be brought into rough quantitative correspondence with some of the library activities, and we can now show, in terms of a specific example, how they can be used to assist the managing librarian. A detailed history of library operation may be interesting in itself and may at times be useful, by itself, in persuading fiscal authorities to increase library budgets. However, to the practicing operations research worker mathematical models, corresponding to past operations, are of real value only when they can be extended into the future, to assist management to see more clearly the probable consequences of alternative policies.

The M.I.T. Science Library

The specimen chosen to show how the theory can assist the librarian is the Science Library at M.I.T., housed in the ground and mezzanine floors of the south half of the Hayden building and serving most of the School of Science. Although data have been gathered and analyzed during the past 10 years, only recently has it become possible to present the following, still incomplete description of operations. The reasons for the long delay are threefold. As with most libraries, there was lack of much basic data (book inventories were infrequent and circulation cards were thrown away when completed) so that several years had to elapse during which sample inventories were taken and other data were amassed. Also manpower for data gathering and analysis was limited; much of the work has been carried out by students, either as a special problem or as thesis research. In addition, of course, a great deal of effort was spent in trying out various models (not all of which were successful) and in finding out how to obtain the needed data most easily.

During the 10 years of the study, the library has changed, of course. Books on the earth sciences were moved in for a while, then moved out to the new earth sciences building, and in 1965 a number of older books were moved to stacks in the basement, to make room for accessions, which have been added to the collection each year. Therefore, for the purposes of the present analysis, the data have been adjusted to the year 1962, the time when the most complete set of figures were gathered. The next survey, to bring the data up to date, would avoid many of the earlier false starts, would need less data, and could probably be completed at the cost of 1 or 2 man months of effort. For our present purpose, however, the situation in 1962 is as useful an example as would be an up-to-date one.

The Status in 1962

In 1962, the Science Library had approximately 52,000 volumes in its collection, mostly books, periodicals, and serials. Project reports were also present, but these were so little used that they will be ignored in our discussion; they simply took up space. The library is all open shelf and available to all users. (Since 1962 some older books have been retired to stacks in the basement and more must be retired in the next 5 years or so.) The periodicals, serials, and reserve books are on the shelves on the main floor; they do not circulate, except overnight. The texts and monographs on the shelves in the mezzanine do circulate, with a 2-week limit (not then enforced for the faculty!). Most of the working space for the users is at large tables on the main floor, capable of seating about 200 persons.

In 1962 the mezzanine collection consisted of about 28,000 volumes. The chief holdings were in the fields of biology, chemistry, geology, mathematics, physics, and metallurgy, with minor holdings in food technology, meteorology, chemical engineering, and a miscellany in engineering and general science. These seemed to divide conveniently into seven homogeneous classes, in regard to circulation behavior:

Class	Dewey Classification
Biology	570 — 619
Chemistry	540 — 549
General Engineering plus some General Science	0 — 509, 620 — 629
Geology, Earth Sciences	550 — 569
Mathematics	510 — 519
Metallurgy, plus some Food Technology and Chemical Engineering	630 — 900
Physics	520 — 539

In very rough numbers, Table 6.1 shows the sizes of the collections at three dates: in 1955, 2 years after the Science Library opened and

Table 6.1 Approximate Number of Circulatable Volumes of Texts and Monographs in the M.I.T. Science Library

Class	1955 Mezzanine	1962 Mezzanine	1966 Mezzanine	1966 Basement	1966 Total
Biology	3000	5000	600	4900	5500
Chemistry	1400	2800	1200	2300	3500
Engineering	700	1400	800	1000	1800
Geology	5500	6700	—	—	—
Mathematics	2400	4900	1600	4400	6000
Metallurgy	1500	3500	800	3600	4400
Physics	1500	3700	1400	3600	5000
Total	16,000	28,000	6400	19,800	26,200
Total without Geology	10,500	21,300			26,200

took over collections from the Eastman Library (chemistry, mathematics, physics), the Lindgren Library (geology, metallurgy, and earth sciences), and the biology collection from what had been called the Central Library (which then became the Engineering Library); in 1962, the date we will use for our exposition; and in 1966, by which time the Science Library had overflowed its open-shelf space in the mezzanine, and the older books had to be "retired" to stacks in the basement. To add to the complexity of analyzing growth and change, between 1962 and 1966 the geology-earth-sciences collection was moved to the new Lindgren Library. Also, starting in 1963 all accessions (plus some of the older books) were given Library of Congress numbers and the rest, still with the Dewey classification, were relegated to the stacks in the basement, where users still have access to them but at the cost of a search through a much larger and less accessible set of shelves.

The total number of accessions to the collection in 1962 was about 2300 volumes, about $1/12$ of the total. As seen in Table 6.1, the average growth of the library in the 7 years between 1955 and 1962 accords well with the assumption that each year the collection was $13/12$ of its size the year before, since $(13/12)^7 = 1.75$ and $28,000 = 1.75 \times 16,000$. The collection without geology had a rather larger growth rate, about 10 per cent a year, corresponding to an increase of a factor of 2 in 7 years and a factor of 2.8 in 11 years, since $(1.1)^7 = 1.95$ and $(1.1)^{11} = 2.83$.

In addition to these circulatable volumes, there was (and is) a nearly equally large periodical collection, which may not be taken from the library. In 1962 there were about 23,000 journal volumes, corresponding to about 1200 different journals, distributed among the fields in about the same proportion as the books (except that there were proportionally somewhat more chemistry journals and somewhat fewer geology journals). Each year about 1700 periodical and serial volumes were added to the main-floor stacks, again roughly in proportion to the holdings.

There were, on the average, about 1000 persons who came into the library a day in 1962 (though this number varied somewhat according to the day of the week and by season), about 450 of these used the library as a study hall, and the other 550 used the library facilities (or at least tried to, see Chapter 2). As we have seen (see Fig. 2.6), the average stay was about 80 minutes and the library was open about 800 minutes a day, so there were, on the average, 100 persons in the library at any one time (see Eq. 3.3 and Fig. 3.1 for greater detail). Since the tables accommodate 200 persons, on the average, only rarely did an attendee have to stand. About 300 persons consulted the card catalogue each day, on the average.

Circulation Data

During the fall of 1961, three samples of circulation records were taken and analyzed, as the basis for a series of term papers in a graduate course in operations research. In each case books were taken at random from the portion under study of the collection in the mezzanine, and a proportional number of books of the same class then circulating or being repaired were also chosen at random. Title, author, date of accession, and dates of circulation were recorded, together with notes on whether the book was duplicated, reasons for its acquisition, etc., when appropriate and known. The largest[5] sample, of 876 titles taken from the whole collection of circulatable books (about 1 title in every 30 of the whole) was put on punch cards for easy manipulation. The second[6] sample was a study of 204 circulatable books with accession dates in the year 1957 (about 1 in 10 of the accessions that year). The third sample was a listing of 97 circulatable books[9] that had been in the library for 4 or more years. Both of these last 2 samples were listed on cards which could be sorted by hand. These 3 samples served as the basis for verifying the Markov model discussed in the previous chapter and will be used in this chapter to answer other questions. Other more specialized samples were taken then and since that time; they will be described as they become pertinent.

It should be noted that, if the Markov model were taken to be valid, a random sample of about 100 per subject field (i.e., about one book in 50) would have been sufficient for the analysis of this chapter. The manpower that went into collecting the data reported here was a few man months; it should be an automatic by-product of any adequately designed computerization of the circulation process. The analysis of the data, of course, took additional time, but this was because the models were being tested; duplication of the tables and calculations reported in this chapter could be carried out in a man month or so.

The values of α and β for the whole collection and for its major portions are given in Table 5.6. However, many questions concerning the characteristics of the collection can be determined without knowing the values of these parameters, if we know the circulation properties of the collection as a whole and the corresponding properties of the yearly accessions. This was not difficult to obtain from the sample circulation history[5] just mentioned. The most useful way of presenting the data is to write down the fraction $F(\geq m)$ of each class of book (as well as of the whole collection) that circulated m or more times during the year, plus the average yearly circulation

$$\begin{aligned}
\overline{R} &= F(\geq 1) + F(\geq 2) + F(\geq 3) + \cdots \\
&= 1(F_1) + 2(F_2) + 3(F_3) + 4(F_4) + \cdots \\
F_m &= F(\geq m) - F(\geq m + 1)
\end{aligned} \tag{6.1}$$

where $F(\geq m) = F_m + F_{m+1} + F_{m+2} + F_{m+3} + \cdots$ and F_m is the fraction of books in a class that circulated precisely m times during the year. The cumulative $F(\geq m)$ are given in Table 6.2.

We note in Table 6.2 that, book for book, physics books circulate

Table 6.2 Number of Circulatable Volumes, Fraction $F(\geq R)$, and the Mean Circulation $\bar{R}$, for the Science Library in 1962

Class	No.	$R = 1$	2	3	4	5	6	7	8	9	10	$\bar{R}$
Biology	5000	0.31	0.12	0.06	0.06	0.02	0.02	0.01	0.01	0.01	—	0.62
Chemistry	2800	0.49	0.29	0.23	0.18	0.14	0.09	0.07	0.05	0.04	0.03	1.63
Engineering	1400	0.14	0.05	0.01	0.01	—	—	—	—	—	—	0.21
Geology	6700	0.12	0.04	0.03	0.02	—	—	—	—	—	—	0.21
Mathematics	4900	0.50	0.28	0.21	0.16	0.15	0.12	0.09	0.07	0.06	0.04	1.95
Metallurgy	3500	0.27	0.11	0.09	0.07	0.05	0.03	0.02	0.01	0.01	0.01	0.67
Physics	3700	0.61	0.47	0.36	0.25	0.22	0.19	0.16	0.09	0.06	0.04	2.44
Total	28,000	0.34	0.18	0.13	0.10	0.08	0.06	0.04	0.03	0.02	0.01	1.10

10 times more often than geology books and 4 times more often than biology books. We also note that nearly two-thirds of the collection as a whole does not circulate at all during a year, since $F(\geq 1)$ is the fraction which has circulated at least once during the previous year and $1 - F(\geq 1)$ (which is equal to $1 - 0.34 = 0.66$ for the whole collection) is the fraction that did not circulate at all in the past year. As a rough figure to use later in our discussion, the total yearly circulation of this collection is approximately equal to the total number of books in the collection; in other words each book, on the average, circulated a little more than once a year. Of course, this is an average over books of many kinds, including old ones that have not circulated for 10 years as well as recent books that circulated 10 or more times during the year. Nevertheless the fact that $\overline{R}$ equals about unity, rather than 10 or 1/10, will enable us to put approximate values to a number of other quantities of interest.

One other important sample of circulation data was taken on the books that were out on loan at any given time. On 2 weekends during the fall of 1961 all the book cards from books out on loan, being repaired, on reserve, or removed for other reasons were counted and analyzed.[10] The numbers and distributions by categories were remarkably similar for the 2 counts, indicating a high degree of stability of these quantities. If circulations are random events, in accord with the Poisson distribution of Eq. 3.5, a collection of several hundred cards would be expected to exhibit such stability. The data are shown in Table 6.3. We have brought over, from Table 6.2, the values of N and $\overline{R}$, in order to compare various quantities more easily.

Computing the Mean Loan Period

The data in Tables 6.2 and 6.3 enable us to determine the mean loan period $1/\mu$ and the fraction of those, wishing to withdraw a book and finding it out of the library, who fill out a reserve card for the book; both are quantities of utility in determining when to order a duplicate of a popular book. The mean loan period $1/\mu$ is the mean fraction of a year a book is off the shelf for a single circulation. This, times the number of its circulations per year, must equal the fraction of the year the book is not in the library; therefore the mean circulation $\overline{R}$ times $1/\mu$ is the mean fraction of the books out of the library at any time. But the fraction of books not in the library at any given time is the number J of books on loan at a given time, divided by the total number of books in the collection. In other words $(\overline{R}/\mu) = (J/N)$ or

Table 6.3 1962 Data on Mean Yearly Circulation $\bar{R}$ per Book, on Mean Number L on Loan at Any Time, and on Reserve Cards and Overdue Books

Class of Book	Biology	Chemistry	Engineering; General Science	Geology	Mathematics	Metallurgy; Food Technology	Physics	Total
N Total number circulatable	5000	2800	1400	6700	4900	3500	3700	28,000
$\bar{R}$ Mean yearly circulation per book in class	0.62	1.62	0.21	0.21	1.95	0.67	2.44	1.081
J Mean number out on loan at any time	287	326	45	106	524	190	671	2149
J/N Mean fraction of class on loan at any time	0.057	0.116	0.032	0.016	0.107	0.054	0.181	0.077
μ Mean return rate per year for all books in the class	10.8	14.0	6.5	13.3	18.2	12.4	13.5	14.1
$T_L = 52/\mu$ Mean loan period in weeks	4.8	3.7	8.0	3.9	2.9	4.2	3.8	3.6
Fraction overdue of books out	0.52	0.37	0.33	0.51	0.33	0.41	0.38	0.39
N_W Mean number reserve cards on hand at any time	5	22	1	4	8	4	32	76
$W = N_W/N$ Reserve cards per book of class	0.0010	0.0078	0.0007	0.0006	0.0016	0.0011	0.0087	0.0027

$$\mu = \frac{\overline{R}N}{J} \tag{6.2}$$

Since we have values of $\overline{R}$, J, and N, we can calculate μ and thence $52/\mu$, the mean number of weeks a book is away from the library during one circulation, which we call the *mean loan period*. (Incidentally one could deal separately with those books that had been renewed from those not renewed, if there is any point in making the distinction; however, ordinarily one wishes to know how long the book will be away from the library, irrespective of its renewal status, so this refinement is usually not worth the trouble.) Reference to Eq. 4.3 will remind us that μ, called the *mean return rate*, is the number of times a year a book could circulate if the successive borrowers picked up the book as soon as it was returned by the previous borrower, so the book was never in the library during the whole year.

We note that the loan period is well over the statutory 2 weeks, for all classes of books. This is corroborated by the figures on the fraction of overdue books. Whenever this fraction is large, the loan period is large and vice versa (except for the small collection in General Science and Engineering, where there were few overdue books but these were out for very long periods). The probable reasons for the loan periods being longer than 2 weeks were (1) faculty were sent overdue notices only when someone else asked for the book and (2) there was some delay in sending out those overdue notices that were sent out. Faculty were responsible for only 40 per cent of the books overdue from 1 to 30 days but were responsible for 65 per cent of the books overdue from 31 to 60 days and for 80 per cent of those overdue more than 60 days.

The differences in the length of mean loan periods for the different classes of book must depend in some way on the nature of the books in the class and also on the nature of the borrowers of the different classes. We notice that in Table 6.3 the three heavily used collections (Chemistry, Mathematics, and Physics have $\overline{R} > 1$) have shorter loan periods than do the lesser used collections (for $\overline{R} < 1$). Is this because the greater demand for the chemistry book, for example, has habituated the chemistry user to a shorter loan period than that required for the biology-book borrower? Or does the borrower of the chemistry book use the book in a way that requires less time than would be required for a biology book? The latter effect must be present to some extent, because the mean loan period for mathematics books is considerably shorter than that for physics books, in spite of the fact that the physics books are more heavily used. The difference in loan periods between the books in engineering and general science and those in geology, both of which have the same mean yearly circulation, also must depend on the difference in the type of book and thus on how it is used. Further investigation of these interesting differences might shed considerable light on borrower habits.

7 Satisfying Circulation Demand

It is a useful exercise to show what can be learned about the library and how it can be improved in service to its users from the data reported in the previous chapter, without bringing in further facts. We can, for example, investigate the effects of circulation interference, can calculate the degree to which the collection satisfies borrowers' demands, and can compare the possible ways by which this demand is better satisfied. Tables 6.2 and 6.3 indicate, for example, that the average mathematics book was out of the library about a tenth of the time ($J/N = 0.107$) and the average physics book was out more than a sixth of the time. Some of these books, of course, were on the shelf all year and others were out more than half the time; the average fraction of time out of the library for the physics books was 0.181.

At this rate of usage there must have been an appreciable number of times when a person came into the library to borrow a specific book and found it already out. To estimate the magnitude of this "frustrated demand" and to develop a measure by which to compare possible improvements in this respect, we need to develop approximate formulas in order to calculate the number of these "disappointed customers," to see whether their number is large enough to warrant taking action, and to see how much the number would be reduced if various actions were taken. The results of the alternative actions may then be compared with their cost and feasibility in order to determine their relative cost effectiveness.

Estimating the Demand

The small number of reserve cards, in comparison with the number of books out on loan, indicates that most persons, finding a book out of the library, give up. (We shall document this more fully later.) Thus the simple model of circulation interference, represented by Eqs. 4.3, 4.4, 4.7, and 4.8, should be adequate for our analysis. The calculation would be simple if probability formulas were easily inverted. Equations 4.4 state that if the expected demand for a given, unduplicated book is λ, then the expected circulation is $R_1 = \mu\lambda/(\mu + \lambda)$ and the expected unsatisfied demand is $U_1 = \lambda - R_1 = \lambda^2/(\lambda + \mu)$. In other words, if we had a collection of books, all subject to an equal demand λ per book per year, then their average circulation, per book per year, would be R_1. But this does *not* say that if a book's circulation last year was R_1 (and its mean return rate was μ) that the demand for the book last year was λ.

Introductory texts on probability define the pertinent relationships, which can be paraphrased here (see also the discussion in Chapter 2). The *conditional probability* that a book circulates m times in a year if the demand for it is λ per year may be written $P(m \mid \lambda)$ (which is the probability of m, given λ). The conditional probability that the demand for the book was λ per year if it circulated m times in the year may be written as $P(\lambda \mid m)$ (which is the probability of λ, given m). These two are related through the *unconditional probability* $P(\lambda)$, the probability that the demand is λ irrespective of the value of m, and $P(m)$, the probability that the circulation is m independent of the value of λ. The relationship is

$$P(m \mid \lambda) \, P(\lambda) = P(\lambda \mid m) \, P(m) = P(\lambda,m) = P(m,\lambda) \qquad (7.1)$$

where $P(m,\lambda) = P(\lambda,m)$ is the *joint probability* that a book both has demand λ and also circulates m times a year. This was demonstrated in the discussion of Eq. 2.6. The joint probability $P(\lambda,m)$ must equal the conditional probability $P(m \mid \lambda)$ that the circulation is m *if* the demand is λ times the chance that the demand does happen to be λ.

Using this relationship, we can go from a formula giving expected circulation in terms of demand to one giving estimated demand in terms of known (or predicted) circulation. Some of the things we would like to know, for each homogeneous class of book, are: the expected value of the demand for those books of a class that circulate

m times a year; the mean value $D = \bar{\lambda}$ of the per-book demand, averaged over all books of the class; and thus, by subtraction, the mean
unsatisfied demand $\bar{U} = D - \bar{R}$ per book for all the books in the class.
We also would like to know how this unsatisfied demand would change
in value if some of the books were duplicated or if the loan period $1/\mu$
were changed in value.

These calculations are not easy, for several reasons. In the first place
λ is not a definite number, the exact number of would-be borrowers
who come to the library for a given book during the year. It is the
expected demand, the quantity to be inserted instead of *N* into the
Formula 3.5 for the Poisson process, to give the probability that *n*
actual persons arrive, looking for the book, during the year. Since λ is
a continuous variable, $P(\lambda \mid m)$ and $P(\lambda)$ are probability *densities*,
chances that demand is between λ and $\lambda + 1$, the summations become
integrations over λ. Second, the conditional probability $P(m \mid \lambda)$ for
circulation *m*, given λ, is a quite complicated function of *m*, λ, and μ,
even for a queuing model as simple as the one producing Eqs. 4.3 and
4.4. However it is not a bad approximation to use the Poisson formula
of Eq. 3.5,

$$P(m \mid \lambda) \simeq P_m\left(\frac{\mu\lambda}{\mu + \lambda}\right) = \frac{1}{m!}\left(\frac{\mu\lambda}{\mu + \lambda}\right)^m \exp\left(\frac{-\mu\lambda}{\mu + \lambda}\right) \qquad (7.2)$$

for the conditional probability that the circulation is *m*, given that the
demand is λ. Function $\exp(-z)$ is another way of writing the exponential e^{-z}, tabulated in Table 2.4. We know from Eq. 4.4 that the
expected circulation, the *N* of Eq. 3.5, is $\mu\lambda/(\mu + \lambda)$. The approximation
involved in using the Poisson formula for $P(m \mid \lambda)$ is better than some
others we shall have to make and is certainly adequate for the uses we
propose to make of the model in view, as well, of the inaccuracies of
the data.

The second difficulty is that we do not have any direct way of measuring the distribution of demand $P(\lambda)$ for a class of books. We *can*
measure the distribution of circulation. In fact the recorded fractions
$F(\geq m)$ of Table 6.2 should enable us to obtain a rough approximation
for the unconditional probability $P(m)$. The data of Table 6.2 indicate
that this distribution is roughly geometric (see Eq. 2.21) though a semilog plot suggests a slight downward curvature, rather than a straight
line. In addition though $P(m)$ is proportional to γ^m, as stated in Eq.
2.21, the proportionality constant is not $1 - \gamma$ and thus $P(0)$ is not
$1 - \gamma$. In other words the nearly straight line of $P(m)$ on a semilog
plot does not extend back to $P(0)$. (See Fig. 8.3.) However a knowledge

of $P(m \mid \lambda)$ and $P(m)$ alone does not enable us to find $P(\lambda)$ and $P(\lambda \mid m$ of Eq. 7.1. We will have to guess the form of $P(\lambda)$ and then verify our) guess indirectly (a procedure often used in physical science).

An obvious assumption is that $P(\lambda)$ is exponential (see Eq. 2.32), which is an extension of the geometrical distribution of Eq. 2.21 to the continuous variable λ. If m is distributed geometrically, then perhaps λ should be exponential. Thus we try

$$P(\lambda) = (1/D)\, e^{-\lambda/D} \qquad \int_0^\infty P(\lambda)\, d\lambda = 1 \qquad (7.3)$$

as the probability that the demand for a randomly chosen book of the class is between λ and $\lambda + 1$ and see whether this will result in a distribution of circulation that is reasonably close to that given by the data of Table 6.2. If it does, we can then work backward to find the value of D in the formula from the known circulation distribution. This will then be the mean *demand per book* of the class,

$$D = \int_0^\infty \lambda P(\lambda)\, d\lambda \qquad (7.4)$$

The circulation distribution, by Eqs. 7.1, 7.2, and 7.3 is

$$P(m) = \int_0^\infty P(m \mid \lambda)\, P(\lambda)\, d\lambda$$

$$= \frac{1}{m! D} \int_0^\infty \left(\frac{\mu\lambda}{\mu + \lambda}\right)^m \exp\left(-\frac{\lambda}{D} - \frac{\mu\lambda}{\mu + \lambda}\right) d\lambda \qquad (7.5)$$

since the integral of $P(\lambda \mid m)$ over all λ equals 1.

An Approximate Formula

Numerical calculation of the integral, for various values of m, λ, and D, produces a distribution $P(m)$ that is nearly geometric but does curve downward when plotted against m on semilog graph paper, as do plots of the F of Table 6.2 (see Figs. 8.3, 8.4, and 8.5). The curvature is not great in the curves from either data or formula. Therefore the ease of use of the geometric distribution makes it advisable to sacrifice a little accuracy in the interests of simplicity and convenience (see the discussion on page 94). We thus will approximate $P(m)$ with a geometric distribution designed to produce the same mean circulation as does the "exact" formula of Eq. 75, which can be set equal to the $\overline{R}$ of Tables 6.2 and 6.3.

A modified geometric distribution that fits both data and Formula 7.5 reasonably well (see, for example, the dashed curve of Fig. 8.3) and automatically produces a mean value equal to $\overline{R}$ is

$$P(m) \simeq \frac{1}{D+1}\left(\frac{Q}{Q+1}\right)^m \qquad \text{when } m > 0$$

$$P(0) = \frac{D+1-Q}{D+1} = \frac{Q+1-\overline{R}}{Q+1} \qquad (7.6)$$

$$P(\geq m) = P(m) + P(m+1) + P(m+2) + \cdots \simeq \frac{Q+1}{D+1}\left(\frac{Q}{Q+1}\right)^m$$

where we set Q so that

$$\overline{R} = P(1) + 2P(2) + 3P(3) + \cdots = \frac{Q(Q+1)}{D+1}$$

in other words

$$Q = [\overline{R}(D+1) + \tfrac{1}{4}]^{1/2} - \tfrac{1}{2}$$

Quantity $P(m)$ is the probability that a book of the class circulates m times a year, $P(\geq m)$ is the probability that it circulates m *or more* times during the year, and $\overline{R}$ is the mean circulation per book of the class. Constant Q is the parameter of the modified geometric distribution, chosen so as to best approximate the actual distribution of Eq. 7.5. Note that $P(m)$ is not the usual geometric distribution; for the relation between $P(0)$ and the other $P(m)$ depends on a second parameter D.

The value of the mean circulation $\overline{R}$ can be computed from Eq. 7.5 exactly, though the individual $P(m)$ cannot. Using the series expansion $e^x = 1 + x + (x^2/2!) + (x^3/3!) + \cdots$, we have

$$\overline{R} = \frac{1}{D}\int_0^\infty \left[\frac{\mu\lambda}{\mu+\lambda} + \frac{2}{2!}\left(\frac{\mu\lambda}{\mu+\lambda}\right)^2 + \frac{3}{3!}\left(\frac{\mu\lambda}{\mu+\lambda}\right)^3 + \cdots\right]$$

$$\times \exp\left(-\frac{\lambda}{D} - \frac{\mu\lambda}{\mu+\lambda}\right)d\lambda$$

$$= \frac{\mu}{D}\int_0^\infty \left(1 - \frac{\mu}{\mu+\lambda}\right)\exp\left(-\frac{\lambda}{D}\right)d\lambda = \mu\left[1 - \frac{\mu}{D}e^{\mu/D}E_1\left(\frac{\mu}{D}\right)\right]$$

$$\frac{D-\overline{R}}{\mu} \simeq 1.11\left(\frac{D}{\mu}\right)^{1.87} \simeq 2.5\left(\frac{\overline{R}}{\mu}\right)^{2.06} \qquad (7.7)$$

where $E_1(x)$ is the exponential integral of x, values of which may be found in many tables of functions. The approximate formulas given in the last line of Eq. 7.7 are good to within 5 per cent over the ranges of μ and $\overline{R}$ encountered in our present study. More accurate values can be calculated using Fig. 7.1.

Thus, given $\overline{R}$ and μ, then D can be calculated by use of a table of exponential integrals or by use of the approximate formulas. Once D

is known, the values of the parameter Q can be calculated and approximate values of the probabilities $P(\geq m)$ obtained.

Since the assumption of Eq. 7.3 produces a circulation distribution that, within the accuracy of the data, can be made to fit the measured

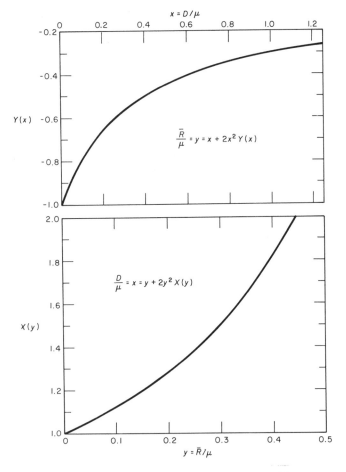

Fig. 7.1.   Curves for computing $\bar{R}$, given D and μ, or D, given $\bar{R}$ and μ.

values, one hopes that Eq. 7.5 corresponds approximately to the demand distribution. In particular, one hopes that D is a good approximation to the average demand.

Quantity $D - \bar{R}$ is, of course, the mean value of the unsatisfied demand per book of the class, since D is the estimated value of the mean demand, the average value of λ, and $\overline{R}$ is the mean circulation. Thus $D - \overline{R}$ is the best estimate we can obtain, from the model and from the data of Tables 6.2 and 6.3, of the average unsatisfied demand $\overline{U}$ per book. Multiplied by N, the number of circulatable books in the class, it gives the best estimate of the total number of persons who looked for a book of the class during the year and did not get it because someone else had the book out. Since some of the books that were borrowed were picked out by a person who was "browsing," who had not specifically gone to the library to get it, perhaps it is more accurate to define $\overline{U}$ as the estimated number of persons who would have borrowed the book if it had been on the shelf when they went to the library.

It may seem presumptuous, and slightly mysterious, to be able to work out how many people did *not* get books from data on how many people *did* get books. Perhaps it becomes less mysterious if we realize we are saying that as long as library users look for a book when *they* want it and not when someone tells them the book is available, i.e., as long as the users are independent individuals, then their very independence creates a definite relationship between the number who come by when the book is on the shelf and those who come by when the book is out on loan, as was explained in Chapter 4. Our choice of a simple model and the approximations we have made may result in the values of D, given in Table 7.1, being off by 10, or even by 30 per cent; this does not matter for our needs. We will be interested in whether D is 2 or 200 and in whether some action increases or decreases $D - \overline{R}$ by factors of 2 or more. And our formulas should be adequate for such purposes.

We could of course have tried to use the very simple Formulas 4.4 to try to deduce λ, given R_1. But we would very soon realize that the values obtained from the equation $\lambda = \mu/(\mu - R_1)$, which is Eq. 4.4 solved for λ in terms of μ and R_1, turn out to be unrealistically large for R_1 nearly equal to μ. In actual fact, we find books with circulations R greater than the μ for their class, which would result in a negative λ if Eqs. 4.4 were to be used. The difficulty with using the simple formulas 4.4 to estimate demand from circulation is that Eqs. 4.4 are formulas for calculating average circulation, given average demand λ and average return rate μ; they are not formulas for computing average demand D, given circulation R and average return rate μ. In fact this latter relation of Eq. 7.7, depends on the range of popularities of the class of books one averages over. Thus, we have had to go to the greater complication of Eqs. 7.6 and 7.7.

Table 7.1 shows the results of these calculations for the seven different

Table 7.1   Estimated Demand, Unsatisfied Demand and Other Inferred Properties of Classes of Books in the Science Library in 1962

Class of Book		Biol.	Chem.	Eng.	Geol.	Math.	Met.	Phys.	Total
N Number books in class		5000	2800	1400	6700	4900	3500	3700	28000
$\overline{R}$ Mean circulation per book in class		0.62	1.62	0.21	0.21	1.95	0.67	2.44	1.081
μ Average return rate		10.8	14.0	6.5	13.3	18.2	12.4	13.5	14.1
$D - \overline{R}$ Inferred unsatisfied demand per book		0.07	0.43	0.01	0.01	0.47	0.08	1.11	0.30
D Inferred demand per book		0.69	2.05	0.22	0.22	2.42	0.75	3.55	1.38
Q Distribution parameter		0.636	1.783	0.210	0.214	2.128	0.691	2.871	—
$N\overline{R}$ Total circulation per year of class		3080	4550	290	1420	9540	2340	9040	30270
$N(D - \overline{R})$ Total unsatisfied demand		370	1200	20	50	2310	270	4090	8310
ND Total demand		3450	5750	310	1470	11850	2610	13130	38580
Calculated	$P(\geq 1)$	0.38	0.58	0.17	0.18	0.62	0.40	0.63	0.42
probability of	$P(\geq 2)$	0.15	0.37	0.03	0.03	0.42	0.16	0.47	0.23
circulation m or	$P(\geq 3)$	0.06	0.24	0.01	0.01	0.29	0.07	0.35	0.14
more times	$P(\geq 4)$	0.02	0.15	—	—	0.20	0.03	0.26	0.09
$P(\geq m)$	$P(\geq 6)$	—	0.06	—	—	0.09	0.01	0.14	0.04
	$P(\geq 8)$	—	0.03	—	—	0.04	—	0.08	0.02
Inferred	$U(0)$	0.03	0.06	0.01	0.01	0.05	0.03	0.09	0.04
unsatisfied	$U(2)$	0.16	0.36	0.04	0.04	0.31	0.17	0.52	0.22
demand $U(m)$	$U(4)$	0.40	0.90	0.10	0.10	0.78	0.43	1.29	0.55
for average	$U(6)$	0.75	1.68	0.19	0.19	1.46	0.80	2.41	1.03
book with	$U(8)$	1.20	2.70	0.31	0.31	2.34	1.29	3.87	1.66
circulation m	$U(10)$	1.76	3.97	0.45	0.45	3.42	1.89	5.68	2.43

classes of books in the Science Library in 1962, together with the overall result for the whole circulating book collection. The first three rows (N, $\overline{R}$, and μ) constitute the data, obtained from Tables 6.2 and 6.3, all that are needed for this model; the rest of the table represents the implications of the data, assuming the model to be a fair representation of the library's behavior.

We see that the different classes had very different demands placed upon them; in fact there are differences of factors of 100 in the estimates of unsatisfied demand, differences too large to be attributable to inaccuracies of the model. The geology collection, the largest in numbers, was very little used; only 1 book in 6 circulated at all during the year $[P(\geq 1) = 0.18]$. Also, since these books were nearly always in the library, all but about 50 of the nearly 1500 persons wishing to borrow a geology book during the year found the book they wanted and borrowed it. On the other hand the physics collection, though among the smallest in size, had the largest circulation per book $\overline{R}$ and was thus subjected to the largest total demand of any class present. As a result the estimated total unsatisfied demand $N(D - \overline{R})$ per year for physics books was by far the largest of any class, being actually larger than the total size of the physics holdings. If the library were to spend any of its limited budget on buying duplicates, certainly the money would be most efficiently spent on physics books.

The total unsatisfied demand, representing about 8000 instances, during the year (160 per week or about 30 per weekday), when a person looks for a particular book and finds that someone else has it out, certainly seems large enough to warrant consideration of various measures to alleviate the situation. Even if the approximations in the formulas were off by 30 or 40 per cent, the gap between supply and demand would still be very large. Certainly such inaccuracies would not have altered the rank order of the results. The conclusion is unavoidable that the physics, chemistry, and mathematics books were so heavily used that circulation interference was serious for them; on the other hand the other classes were so lightly used that very few potential borrowers were disappointed.

One might say that it was easy to see, without all this calculation, that the 3 classes were more heavily used than the others. But guesses are not good enough; if we wish to choose between various ways to improve the situation, we must know, at least approximately, by *how much* a proposed action reduces the unsatisfied demand, so we can choose the action that does the most good for the least cost or effort.

The probabilities $P(\geq m)$ that a book of the class circulates m or more times, calculated from Eqs. 7.6 and 7.7, are tabulated. These should be compared with the recorded $F(\geq m)$ of Table 6.2, obtained from the data. The check is quite satisfactory (note the agreement for the physics column) considering the facts that the model is approximate and the data is obtained from relatively small samples. The figures for the whole collection, in the last column, are not calculated from a Q for the whole collection but are weighted means of the values in the other columns; the whole collection is not a homogeneous class (see page 35) and should not be expected to have a geometric circulation distribution.

Demand Inferred from Circulation

Finally, to illustrate the nature of the inversion of probabilities, we have listed in Table 7.1 the expected values of $U(m)$, the best estimate we can make, from the data, of the average number of unsatisfied borrowers per year per book for those unduplicated books of a class that have circulated precisely m times in the year. The inferred value of the total average demand for such a book would thus be $m + U(m)$, if the book were a single copy. This is the probabilistic inverse of $R_1(\lambda) = \mu\lambda/(\lambda + \mu)$ of Eq. 4.4, the expected circulation of those books which have a total yearly demand λ. In line with Eqs. 7.3 to 7.7 the formula for $U(m)$ and a reasonable approximation to its value are (see Eq. 2.6)

$$U(m) = \int_0^\infty \frac{\lambda^2}{\lambda + \mu} P(\lambda \mid m) \, d\lambda = \int_0^\infty \frac{\lambda^2}{\lambda + \mu} \frac{P(\lambda)}{P(m)} P(m \mid \lambda) \, d\lambda$$

$$\simeq \frac{D+1}{m!\,D} \left(\frac{Q+1}{Q}\right)^m \int_0^\infty \frac{\lambda^2}{\mu + \lambda} \left(\frac{\mu\lambda}{\mu + \lambda}\right)^m \exp\left(-\frac{\lambda}{D} + \frac{\mu\lambda}{\mu + \lambda}\right) d\lambda$$

$$\simeq \frac{1}{2}(m+1)(m+2)\frac{(D - \overline{R})(D+1)}{D - Q + (Q+1)^3} \tag{7.8}$$

where $U(0)\,P(0) + U(1)\,P(1) + U(2)\,P(2) + \cdots = D - \overline{R}$ and where we have used the same degree of approximation to obtain the last line as was used to obtain Eq. 7.6 for $P(m)$.

Examination of this part of Table 7.1 brings to light several properties of probabilistic inference. In the first place $U(0)$, the inferred, mean, unsatisfied demand for a book that did not circulate at all in the year is not zero (though it is quite small). This comes about because λ, the *expected* demand for a book, is not always equal to the actual number of persons per year coming to borrow the book; the actual number who come may be greater or less than λ, according to the Poisson distribution of Eq. 3.5. Even if a book did not circulate during the year, the expected demand for it may not be exactly zero. Such "fuzziness" always occurs when we have to invert conditional probabilities. In the present case, it is small; we see that, for the Science Library books, the inferred unsatisfied demand for those books that did not circulate is effectively zero.

This unsatisfied demand rises rapidly for books with larger circulation rate m of course, as a retrospective glance at Eqs. 4.4 will verify. Constant m here is related to R_1 in those equations and $U(m)$ is related to U_1 there. There λ and μ were assumed known and R_1 and U_1 were inferred average values; here μ and m (where $m = R$) are assumed known and $U(m)$ and D are inferred averages. Here we have picked out all the books in the class (i.e., with a given μ) that circulated exactly m times in the year and have asked what the mean value of the excess demand per book would be for such books. In Chapter 4 we picked all those books that had an *expected* total demand λ per year and asked what would be the average excess of demand over actual circulation.

In the case of Eqs. 4.4 our result was independent of the statistical properties of the class of book (aside from the value of μ); it depended on the statistics of arrival of prospective borrowers, which we said was Poisson, was independent of the class of book and only dependent on the value of λ. In the case of Eqs. 7.8 and the $U(m)$ of Table 7.1, on the other hand, the result does depend on the demand distribution of the book class (on the value of D) as well as on μ. For example, our inferred value of $U(m)$ is smaller for those classes that have few popular books than for the higher circulation classes. If a geology book happens to have circulated 10 times last year, we are reasonably sure this is a statistical fluctuation, which will be unlikely to occur next year (or to occur for another geology book), rather than an effect of large, continuing demand. Thus we infer a smaller unsatisfied demand for the geology book than for a physics book that circulated 10 times. The values of $U(m)$ given in Table 7.1 are the best estimates we can make of the unsatisfied demand, given the fact that we cannot measure total demand directly, but we must infer it from the statistical model of circulation and from the values of $\overline{R}$ and μ for the class.

If we had tried to use Eqs. 4.4 to find $U(m)$, given μ and $m(= R_1)$, by solving for λ in terms of μ and m and subtracting R_1 $(= m)$, we would obtain the improper equation $U(m) = m^2/(\mu - m)$. Using this equation, we would have calculated, for chemistry books where $\mu = 14$, that $U(2) = 0.3$, $U(4) = 1.6$, $U(6) = 4.5$, $U(8) = 10.7$, and $U(10) = 25$. These values are larger than the values given in Table 7.1 for m equal to 4 or more. In fact, according to this improper formula, $U(m)$ goes to infinity when $m = 14$. The *mean* circulation of a class of books, all with the average return rate μ, *cannot* be larger than μ; thus Eqs. 4.4 might seem to require that we never find books with circulation greater than μ. But this is wrong. Individual books *are* found that have circulation greater than μ; they happened to be returned more quickly than the average rate μ. If we do not know λ but do know μ and m for a book, we have to allow for the fact that circulation sometimes can be larger than μ and a popular class of books is more likely to have unsatisfied demands than is a less-used class.

Parenthetically, it probably would have been more logical to devise a Markov-process model for circulation history, to go from the demand $\lambda(t)$ of 1 year to expected demand $\lambda(t + 1)$ next year, rather than the model we chose, which goes from known circulation $m(t)$ to expected mean circulation $\bar{m}(t + 1) = \alpha + \beta m$ for next year (and thence, by the Poisson distribution, to next year's circulation for each book). However, circulation is the quantity which is measured; demand must be inferred. Though it might have been more logical to go from demand to demand, it is more immediately useful to have a dynamical model that goes from circulation to circulation.

Effect of Reducing the Loan Period

Since the mean loan period for all the classes in the Science Library is considerably longer than 2 weeks, it might be suggested that a way to satisfy more of the demand is to have the books returned more quickly, in other words to increase the value of μ. As an illustration of the effect, suppose an extra effort had been made to have the books returned on time, so that the mean return rate μ was 25 for all books, instead of being much less than 25 as it actually was; what then would be the circulation and the unsatisfied demand? To compute this we assume that the value of D stays the same and recalculate $\bar{R}$ for $\mu = 25$ (call it $\bar{R}'$) and the corresponding unsatisfied demand $D - \bar{R}'$) per book as well as the total $N(D - \bar{R}')$ and the gain in circulation (or reduction of unsatisfied demand) $N(\bar{R}' - \bar{R})$ produced by the increased return rate μ'.

This is shown, for each class, in Table 7.2 on the line $N(\bar{R}' - \bar{R})$. We see that the increase in return rate increases the total circulation (or decreases the unsatisfied demand) by nearly 3000 borrowings per year. Most of this comes in the chemistry, mathematics, and physics classes of books. Tightening up the return of books hardly changes the geology or the general engineering book circulation; the demand is not there to take advantage of the increased availability of the book on the shelf. The gain in circulation is large but is only a third of the way to complete satisfaction of the demand; some 5600 potential borrowers would still be unsatisfied. Also the cost of increasing the return rate μ might be

Table 7.2   Total Unsatisfied Demand $N(D - \overline{R})$ and Estimates of Its Reduction If All Books in Class with Circulation M or Greater Had Shorter Loan Periods $NS(M)$ or Were Duplicated $NG(M)$

Class of Book		Biol.	Chem.	Eng.	Geol.	Math.	Met.	Phys.	Total
$N(D - \overline{R})$ Unsatisfied demand		370	1200	20	50	2310	270	4090	8310
Number	$NP(\geq 1)$	1880	1630	240	1170	2430	1390	2340	11080
circulating	$NP(\geq 2)$	730	1050	43	210	2080	570	1730	6410
M or more	$NP(\geq 4)$	110	430	7	6	960	100	950	2560
times	$NP(\geq 6)$	17	180	—	—	450	16	520	1180
$NP(\geq M)$	$NP(\geq 8)$	3	70	—	—	210	3	290	580
$Ne^{-\mu/2D}$, Number with $U \geq \frac{1}{2}R$		2	95	—	—	114	1	552	764
$N(\overline{R}' - \overline{R})$ Gain if $\mu' = 25$		200	440	10	20	500	120	1410	2700
$N(\overline{R}'' - \overline{R}) = NS(0)$, $\mu'' = 33$		240	640	15	25	960	130	2040	4050
Gain $NS(M)$ if	$NS(1)$	170	540	6	9	830	90	1960	3610
$\mu'' = 33$ only	$NS(2)$	110	470	2	7	740	60	1560	2930
for those	$NS(4)$	34	320	—	3	540	26	1270	2200
circulating	$NS(6)$	12	200	—	—	370	8	970	1560
M or more									
$NG(6) + N[S(6) - S(2)]$		120	590	2	9	1140	70	2160	4090
Gain if books	$NG(0)$	350	1040	19	30	2020	250	3310	7020
circulating	$NG(1)$	250	880	8	13	1740	180	2710	5780
M or more	$NG(2)$	160	760	2	10	1560	120	2530	5130
times were	$NG(4)$	50	520	—	7	1140	40	2060	3820
duplicated	$NG(6)$	17	320	—	3	770	16	1570	2690
$NG(M)$	$NG(8)$	3	180	—	—	490	3	1150	1830

high; it would involve greater promptness in sending overdue notices, and it would require that faculty borrowers not be given a privileged position.

The circulation could be increased even more by further reducing the loan periods on high-circulation books, for example by making 7-day books all those that circulate 4 or more times a year. This gain can be estimated by the method discussed in the next section, so we postpone further discussion till then.

We should emphasize again that the quantities tabulated in Tables 7.1

and 7.2 are fairly crude approximations to the "true" values, in part because the data on which they are based come from small samples and in part because the Formulas 7.2 through 7.8 are approximations to the "true" formulas. Note, however, that we are not dependent, for our decisions, on the exact values of D, $D - \bar{R}$, and $\bar{R}' - \bar{R}$. We are interested in whether $N(D - \bar{R})$, the total unsatisfied demand, for a whole class of books, is less than 100 or more than 1000 and we are interested in which classes of books have values conspicuously larger than others. The value of $N(D - \bar{R})$ for physics books tabulated in Table 7.1 may be 30 per cent too large or 40 per cent too small; there is no question that the "correct" value is somewhat larger than the "correct" values for chemistry and mathematics books and that it is considerably larger than that for geology. In fact relative values are likely to be more accurate than absolute values; it is more certain that the unsatisfied demand for mathematics books is two-thirds that for physics books than it is that the unsatisfied demand for physics books is between 3500 and 4500 a year, for example. In other words, the numbers tabulated in Table 7.1 and later tables are of considerable utility in picking between alternative policies and in regard to relative magnitudes of entries, but their absolute magnitudes may all be too large or too small by a factor of 1.5 or so. This is a situation often encountered in operations research; inaccurate numbers are better than no numbers at all, if the numbers are used with appropriate caution and forbearance.

Effect of Duplicating Some Books

Another way of avoiding circulation interference and of decreasing unsatisfied demand is to buy duplicate copies of the more popular books. As was shown in Chapter 4, if the demand rate for a book is λ and its return rate is μ, the mean unsatisfied demand is U_1 if the book is a single copy and U_2 if there are two copies. The net reduction $U_1 - U_2$ in unsatisfied demand by duplicating the book is

$$U_1 = \frac{\lambda^2}{\mu + \lambda} \qquad U_2 = \frac{\frac{1}{2}\lambda^3}{\mu^2 + \mu\lambda + \frac{1}{2}\lambda^2}$$

$$U_1 - U_2 = \frac{\mu^2\lambda^2 + \frac{1}{2}\lambda^3\mu}{(\mu + \lambda)\left[\mu(\mu + \lambda) + \frac{1}{2}\lambda^2\right]}$$

(7.9)

The mean unsatisfied demand per book for a class of books with mean demand D and mean circulation $\bar{R}$, related by Eq. 7.7, is $\bar{U}_1 = D - \bar{R}$, which has already been tabulated in Table 7.1.

Using the model represented in Eqs. 7.4 to 7.7, the reduction in the mean unsatisfied demand, the gain in per-book circulation if *all* of the books of the class were duplicated is

$$G = \int_0^\infty (U_1 - U_2)P(\lambda)\,d\lambda \simeq \frac{1}{D}\int_0^\infty \frac{\mu\lambda^2 + \frac{1}{2}\lambda^3}{(\mu + \lambda)^2}\,e^{-\lambda/D}\,d\lambda$$

$$\simeq \frac{1}{2D}\int_0^\infty \left[\lambda - \frac{\mu^2}{\mu + \lambda} + \frac{\mu^3}{(\mu + \lambda)^2}\right] e^{-\lambda/D}\,d\lambda$$

$$= \frac{1}{2}\left[D + R\left(1 + \frac{\mu}{D}\right) - \mu\right] = G(0) \qquad (7.10)$$

where R is given in terms of μ and D in Eq. 7.7. This, or rather NG, the increase in total circulation during the year to be expected if all the books were to be duplicated, is given in Table 7.2. We see that it is nearly equal to the total unsatisfied demand in all but the few heavily used classes. In all but chemistry, mathematics, and physics there is a negligible fraction of the books that circulate so much that a duplicate will not satisfy the excess demand. In the three heavily used classes, there are an appreciable number of books that circulate 6 or more times a year. (In Table 7.2, the row for $NP(\geq 6)$ shows that these number about 1000.) When a book circulates 6 or more times a year, it is out of the library about half the time (with μ averaging 14, the fraction of time out of the library is $6/14 \simeq 1/2$), so half the demand is unsatisfied and some of this would still be unsatisfied even with the presence of a duplicate copy (see Table 4.1).

A better picture is obtained if we ask how many books have a demand λ such that a third or more of the demand is unsatisfied. Reference to Eqs. 4.4 and 4.7 shows that if λ is equal to $\frac{1}{2}\mu$ or greater then the unsatisfied demand U_1, for a single copy, is $\frac{1}{3}\lambda$ or greater and that still unsatisfied if two copies are present is $U_2 = (1/13)\lambda$ or greater. From Eqs. 7.3, we see that the fraction of books of a class which have a demand rate λ equal to $\frac{1}{2}\mu$ (i.e., about 7 per book per year) or greater is $e^{-\mu/2D}$. This quantity times the number N of books in the class is thus the number of books for which the unsatisfied demand per year is greater than $\mu/6$ (about 2 persons per book) if the book is a single copy and for which the unsatisfied demand is greater than $\mu/25$ (about 3/5 of a person per book) if there are two copies available. The numbers $Ne^{-\mu/2D}$ of these books, for which duplication is advisable, are given in Table 7.2. The great majority of them are in the 3 classes, chemistry, mathematics, and physics; in fact the 550 physics books with λ greater than 7 per year constitute more than two-thirds of all of these heavily used books.

It would manifestly be inefficient (and also too costly) to duplicate all the 28,000 books in the collection. Remember that more than half of the books did not circulate at all; adding extra copies of these books would satisfy no one. We might ask how efficient it would be to duplicate only those books that circulate more than M times a year. (The problem of how we locate these books so as to order an extra copy in time to satisfy the extra demand will be discussed later.) What is needed is an estimate of the number of books of each class that circulate M or more times, to see whether the cost of duplication is within the budget, plus an estimate of the gain in circulation (the reduction of the unsatisfied demand) that would be achieved if extra copies of these books were bought.

The number of books with circulation M or more is $NP(\geq M)$, where $P(\geq M)$ is given in Eqs. 7.6. These values are given in Table 7.1 for $M = 1, 2, 4, 6, 8$. We see, as expected, that it would be beyond the budget limitations to duplicate all the 6400 books that circulate 2 or more times during the year, even though the number to be duplicated the following year would be considerably less than this (in fact it would be approximately equal to the same fraction of the acquisitions, roughly one quarter of 2300, or about 600 books). However it might be possible to duplicate the 1000 books circulating 6 or more times or the 600 that circulate 8 or more times (if we could locate them soon enough).

To see how much of the unsatisfied demand $N(D - R)$ would be satisfied by this action we need to compute the expected gain in circulation if these books are duplicated. As indicated in Eqs. 7.2, 7.6 and 7.10, the expected gain in circulation produced by duplicating those books that circulate m times a year is

$$
\begin{aligned}
G_m &= \int_0^\infty (U_1 - U_2) P(\lambda \mid m)\, d\lambda \\
&\simeq \frac{D+1}{m!\,D} \left(\frac{Q+1}{Q} \right)^m \int_0^\infty \left[\frac{\mu\lambda^2 + \frac{1}{2}\lambda^3}{(\mu + \lambda)^2} \right] \left(\frac{\mu\lambda}{\mu + \lambda} \right)^m \\
&\quad \times \exp\left(-\frac{\lambda}{D} - \frac{\mu\lambda}{\mu + \lambda} \right) d\lambda
\end{aligned}
\tag{7.11}
$$

The fractional gain per book of the whole class, if all books with circulation M or greater are duplicated, is

$$
G(M) = G_M P(M) + G_{M+1} P(M + 1) + G_{M+2} P(M + 2) + \cdots
\tag{7.12}
$$

where $P(m)$ is given in Eqs. 7.6. An approximate formula for $G(M)$, obtained by use of methods analogous to those used to obtain the approximate formulas for $P(m)$ and $P(\geq m)$ given in Eqs. 7.6 (where G is given in Eq. 7.10) is

$$G(M) \simeq G \frac{(2Q + M + 1)(2Q + M + 2)}{(2Q + 1)(2Q + 2)} P(\geq M) \qquad (7.13)$$

This quantity, when multiplied by M, the total number of books in the class, is our best estimate, from the data of Table 6.3, of the gain in circulation resulting from a duplication of all books in the class having circulation M or more. In other words, if $N(D - R)$ is the total unsatisfied demand if all books in the class are single copies, then $NG(M)$ is the extra amount by which this demand is satisfied, if all books with circulation M or more were duplicated.

These quantities are also given in Table 7.2; they exhibit several interesting properties of the system. In the first place, the "efficiency" of extra copies of the higher circulation books, in satisfying extra demand, is apparent. For example, for the mathematics books, if all the 2000 books that circulate 2 or more times were duplicated, then about 1600 of the 2300 unsatisfied demands would be satisfied but at the cost of buying 2000 books. Each extra copy, on the average, would be borrowed about three-fourths of a time per year. On the other hand, if only the 450 books that circulated 6 or more times were duplicated, this would satisfy only about a third of the unsatisfied demand, but the extra copies bought would circulate about twice a year; each duplicate copy would satisfy nearly 2 otherwise unsatisfied, would-be borrowers. Referring to the discussion at the end of Chapter 4, if the librarian should decide that it is "worth" buying a book to "satisfy" 2 persons a year (and the Science Library as a whole "satisfies" about 1.1 persons per year per book, in regard to circulation), then he should get extra copies of all books that circulate more than about 5 times a year.

In the second place, it is apparent that this gain in effectiveness of duplicates only applies to the heavily used classes. For the biology and metallurgy books the high-demand books are so rare that those few that happen to circulate 6 or more times are more likely to be chance fluctuations rather than evidence of a "permanent" high demand. However, the numbers involved are so minute that it would be easier to make a uniform rule that all books with circulation greater than, say 5 times a year, should have duplicate copies bought. At the cost of buying about 1200 volumes, approximately 2700 additional circulations could be attained, about one-third of the estimated unsatisfied demand per year.

To return to the effects of reducing the loan period on some books, we have already seen how to calculate the effect of changing μ for all books. We should also calculate the effect of increasing μ for just the high-circulation books. Since the gain in mean circulation (i.e., the reduction of unsatisfied demand) for a book with expected demand λ, if the return rate is changed from μ to μ'', is

$$S(\lambda) = \frac{\mu''\lambda}{\mu'' + \lambda} - \frac{\mu\lambda}{\mu + \lambda} \simeq \frac{\mu'' - \mu}{(\mu''/\mu)} \frac{\lambda^2}{(\mu + \lambda)^2}$$

one can calculate the expected gain in circulation if the books with circulation m have return rate changed from μ to μ'. This gain is

$$S_m = \int_0^\infty S(\lambda)P(\lambda \mid m) \, d\lambda$$

By methods similar to those used in obtaining Eqs. 7.6 and 7.12, the approximate formula for the gain in circulation per book produced when the mean loan period of all books of a class that circulate M or more times is changed from $1/\mu$ to $1/\mu''$ is

$$S(M) = S_M P(M) + S_{M+1}P(M + 1) + S_{M+2}P(M + 2) + \cdots$$
$$\simeq \frac{(2Q + M + 1)(2Q + M + 2)}{(2Q + 1)(2Q + 2)} SP(\geq M) \tag{7.14}$$

where $S = (\overline{R}'' - \overline{R})$, and $\overline{R}''$ and $\overline{R}$ are computed from Eq. 7.7 for the same value of D but using μ'' for $\overline{R}''$ and μ for computing $\overline{R}$. Parameter Q is, to the first approximation, given by Eq. 7.6, using $\overline{R}$, since we make our decision to change μ on the basis of the book's record when its return rate is μ.

Values of $NS(M)$, the total gain in circulation for the class when books circulating M or more times a year have their return rate changed from μ to $\mu'' = 33$ (roughly a 7-day period, allowing for some delays in return), are shown in Table 7.2. The row for $N(\overline{R}'' - \overline{R}')$ shows the gain if all books are made 7-day books; it is little less than half the total unsatisfied demand. If only the books with circulation 4 or more have their loan period reduced (this constitutes less than 10 per cent of the books; $NP(\geq 4) = 2560$), the gain is cut to 2200, about a quarter of the total unsatisfied demand. However, this is nearly as effective as buying duplicates of all books with circulation greater than 6, and it may be less expensive.

To show how these various calculations may be combined, row labeled $NG(6) + N[S(6) - S(2)]$ in Table 7.2 shows the gains if books with circulation between 2 and 5 inclusive are changed to 7-day books and those with circulation 6 or over are duplicated but left with unaltered μ (this is not a recommended policy, but serves to show what can be calculated!). Nearly half of the unsatisfied demand is taken care of, at the cost of buying about 1200 books and tightening up the book returns. But perhaps these are enough examples of the way the model works; we should turn our attention to other matters.

Comments on the Model

In conclusion, we should anticipate comments that are sure to be made about the cavalier way we have handled the model and the data. We have, for example, ignored the fact that some of the books in the collection did have duplicates and that some books were not on the shelves because they were being repaired or were simply lost. The answer is that these complications are not large enough to modify the order of magnitude of the result nor the relative magnitudes of the various effects. Our object was to arrive at a model simple enough so results could be obtained graphically or by slide rule. Accuracy is not often important in reaching policy decisions; order-of-magnitude figures are far better than none. Any modifications of the data that change the figures used here by less than 25 per cent are not worth including, particularly if it further complicates the model. We are seeking assistance in deciding how to act, not working out a problem in mathematics.

One could also complain that the model really tells what *should have* been done, not what should be done now. Our estimates in Table 7.2, for example, tell what increase in circulation *would have* occurred this year *if* we had duplicated a number of books last year. This is a valid criticism; we still have to bring in our Markov model before we can predict next year's circulation. This will be done in the next chapter. We also have neglected the effects of in-library use of the books and the problems connected with lost books; these topics will be touched on later.

Finally, it should be pointed out that, at present, there is no simple way to spot all the high-circulation books, even when we have decided what should be done with them. One way is through reserve cards, though we will shortly demonstrate that this is an inefficient way in most university libraries. But it brings us to one of the reasons why this book is being written just now. Data of the sort we have been using so freely in the past two chapters are at present not easy to obtain in most libraries. The gathering requires tedious counting and copying by hand plus an experience with sample counts that most library personnel do not now have. But, as the library becomes more "mechanized" or "computerized," these data will become enormously easier to collect, *if the computer system is designed to gather the needed data.*

It is the author's belief, based on discouraging experience, that neither the computer experts nor the librarian (for different reasons) really know what data would be useful for the librarian to have collected, analyzed, and displayed, so he can make decisions with some knowledge of what the decision implies. What is needed *before* the computer designs are frozen is for models, of the sort developed in this book, to be played with, to see which of them could be useful and to see what data are needed and in what form, in order that both models and computers can be used most effectively by the librarian.

If it is so designed, the computer not only can gather the needed data but also can efficiently help to carry out the operating policy, once decided on. For example, if the computer keeps records of book circulation, it can quickly bring to the librarian's notice that a particular book has been borrowed several times in the past 2 months and perhaps an extra copy should be ordered. Likewise it can, from its records, spot overdue books and can, if so designed, prepare the overdue notice the day the book is due, thereby effectively reducing the mean loan period. Again what is needed is some experimenting with models of operation of the sort discussed in this book, so as to ensure that the computer will utilize, as completely as possible, the data it gathers and stores and also to prevent the system from being overdesigned to do things that turn out to be inutile or vacuous.

But before we return to the Markov model, we should see how, before the computers are installed, one can spot the high-circulation book, in order to do something about it before it is too late.

Reserve Cards

Let us now extend our circulation model to include consideration of that small number of unsatisfied borrowers who want the book so much that they leave a reserve card for it. These persons, of course, eventually get the book they want, so they are to be subtracted from the "unsatisfied demand" term and added to the circulation figure. The only reason the simple model can be used successfully (as it has in the preceding pages) is because, in most libraries, a very small fraction of the persons who don't find the book of their choice take the trouble to turn in a reserve card. This fraction is so small that it can be neglected in a first survey. Nevertheless it is desirable now to investigate its effects to verify that these effects really are small and to see whether increased use of reserve cards would be detrimental or advantageous (or neither).

The model to use was discussed in Chapter 4 and summarized in Eqs. 4.10; we will rewrite them here. For a single-copy book, for which there is an expected demand λ per year and which has a mean return rate μ, the probability that the book is on the shelf is P_0; the probability that the book is on loan and q reserve cards are waiting is P_{q+1}; the mean circulation rate is $R(\lambda)$; and the mean number of reserve cards on hand for the book is $W(\lambda)$; where

$$P_0 = \frac{\mu - \delta\lambda}{\mu + (1 - \delta)\lambda} \qquad P_{q+1} = \frac{\mu - \delta\lambda}{\mu + (1 - \delta)\lambda} \delta^q \left(\frac{\lambda}{\mu}\right)^{q+1}$$

$$R(\lambda) = \frac{\lambda\mu}{\mu + (1 - \delta)\lambda} \simeq \left(\frac{\lambda\mu}{\mu + \lambda}\right)\left[1 + \frac{\delta\lambda}{\mu + \lambda} + \left(\frac{\delta\lambda}{\mu + \lambda}\right)^2 + \cdots\right]$$

$$W(\lambda) = \frac{\delta\lambda^2}{(\mu - \delta\lambda)[\mu + (1 - \delta)\lambda]} \qquad (7.15)$$

$$\simeq \left[\frac{\lambda^2}{\mu(\mu + \lambda)}\right]\left[1 + \delta\frac{\lambda^2 + 2\mu\lambda}{\mu(\mu + \lambda)} + \delta^2\frac{\lambda^4 + 5\lambda^3\mu + 5\lambda^2\mu^2}{\mu^2(\mu + \lambda)^2} + \cdots\right]$$

In Chapter 4 as indicated, δ is the fraction of persons, looking for a specific book and not finding it, who leave a reserve card; we might call it the *reserve card utilization factor*. The approximate formulas for $W(\lambda)$ and $R(\lambda)$ are valid for δ smaller than about one-fifth.

Note that an increase in δ does increase the book's circulation (and thus reduces the unsatisfied demand $\lambda - R$), and the effect is larger the more popular the book is (the larger λ is). An unpopular book is usually in the library; one does not need to use a reserve card to borrow it. Note also that with very popular books (λ larger than μ) an unstable situation can arise if too many leave reserve cards. If $\delta\lambda/\mu$ is greater than unity, no equilibrium can be reached. The book will be out on loan all the time and the number of reserve cards will increase continually; more people ask for and wait for the book than can be taken care of by one book. Usual values of δ and λ are far too small for this to happen, however.

Our first task is to determine the mean value of δ for a homogeneous class of books having the geometric distribution of demand characterized by Eq. 7.3. We have already seen how to calculate the mean demand D from the mean circulation $\overline{R}$ and mean return rate μ of the class. The only other piece of data we need, in order to find the mean value of δ, is the mean number N_w of reserve cards on hand for books of the class; this divided by the number N of books in the class equals $\overline{W}$, the mean number of reserve cards per book of the class. To assure ourselves that there is a statistical constancy of behavior of library users with respect to the use of reserve cards for books of a class, we need to verify that N_w remains reasonably constant in value from week to week. In 1962 for example, N_w for physics books[10] was 31 on 1 weekend and was 32 several weekends later, which indicates that the fraction δ of persons who left reserve cards for physics books they wanted is a meaningful statistical measure of these users' behavior with respect to this class of books. The 32 cards were not for the same books as were the 31 cards; the two surveys were enough separated in time so that most of the first cards had already been honored and the second batch were for other books. Nevertheless, on the average, about the same fraction of the users were leaving cards at one time as at another; the population of physics book borrowers was large enough so that we are able to deal with averages and to predict from them. This was not the case with the geology books, which had 6 cards on 1 weekend and 1 on the other. One can usually expect large fluctuations in such small samples; more surveys, on other weekends, would be needed to determine a reasonably stable average value for this and the other less used classes.

From Eqs. 7.3 and 7.15, the mean number of reserve cards per book of the class is

$$\overline{W} = \int_0^\infty W(\lambda)P(\lambda)\,d\lambda \simeq \frac{1}{D}\int_0^\infty \frac{\delta\lambda^2 e^{-\lambda/D}\,d\lambda}{(\mu - \delta\lambda)[\mu + (1 - \delta)\lambda]}$$

$$\simeq \delta\left(\frac{D - \overline{R}}{\mu}\right) + \delta^2\left(2\,\frac{D^2 - \mu\overline{R}}{\mu^2} + \frac{D - \overline{R}}{D}\right)$$

$$+ \delta^3\left[\frac{6D^3 - \mu^3 - 3\mu^2\overline{R}}{\mu^3} + \left(\lambda + \frac{\mu}{2D}\right)\frac{D - \overline{R}}{D}\right] + \cdots \quad (7.16)$$

Values of $\overline{W}/\delta$ are plotted in Fig. 7.2 as functions of $\overline{R}/\mu$ for several different values of δ. If every third person, not finding the book he wanted, should leave a reserve card ($\delta \simeq 0.3$) then, if mean circulation is one-fifth of the maximum rate μ (where $\overline{R}/\mu = 0.2$) there would be, on hand at any time, reserve cards for about one-twentieth ($\overline{W}/\delta = 0.15$, $\overline{W} = 0.05$) of the books of the class. Reducing the circulation to half this value ($\overline{R} = \mu/10$) reduces the mean number of reserve cards by a factor of nearly 5 (or $W \simeq 0.01$); only about 1 in a 100 of the books of the class would have a reserve card waiting for it. As circulation falls below this, fewer and fewer books are out on loan and the number of reserve cards on hand reduces even more precipitously.

With the curves of Fig. 7.2 and by means of the values of $\overline{W}$, $\overline{R}$, and μ for the different classes of books given in Table 6.3, we can quickly determine the reserve-card utilization factor δ for the cases where $N_w = N\overline{W}$ is large enough so that two readings would result in a meaningful average value. These values are shown in Table 7.3 for the

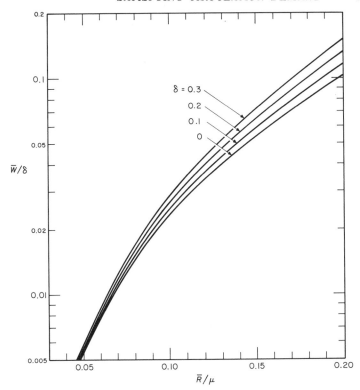

Fig. 7.2.   Mean number $\overline{W}$ of reserve cards per book as a function of mean circulation rate $\overline{R}$, mean reserve card utilization factor δ, and mean return rate μ.

Science Library in 1962.[10] Leaving out the low-circulation cases, the
3 high-use classes indicate that only about 1 person in 8 (or $\delta \simeq 0.13$),
having missed finding a book on the shelf, bothered to fill out and
leave a reserve card. Knowing the habits of users of the library, this
value is not unreasonable. The mean value of the correction term
$\delta\lambda/(\mu + \lambda)$ in Eq. 7.15 for R is less than 0.01, so our earlier formulas
for $\overline{R}$ and D need not be corrected.

To display the degree of accuracy of the determination of the value
of δ and also to indicate what would happen if a larger fraction of users
turned in reserve cards, the bottom row of Table 7.3 gives the expected
number of cards that would be on hand if δ were equal to 0.3 for all
classes. The numbers for the low-use classes would not change very
much, but the cards on hand for the 3 high-use classes would be increased considerably more than could reasonably be accounted for by

Table 7.3   Reserve Cards as Indicators of Circulation*

Class of Book	Biol.	Chem.	Eng.	Geol.	Math.	Met.	Phys.	Total
N Number in class	5000	2800	1400	6700	4900	3500	3700	28000
$\overline{R}$ Circulation per book	0.62	1.62	0.21	0.21	1.95	0.67	2.44	1.081
μ Mean return rate	10.8	14.0	6.5	13.3	18.2	12.4	13.5	14.1
$\overline{R}/\mu$	0.057	0.116	0.032	0.016	0.107	0.054	0.181	—
Q Dist. Parameter	0.636	1.783	0.210	0.214	2.128	0.691	2.871	—
$\overline{W}$ Reserve cards per book	0.0010	0.0078	0.0007	0.0006	0.0016	0.0011	0.0087	0.0027
$N\overline{W}$ Number reserve cards	5	22	1	4	8	4	32	76
δ Reserve card utilization factor	0.10?	0.23	—	0.30?	0.06	0.20?	0.10	0.13
Circulation 2 or more Total number	730	1050	43	210	2080	570	1730	6410
Number with reserve cards	1 (3)	13 (20)	—	—	5 (31)	1 (2)	23 (93)	43 (149)
Circulation 4 or more Total number	110	430	7	6	960	100	950	2560
Number with reserve cards	—	7 (10)	—	—	3 (18)	—	16 (65)	26 (93)
Circulation 6 or more Total number	17	180	—	—	450	16	520	1180
Number with reserve cards	—	4 (6)	—	—	2 (12)	—	11 (45)	17 (63)
Circulation 8 or more Total number	3	70	—	—	210	3	290	580
Number with reserve cards	—	2 (3)	—	—	1 (6)	—	7 (28)	10 (37)
If $\delta = 0.3$, the Number $N\overline{W}$ of reserve cards would be	(11)	(33)	(1)	(4)	(49)	(7)	(130)	(235)

* Numbers not in parentheses are for the δ given in the eighth row. Numbers in parentheses are for $\delta - 0.3$. Question marks follow estimates of δ for which the sample data is too small to yield dependable results.

chance fluctuations; the total number on hand would be roughly tripled.

Indicators for High-Use Books

The ideal way to decide which books need duplicates is to use professional judgment. One could request some expert in the field, once or twice a year, to examine the circulation records of all the books in a class and to decide, on the basis of the records plus his special knowledge (of the importance of the book or of its likelihood of being used as a reference in class or whatever), which books need duplication. If this could be done regularly, it would of course be the best way to ensure having enough copies to satisfy demand and to avoid wasting money buying duplicates that will not be needed. But any librarian knows that this is a council of perfection; in fact one can question whether this would be an economic (or a popular) way of using valuable advisory talent.

Lacking expert talent of this sort and in this profusion, what is needed is an *operating rule* to be used by the *library personnel* that *on the average* will spot *most* of the books needing duplication, will spot them in time to avoid frustrating many potential borrowers, and will waste neither the time of highly skilled people nor the money spent on books that do not need to be duplicated. We indicated in Chapter 4 that a possible operating rule is that a book is to be duplicated whenever its circulation rate R is greater than some limit. We suggested this limit might be $\mu/2$, but the value must be chosen by the librarian, in the light of his budgetary limitations.

When the library circulation process is *adequately* computerized, the circulation record of each book will be recorded in machine-readable form and it will be simple to determine periodically those books that have circulated more than a specified number of times in the previous 4 or 6 months. It will then be feasible to use a simple operating rule as to which book is to be duplicated, using the formulas to balance between cost and unsatisfied demand. But in present libraries a search through the whole collection to find the books that have circulated more than the assigned limit would be more time-consuming than a full-scale inventory — and few libraries have the manpower to inventory more than once in 10 years. Until computerization is general, it would be useful to find some other means to spot books that need duplication before the need is long past.

One possibility, which may not require too much additional work by the circulation-desk personnel, is to scan each book card after it has accumulated its first 6 or 8 due dates (the first book card in a new book could be one with only 6 or 8 places on it, for example, so attention is automatically required when these have been used up). If the accumulated due dates are entirely in the previous 6 months, for example, then the book's circulation has been large enough to consider ordering a duplicate; whereas if the due dates are spread over the previous several years, no action need be taken. This procedure, of course, spots only those books that are initially popular and would not find those that became popular later (as with Book C of Table 5.1), but it would be a simple procedure that would be more effective than the hit-or-miss methods presently in use.

Another indication of high circulation, one that might be utilized, is the occurrence of reserve cards (which is of course the reason this discussion occurs here). It is thus of interest to use the models of circulation distribution of Eqs. 7.2 and of circulation interference of Eqs. 7.5 to see whether (and when) reserve cards can be used to spot books that should be duplicated. The procedure would be to examine periodically all the book cards that have reserve cards attached and to order duplicates (or to take some other appropriate action) for those indicated that have circulated more than a specified number of times in the previous 6 months. The questions that should be answered in order to evaluate this procedure include: how much work is it, i.e., how many cards must be looked at per pass (we will call each examination of all book cards having reserve cards a *pass*); how efficient is it, i.e., how many passes must be made a year in order to spot a majority of high-use books; and how accurate is it, i.e., what fraction of book cards looked at during a pass are for high-use books?

To answer these questions we need to use our models to calculate (1) the expected number of reserve cards present at the time of a pass, (2) the fraction of the books needing duplication that happen to have a reserve card present at the time of a pass, and (3) the fraction of the reserve cards present during a pass that are for books needing duplication.

Reserve Cards as Use Indicators

By the approximate methods we have already used to get Eqs. 7.8 and 7.13, we can show that the joint probability $P(k, m)$ that a book of a class circulates m times a year and, at the same time, has k reserve cards on hand at some randomly chosen instant of time, is

$$P(k,0) \simeq (k+1)\frac{D+1-Q}{D+1}\left(\frac{Q+1-\eta}{Q+1}\right)^2\left(\frac{\eta}{Q+1}\right)^k$$

$$P(k,m) \simeq \frac{1}{D+1}\frac{(m+k+1)!}{(m+1)!k!}\left(\frac{Q+1-\eta}{Q+1}\right)^2$$

$$\times \left(\frac{\eta}{Q+1}\right)^k\left[\frac{Q(Q+1-\eta)}{(Q+1)^2}\right]^m \quad (m>0)$$

(7.17)

The two quantities D and Q have already been defined and used previously. The joint probability is such that the sum, over all values of k for a given value of m, is equal to the probability $P(m)$ that the book circulates m times, regardless of the number of reserve cards that it generates; this has already been given in Eq. 7.6.

$$P(m) = P(0,m) + P(1,m) + P(2,m) + \cdots \simeq \frac{D+1-Q}{D+1} \quad (m=0)$$

$$\simeq \frac{1}{D+1}\left(\frac{Q}{Q+1}\right)^m \quad (m>0)$$

Likewise the probability $P(k)$ that a book has k reserve cards waiting for it, independent of its circulation, is

$$P(k) = P(k,0) + P(k,1) + P(k,2) + \cdots$$

$$\simeq \frac{Q+1-\eta}{(D+1)(Q+1)}$$

$$\times \left[(k+1)(D-Q)\frac{Q+1-\eta}{Q+1} - \frac{Q+1}{Q}\right]\left(\frac{\eta}{Q+1}\right)^k$$

$$+ \frac{(1+Q)^2}{Q(D+1)}\frac{Q+1-\eta}{Q+1+\eta Q}\left[\frac{\eta(Q+1)}{Q+1+\eta Q}\right]^k \quad (7.18)$$

The parameter η is chosen so that the mean number of reserve cards on hand, per book of the class, is $\overline{W}$, as defined in Eq. 7.16,

$$\bar{k} = 0 \times P(0) + 1 \times P(1) + 2 \times P(2) + 3 \times P(3) + \cdots$$

$$\equiv \overline{W} \simeq \eta\frac{\overline{R}+2}{Q+1-\eta} \simeq \delta\frac{D-\overline{R}}{\mu} \quad (7.19)$$

Because the formula for $P(k,m)$, given in Eq. 7.17, is an approximate one, it is not worthwhile to include more than the first orders of the small quantities η and δ. To this order of approximation, therefore,

$$\eta \simeq \overline{W}\frac{Q+1}{\overline{R}+2} \simeq \delta\frac{D-\overline{R}}{\mu} \simeq \overline{W} \quad (7.20)$$

To answer the questions raised at the end of the previous section, we need to calculate the joint probability that a book circulates M or more times a year $(M > 0)$ and, in addition, on the average, 1 or more reserve cards are on hand for it,

$$P(k > 0, m \geq M) = P(m \geq M) - P(k = 0, m \geq M)$$

$$\simeq \frac{Q+1}{D+1}\left[1 - \frac{(Q+1-\eta)^{M+2}}{(Q+1+\eta Q)(Q+1)^{M+1}}\right]\left(\frac{Q}{Q+1}\right)^M$$

$$\simeq \eta\,\frac{Q+M+2}{Q+1}\,P(m \geq M)$$

$$\simeq \overline{W}\,\frac{Q+M+2}{R+2}\,P(m \geq M) \tag{7.21}$$

The expected number of reserve cards on hand for all the books of a class that circulate M or more times a year is, to this degree of approximation, equal to $P(k > 0, m \geq M)$ times N, the total number of books in the class. Values of this quantity are given in Table 7.3, under the headings "Number with reserve cards" (the numbers *not* in parentheses); just above them are the expected numbers $NP(\geq M)$ of books in the class with circulation equal to M or more, for comparison.

We see that any particular inspection of the reserve cards on hand (one "pass") does not locate very many high-circulation books. Even with the physics books, only about 23 of the roughly 1730 books having circulation 2 or more per year (i.e., about one out of 75 of these books) would come to light in one pass. Thus more than 100 passes would have to be made during the year to spot most of the books with circulation 2 or more. This improves somewhat if we look at the higher circulation books; about a fortieth of the books (7 out of 290) circulating 8 or more times a year would be spotted on one pass, so one pass a week would locate most of them by the end of the year.

Nor is the individual pass very efficient; only a third of the reserve cards (11 out of 32) are for books with circulation 6 or greater. The efficiency is not negligible, of course, since only 1 physics book out of 7 (520 out of 3700) circulates 6 or more times a year and yet these books generate a third of the reserve cards. If reserve cards were studied each week (less than 100 would have to be examined per pass, which should be easy if they were easy to spot), we would have spotted (per pass) 1 out of 74 (17 out of 1180) of all the books in the Science Library that circulated 6 or more times in 1962. Thus somewhat more than half of these books would have been spotted in 52 passes.

Because several passes will "respot" some books already spotted earlier, the fraction of books spotted is *not* the number p of passes times the ratio between $N_w(M)$, the number spotted per pass (the 17 in the example), and $N(M)$, the total number to be spotted (the 1180 in the example); the fraction spotted in p passes turns out to be $1 - \exp[-pN_w(M)/N(M)]$ and in the example this is $1 - \exp[-52(17/1180)] = 0.53$. The procedure of weekly passes therefore is possible without undue effort, and is probably worth the effort, though it certainly is not very efficient, compared with an automatic tabulation of all books with circulation 6 or greater, which a computer could be programmed to deliver whenever it was required (*if* the data on J, R, and thus μ were stored in its memory).

It should be noted that a campaign to induce more people to turn in reserve cards would improve the efficiency of the reserve card as a high-circulation indicator. As an example, the figures in parentheses are computed assuming that $\delta = 0.3$ (i.e., about 1 frustrated borrower in 3 turns in a card) rather than the $\delta = 0.12$ which was the case. The task per pass would be tripled (235 cards to look at rather than 76) but would not be impossibly large. A quarter of these cards (63 out of 235) would spot one-nineteenth of the books circulating 6 or more times a year (63 out of 1180), and thus 1 pass a week would spot 95 per cent of these books by the end of the year and would spot 75 per cent of them in the first 6 months (the second 6 months would spot an additional 20 per cent, in addition to respotting many that had been spotted in the first 6 months). Thus if δ were as large as 0.3, the procedure of looking each week at the circulation records of all books with reserve cards would be a fairly efficient means of spotting high-circulation books; even with $\delta = 0.13$ the procedure is probably worth the trouble, assuming of course that the library can afford to duplicate the books thus spotted.

But we still have not reached a satisfactory conclusion to our analysis; the time element has not yet been introduced. We have shown how we can use statistical knowledge of circulation and of reserve cards to calculate *this year's* mean loan period and circulation for a class of books, and what would result during the current year if these quantities had been changed. To be useful in decision making, we should be able to predict what will happen next year if the quantities were changed at the end of this year. We need, for example, to differentiate between the behavior of this year's accessions and that of the books which have been in the library for several years. When this is done, we can not only estimate the future demand for the whole collection but we can also begin to determine which books should be relegated to less easily available space when the open shelves begin to be crowded. But for this more data must be gathered.

8 Predicting Future Use

To make decisions regarding book purchases and book retirement, we need to know more than the circulation pattern for the present year; we need to be able to predict the future pattern. The predictions need not be accurate for each book. Indeed the random nature of book use by the library clientele makes detailed prediction impossible. As we have already seen, an expected value cannot be an accurate prediction of each event; some outcomes are greater, some are less than the expected value. But with a large enough sample of events, the average outcome will correspond reasonably well to the expected value. Decisions regarding the purchase of duplicate books or their retirement to a less accessible location are usually taken many times during the year. Even though some decisions are not justified by later results, the errors will tend to balance out if we go by expected-value predictions. In addition our model can estimate the degree and magnitude of probable error and thus can indicate whether our predictions are likely to be accurate enough to be of help.

Future Demand

We see from Eq. 5.7 that, if we know the values of α and β of the circulation class of the book or books in question, and if we know the circulation $R(0)$ during the year just ended ($t = 0$), the expected yearly circulation per book next year ($t = 1$), the year after ($t = 2$), or the tth year later is

$$E[R(t)] = \frac{\alpha}{1 - \beta} + \left[R(0) - \frac{\alpha}{1 - \beta} \right] \beta^t \qquad (8.1)$$

In order to estimate the worth of buying a duplicate book, we should consider the number of "lost customers" for the book not only for this year but also for later years. In fact the more important quantity is the estimated number of lost customers in later years; it is too late to satisfy those of the past year.

If the book is one of a collection behaving like those in the Science Library, with a mean return rate μ that has been determined by Eq. 6.2, the relation between mean demand and mean circulation given in Eq. 7.7 should represent the situation reasonably well. In particular, if the expected value of circulation per book in some future year is $E(R)$ for a collection of books having mean return rate μ, then a rough approximation to the expected number of lost customers per book of the collection in that year would be, at least over the range

$$E(U) \simeq 2.5 \, \mu \left[\frac{E(R)}{\mu} \right]^2 \qquad 0 < R < 0.4 \, \mu \qquad (8.2)$$

from the last line of Eqs. 7.7.

Combining these two forecasts, a rough approximation to the expected value of unsatisfied demand per book in the tth year of a number of books that had circulation $R(0)$ in the zeroth year is

$$E[U(t)] = 2.5 \, \frac{\alpha^2}{\mu(1 - \beta)^2} [1 - 2(1 - v)\beta^t + (1 - v)^2\beta^{2t}] \qquad (8.3)$$

where $v = [(1 - \beta)R(0)/\alpha]$. The cumulative number of unsatisfied customers per book for the next T years can then be obtained by using Eq. 2.22,

$$U_T = E[U(1)] + E[U(2)] + \cdots + E[U(T)] = \left[\frac{\alpha^2}{\mu(1 - \beta)^2} \right] u(T)$$
$$(8.4)$$
$$u(T) = 2.5 \left[T - 2(1 - v)\beta \frac{1 - \beta^T}{1 - \beta} + (1 - v)^2\beta^2 \frac{1 - \beta^{2T}}{1 - \beta^2} \right]$$

The function $u(3)$ is plotted in Fig. 8.1 as function of v for different values of β. From it we can estimate the unsatisfied demand per book for the next 3 years, for those books that have circulated $R(0)$ times last year if the books were not duplicated meanwhile. We could, of course, use a different value of T, but $T = 3$ seems a reasonable time

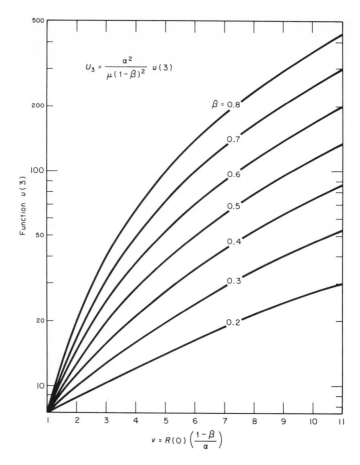

Fig. 8.1. Curves to predict unsatisfied demand U_3 for next three years for books with present circulation $R(0)$ and parameters α, β, and μ.

span; it covers most of the interval in which there is much unsatisfied demand for most books.

Using the values of α, β, and μ given in Tables 5.6 and 6.3 we see that, for the different classes of books in the Science Library,

Biology	$v = 1.37R(0);$	$U_3 = 0.049u(3);$	$\beta = 0.45$
Chemistry	$v = 0.83R(0);$	$U_3 = 0.103u(3);$	$\beta = 0.5$
Engineering; General Science	$v = 1.00R(0);$	$U_3 = 0.154u(3);$	$\beta = 0.7$
Geology	$v = 1.78R(0);$	$U_3 = 0.024u(3);$	$\beta = 0.2$
Mathematics	$v = 1.33R(0);$	$U_3 = 0.031u(3);$	$\beta = 0.6$

Metallurgy; Food

Technology	$v = 1.50R(0);$	$U_3 = 0.036u(3);$	$\beta = 0.7$
Physics	$v = 0.80R(0);$	$U_3 = 0.116u(3);$	$\beta = 0.6$

Thus, for a physics book that had circulated 10 times in the first year, the unsatisfied demand accumulated during the next 3 years would be expected to be about 13 (i.e., $v = 8$, $u(3) = 114$, $U_3 = 114 \times 0.116 = 13.2$); but if $R(0) = 5$, then U_3 would be about 4. On the other hand, if a geology book circulated 10 times last year, the expected 3-year unsatisfied demand would be less than 2 because of the very small value of β, indicating rapid decay of popularity. However, if an engineering and general science book had $R(0) = 10$, then U_3 for it would be about 38, partly because of the slowness with which such books lose popularity (i.e., the large value of β) and partly because these books are kept out a long time ($\mu = 6.5$ and $52/\mu = 8$ weeks). Therefore if there were a book of this class which circulated 10 times in a year, it would be off the shelf most of the time. A chemistry book with $R(0) = 10$ would be expected to have a U_3 of about 9, and so on.

The graphs can be used to set criteria for ordering duplicates (or to put a book on reserve). If we decide, for example, that whenever the expected unsatisfied demand in 3 years is 10 or greater, a duplicate should be ordered; then, working backward, one can find the value of $R(0)$ above which the book should be duplicated. These limiting circulations are listed below, for the different classes of books,

Biology	If $R(0) \geq 13$, then $U_3 \geq 10$; there were 15 of these
Chemistry	If $R(0) \geq 11$, then $U_3 \geq 10$; there were 70 of these
Engineering;	
General Science	If $R(0) \geq 5$, then $U_3 \geq 10$; there were 10 of these
Geology	If $R(0) \geq 25$, then $U_3 \geq 10$; there were none of these (8.5)
Mathematics	If $R(0) \geq 10$, then $U_3 \geq 10$; there were 200 of these
Metallurgy; Food Technology	If $R(0) \geq 7$, then $U_3 \geq 10$; there were 70 of these
Physics	If $R(0) \geq 8$, then $U_3 \geq 10$; there were 330 of these

Because of the different rates at which different classes of books decay in popularity (different value of β) and also because of the different mean lengths of time books are kept out, different values of circulation correspond to the same value of U_3, the 3-year cumulative number of unsatisfied customers. The last statement in each line indicates the approximate number of books of the class in the Science Library in 1962 which circulated this number of times or more (from Table 6.2). Thus if roughly all the 700 books with circulation greater than the noted limit, whether new or old, were duplicated, the majority (but not all, see Fig. 4.4) of about 7000 prospective borrowers would not be disappointed in the following 3 years. If the criterion were $U_3 \geq 13$ instead of $U_3 \geq 10$, the number of books to be duplicated would be about 350 instead of 700.

If and when an adequately designed computer data system is provided for the Science Library, search could easily be made each month for high-circulation books. Whenever a mathematics book shows 5 circulations or more in the previous 6 months, for example, this fact could be noted and, if so desired, a duplicate could be ordered. Popular books could be duplicated during the first year, thus drastically reducing the amount of unsatisfied demand at the time it is greatest. We will discuss the circulation distribution of first-year books in the next section.

Another calculation of use in our later discussions involves a consequence of Eqs. 5.7 regarding the decrease of mean circulation of a collection with time. It was noticed that, for several years after 1962, the mean circulation of the whole collection did not change appreciably with time, remaining approximately 1.1 circulations per volume in the collection per year (see Table 6.2). In order for this to happen, the circulation of the accessions each year should just make up for the decrease in circulation of the books already there. But, from the discussion preceding Eqs. 5.7 we see that the mean circulation, next year, of the collection which had mean circulation 1.1 this year, will be $\bar{\alpha} + 1.1\bar{\beta}$, where $\bar{\alpha}$ and $\bar{\beta}$ are the values of α and β which should be used for the whole collection of all ages. If our previous discussion (see Table 5.12) is correct, the $\bar{\beta}$ for the whole collection should be 0.5 and the $\bar{\alpha}$ should be somewhere between 0.15 and 0.4.

But the year's accessions are about a twelfth of last year's total collection $N = 28,000$ (see Table 6.1), and the mean circulation of these accessions is about 4.4 per book (see Table 8.1). Therefore the total circulation of old and new books next year will be, if we set $\bar{\beta} = 0.5$,

$$28,000(\bar{\alpha} + 0.55) + 2300(4.4) = 28,000\bar{\alpha} + 15,400 + 10,100$$

which should equal 30,300 times 1.1 (the new total number of volumes times the same mean circulation as last year). Therefore

$$28,000\bar{\alpha} = 33,300 - 25,500 = 7800 \text{ or } \bar{\alpha} \simeq 0.28 \qquad (8.6)$$

which is a reasonable average of the values of α given in Table 5.12 for the whole collection.

Circulation Distribution of New Books

During the survey mentioned earlier,[6] the first-year circulation of a random sample of about 300 new books was recorded. This can be analyzed to discover how many new books have a large enough circulation to warrant duplicating as soon as possible. Interestingly enough, the data indicate that the circulation of new books is geometrically distributed (see Eq. 2.21). Figure 8.2 shows some of the data plotted on a

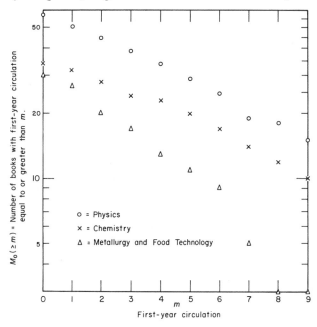

Fig. 8.2. First-year circulation distribution for random samples of accessions for 1958.

semilog chart; the lines are remarkably straight, considering the small size of the sample. The result enables us to work out a number of interesting prognostications, which will be discussed later. But first we must determine the distribution parameters.

Referring to Eqs. 2.21 to 2.27, we see that for such a distribution, the probability P_m^0 that a book of a given class has a first-year circulation

m, the expected number $M_0(\geq m)$ of books of the class which circulate m or more times during their first year on the shelves, and the expected value $\overline{R}_0$ of the average, per-book, first-year circulation are

$$P_m^0 = (1 - \gamma)\gamma^m \qquad P^0(\geq m) = \gamma^m$$
$$M_0(\geq m) = M_0 P^0(\geq m) = M_0 \gamma^m \tag{8.7}$$

$$E(\overline{R}) = P_1^0 + 2P_2^0 + 3P_3^0 + \cdots$$

$$= \frac{1}{M_0} [M_0(\geq 1) + M_0(\geq 2) + M_0(\geq 3) + \cdots]$$

$$= \gamma + \gamma^2 + \gamma^3 + \cdots = \left(\frac{\gamma}{1 - \gamma}\right)$$

all given in terms of γ, the single parameter for the particular class of acquisitions.

To determine γ for one of the book classes, we can use the mean circulation $\overline{R}$. From the last equation we see that γ is approximately equal to $\overline{R}/(\overline{R} + 1)$; the approximation is usually better the larger the sample measured. We can also calculate γ from the first $N + 1$ values of $M_0(\geq m)$, because from Eqs. 8.7,

$$\gamma^p = \frac{M_0(\geq 0)M_0(\geq 1) \cdots M_0(\geq N)}{(M_0)^{N+1}} \tag{8.8}$$

where $p = \frac{1}{2}N(N + 1)$. The closer the data corresponds to the geometric model of Eqs. 8.7 the nearer the two derived values of γ should approach each other. In Table 8.1, the value $\gamma_R = \overline{R}/(\overline{R} + 1)$ and γ_p, obtained from Eq. 8.8, are both tabulated. The correspondence is good; the largest discrepancy is less than 4 per cent of the mean value.

Equations 8.1 to 8.4 work as well for a collection of books with mean first-year circulation $\overline{R}_0$ per book as they do for a set of books all having circulation $R(0)$. Thus we can use Fig. 8.1 to determine $\overline{U}_3$, the mean number per book of persons who have missed borrowing a book of the class during the second, third, and fourth year of the book's life in the library. For the less popular books, of course, there would be few or none such unsatisfied persons. But there are enough high-popularity books among the physics, mathematics, and chemistry accessions so that even the average value of $\overline{U}_3$ for these collections is larger than 3. The estimated total number of unsatisfied persons $M_0\overline{U}_3$ for the whole collection of books introduced during the year is given in the row below this. These are, of course, approximations, but the total number must be well above 3000 for 2 or 3 persons per new book.

Returning to Eqs. 8.7, we can calculate the fraction of the accessions

Table 8.1 First-Year Circulation Data for Accessions of 1960

Class	Biol.	Chem.	Geol.	Math.	Met.	Phys.	Total
M_0 Total accession	290	200	170	360	290	320	1630
Average circulation $\overline{R}_0$	4.64	6.19	2.32	3.47	3.83	5.37	4.33
γ_R from $\overline{R}_0$	0.82	0.86	0.70	0.78	0.79	0.84	—
γ_p from Eq. 8.8	0.856	0.880	0.681	0.792	0.820	0.871	—
β	0.45	0.50	0.60	0.60	0.70	0.60	0.49
$\alpha/(1 - \beta)$	0.727	1.200	0.563	0.750	0.667	1.250	0.784
μ	10.8	14.0	13.3	18.2	12.4	13.5	14.1
$\overline{U}_3$ Mean number unsatisfied in next 3 years	2.21	4.15	0.29	1.44	3.31	4.80	2.79
$M_0\overline{U}_3$ Total unsatisfied	640	830	50	520	960	1540	4540
Probability $\quad P(\geq 2)$	0.711	0.774	0.464	0.627	0.672	0.741	0.673
$P(\geq m)\quad\quad P(\geq 5)$	0.426	0.528	0.147	0.312	0.371	0.473	0.353
that $\quad\quad\quad P(\geq 7)$	0.303	0.409	0.068	0.195	0.249	0.351	0.268
book $\quad\quad\quad P(\geq 8)$	0.255	0.360	0.046	0.155	0.204	0.302	0.224
circulates $\quad P(\geq 10)$	0.181	0.279	0.021	0.097	0.137	0.224	0.158
m or							
more $\quad\quad\quad P(\geq 11)$	0.152	0.245	0.015	0.77	0.113	0.193	0.134
times $\quad\quad\quad P(\geq 13)$	0.108	0.190	0.007	0.048	0.076	0.143	0.095
1st year							
$K = $ Number with $U_3 \geq 10$	31	49	0	35	72	97	280
Mean circulation of these	18	17	—	13	11	13	12.9

of each class that circulate m or more times during the first year. Some of these values are given in Table 8.1. Now we can return to Eq. 8.5. We see that if we bought duplicates of all the 100-odd physics books that circulated 8 or more times in their first year, we would have gone a long way toward satisfying $10 \times 100 = 1000$ or so persons who, otherwise, during the next 3 years, would have missed borrowing these books because they were not on the shelves. Using the value of $P(\geq 8)$, we see that $M_0P(\geq 8)$ corresponds to 97 of the 320 physics books that should be duplicated, according to this criterion. If, during the first 6 months of their life on the shelves, these 97 high-circulation books could have been spotted and another copy of each bought (which perhaps would have arrived by the end of the first year), then an appreciable fraction of the 1500-odd frustrated borrowers would have been satisfied during the following 3 years. (Of course, the librarian could have put these books on the reserved shelves, thus disappointing *all* prospective borrowers but at least keeping such a book available for anyone who can get what he needs by using the book in the library.)

The expected first-year circulation of those physics books that circulate 8 or more times in their first year is, from Eqs. 8.7,

$$K = \left[\frac{1}{P^0(\geq 8)}\right](8P_8^0 + 9P_9^0 + 10P_{10}^0 + \cdots)$$

$$= 8 + \gamma + \gamma^2 + \gamma^3 + \cdots = 8 + E(R_0) \qquad (8.9)$$

Similar equations can be written for the other classes. Values of K are shown in the last row of Table 8.1. These values are entirely too large to allow us to use Eqs. 8.4 or Fig. 8.1 to compute $\bar{U}_3$ for them ($K > 0.4\ \mu$ for them), but we can estimate that they represent more than half of the $M_0\bar{U}_3 \simeq 4500$ unsatisfied borrowers for 3 years after accession, for the whole year's accessions.

Details of Circulation Histories

Though it is not necessary in order to calculate the measures of effectiveness we have been, and will be, using, it nevertheless is of interest to see how closely our Markov model of book circulation corresponds with the rather fragmentary data that have been gathered. In Figs. 5.3 and 5.4, we showed how the Markov model could predict the decline with age in circulation of a collection of books since accession. Data taken from the Science Library are not complete enough to check these curves in detail, year by year. What is available,[6,9] however, is the circulation distribution of relatively small samples of books of the 6 classes during their first year, circulation distributions of books no older than 4 years, plus distributions for random samples of the whole collection, including books of all ages.

For example, in Fig. 8.3 we have plotted, as circles, the first-year circulation distribution of 57 physics books. As indicated in Table 8.1 this initial distribution can be represented by a geometric distribution, and $P_1(\geq m)$, the probability that the book circulates m or more times in its first year, is

$$P_1(\geq m) = \gamma^m$$

with $\gamma \simeq 0.87$. The data indicate a remarkably successful choice of accessions; only 10 percent of the accessions did not circulate at all during the first year $[P_1(0) - P_1(1) \simeq 1.0 - 0.9 = 0.1]$, and half of them circulated 5 or more times.

The crosses on Fig. 8.3 plot the fraction of physics books not more than 4 years old which circulated m or more times during the year. If we assume that accession choice has been as good, during the 4 years, as it was for the year represented by the circles (i.e., that γ remained the same) and that the books aged according to the Markov parameters $\alpha = 0.5$ and $\beta = 0.6$, we can then compute the expected circulation distribution of a mixture of equal numbers of books 1, 2, 3, and 4 years old.

$$F_4(\geq m) = \tfrac{1}{4}[P_1(\geq m) + P_2(\geq m) + P_3(\geq m) + P_4(\geq m)] \qquad (8.10)$$

with the probabilities $P_i(\geq m)$ given by Eq. 5.13 and obtained from the tables in the Appendix. The resulting predicted distribution is shown in

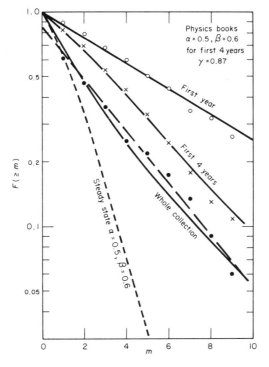

Fig. 8.3.   Fraction $F(\geq m)$ of physics books that circulate m or more times a year (dots, crosses, and circles) compared to theoretical probability $P(\geq m)$, solid lines.

the solid line marked "first 4 years" which checks fairly well with the data, given by the crosses, considering that there were no constants to adjust to "force" the fit; the values of α and β had been determined from other data, γ had been determined by fitting the first-year distribution.

We see that the circulation of the mixture is considerably degraded. Twenty percent of these books did not circulate at all during the year and only a third of them circulated 5 or more times. In fact the majority of the high-circulation books are the first-year books. As Fig. 5.3 indicates, very few of the older books circulate 5 or more times (only 1 in 10 of the 4-year-old books, with $\alpha = 0.5$ and $\beta = 0.6$, circulate 5 or more times).

If α kept its original value throughout the life of the collection, the eventual circulation distribution of the physics books, older than 10 years, would be given by the dotted line, marked "steady state" in Fig. 8.3. We know, from Table 5.12, however, that after about 5 years, α begins to decrease in value, reaching about half its original value (about 0.3 for physics books) after 10 or 12 years. We also know, from Table 6.1, that roughly half of the physics collection is less than 6 years old and less than about a quarter of them are more than 12 years old. Thus a very rough approximation to the circulation distribution of the whole physics collection would be an extension of the first 4-year combination to the first 6 years, and combining this with the steady-state distributions for $\alpha = 0.4$, and 0.3, to represent the older books

$$F(\geq m) \simeq \frac{1}{10} [P_1(\geq m) + P_2(\geq m) + \cdots + P_6(\geq m)]_{\alpha=0.5}$$

$$+ \frac{2}{10} [P_\infty(\geq m)]_{\alpha=0.4} + \frac{2}{10} [P_\infty(\geq m)]_{\alpha=0.3}$$

This is plotted as the solid curve marked "whole collection." The fit with the dots is not particularly good; in fact the dots fit the dashed straight line, corresponding to the approximate Formula 7.3, at least as well. This may be because the data are taken from too small a sample to expect a better fit, or it may be because we have not correctly estimated the change of α with book age; further data would be needed to determine this. The Markov model certainly corresponds well enough to warrant using it to predict average values and aggregate behavior. It need not disturb us that we use 2 different formulas, represented by the solid and the dashed lines, to represent the same data at different stages in our analysis; both formulas are approximations and they do not differ much from each other.

The analysis for the chemistry collection follows a similar pattern; the results are shown in Fig. 8.4. The popularity of the first-year books is slightly better than for the physics accessions, though the numbers of very high-circulation books drop below the geometrical straight line, marked "first year," rather more than for the physics books. If we had been more meticulous than the data warranted (and than is required for our prediction of averages), we would have used a first-year distribution that fell off more rapidly with increasing m than does the straight-line geometric distribution. Such a modified first-year plot, carried through to the next 3 years, would also have fitted the crosses (representing the circulation of books up to 4 years in age) somewhat better in the high m values.

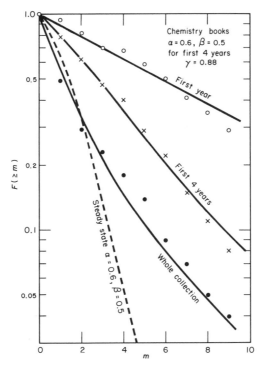

Fig. 8.4. Circulation history of chemistry books comparable to that of physics books in Fig. 8.3.

We should note the much greater reduction in high circulation between the circles and crosses for the chemistry books as compared to the physics books. This is primarily produced by the difference in value of β; as noted in Chapter 5, the smaller the β the more rapidly the book loses popularity. The change from $\beta = 0.6$ to $\beta = 0.5$ means a reduction by a factor of about $2/3$ in the number of books circulating 7 or more times in the 4-year sample, and a factor of nearly $1/2$ in the whole collection. The values of β and α are resultants of the rate at which the field of knowledge progresses (i.e., how rapidly a book gets out of date) and of the reading habits of the population of users of the library (i.e., whether they are interested in the latest developments or are interested in the field as a whole). Comparison of the values of these parameters, for example, for chemistry books in different libraries, will give us some interesting insights into the relative importance of these factors.

A rough approximation to the expected distribution for the whole chemistry collection is not the same as that for the physics books, because in the case of the chemistry books half of the collection is at least 7 years old. We used the combination

$$F(\geq m) \simeq \frac{1}{10} [P_1(\geq m) + P_2(\geq m) + \cdots + P_5(\geq m)]_{\alpha=0.6}$$
$$+ \frac{2}{10} [P_\infty(\geq m)]_{\alpha=0.4} + \frac{3}{10} [P_\infty(\geq m)]_{\alpha=0.2}$$

to produce the line labeled "whole collection," which fits the data, shown by the dots, only moderately well (but well enough for our purposes in the rest of the book).

The circulation history of biology books, as shown in Fig. 8.5, follows much the same pattern. The first-year books do not have as many high-circulation volumes as do the other 2, and the discrepancy between the data and the simple geometrical distribution, for m greater than 6, is still more pronounced. It may be that biology, covering a wider dispersion of subject matter, has fewer books with a general appeal to all biologists, or it may be that the biology accessions were not as carefully chosen as were those for chemistry and physics.

We note that if we had cared to represent the first-year books by a more complicated distribution curve, concave downward, which fit the circles better, then the resulting "first 4 years" curve would have fitted the crosses better also. Because of the more rapid obsolescence of biology books, measured by the smaller value of β, the fraction of high-circulation books in the older parts of the collection is considerably smaller than that for physics and chemistry; only 1 book in 30 of the whole collection circulates 4 or more times a year. The wide gap between "first 4 years" and "whole collection" also comes about because the whole collection has more older books than does the physics collection, for example. The combination represented by "whole collection" is

$$F(\geq m) \simeq \frac{1}{10} [P_1(\geq m) + P_2(\geq m) + \cdots + P_5(\geq m)]_{\alpha=0.4}$$
$$+ \frac{2}{10} [P_\infty(\geq m)]_{\alpha=0.3} + \frac{3}{10} [P_\infty(\geq m)]_{\alpha=0.2}$$

The data fit the curve reasonably well, considering the smallness of the sample.

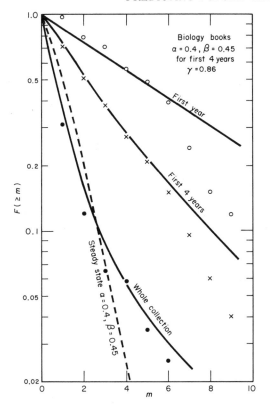

Fig. 8.5. Circulation history of biology books comparable to that of physics books in Fig. 8.3 and chemistry books in Fig. 8.4.

Decisions Regarding Book Retirement

We are now in a position to discuss Question 6, posed in Chapter 1 and related to the "retirement" of books. According to Table 6.1, the mezzanine of the Science Library contained about 28,000 volumes in 1962; this collection was growing at a rate of about 2300 volumes a year. Since the number of volumes that could be comfortably shelved in the mezzanine, for easy access to borrowers, without crowding other collections, was about 34,000, it was obvious that some drastic action had to be taken in the next 2 or 3 years. This action was taken; as noted in Table 6.1, a large number of the older volumes were moved to stacks in the basement. These stacks are somewhat less accessible, but they also have limited capacity.

The action taken in "retiring" books to the basement had to be taken before the surveys and analysis reported in this volume could be completed, because of the rudimentary state of data gathering then in force. If circulation had been computerized at the time, the move could have been planned with greater knowledge of expected results, and also a wider variety of possible actions would have been available to choose between.

To illustrate these statements, we return to 1962 and imagine we have at hand the data and analytic models discussed in this volume. We wish to use them to help decide what action to take. If we don't want to run out of shelf space, we will soon need to retire about 2300 volumes a year from the borrowable collection in the mezzanine, about 7000 volumes (a quarter of the 1962 collection) every 3 years. Suppose we decide to carry out this retirement action every 3 years, instead of every year. Which book out of every 4 will we relegate to less accessible quarters, and what will be the effect of our action on the borrowing public?

Let us review the data at hand to assist in the choice. We have the last row of Table 6.2 to give us the fraction of the collection that circulates m or more times a year. We have the values of α and β, given in Table 5.12, that will enable us to predict circulation in future years, and we have the values of γ, given in Table 8.1, that enable us to estimate the circulation distribution of future accessions. What are the alternative actions, and what will be the measures that will enable us to choose between them?

The obvious action is to retire to the basement the oldest quarter of the books in the mezzanine each 3 years (or the oldest half of the collection every 6 years, or whatever). In the absence of full and easily accessible circulation records of books, this is much the easiest policy, and it certainly should be investigated. An alternative, to retire the quarter of the books that are the oldest of those that have not circulated in the past year would be fairly simple if circulation records were computerized but would require hand examination of each book otherwise. We will also investigate this action, just to see how much better it might be and thus, indirectly, to indicate another advantage of circulation computerization.

To return to the first alternative, to retire the oldest quarter of the collection each 3 years, we can estimate, from Table 6.1, that about a quarter of the 28,000 books are 12 or more years old, by which time the volumes would have reached steady-state circulation (see Fig. 5.3) for the parameters $\alpha = 0.12$ and $\beta = 0.5$ (see Table 5.12). Thus, on the average, each retired book would have circulated $\alpha/(1 - \beta) \simeq 0.25$ times a year (see Eq. 5.17) if it had stayed on the mezzanine. This corresponds to a total of $7000 \times 3 \times 0.25 \simeq 5200$ borrowings for the 3 years, or in general, $7000\, R_r t$ for t years, where

$$R_r = \frac{\alpha}{1 - \beta} \qquad (8.11)$$

and α is for the older books. If instead they are in the basement stacks, either about 5200 library users will have to go to the trouble of going to the basement or else will not borrow the book (probably some of both); in either case the action will cause about 5000 "inconveniences" during the 3 years.

To see how this compares with the borrowing load from the mezzanine, we first calculate the total circulation if all books stayed upstairs. We would ordinarily have to calculate the decrease in average circulation of the books already on hand at the beginning of the 3-year period (till the next retirement) and add to it the effect of the high circulation of the 3 years' accessions. However, as the discussion of Eq. 8.6 indicates, the value of $\bar{\alpha}$ seems to be such that gain in circulation from new additions just about balances loss from aging of the older books. In other words, it appears that mean circulation, per book, of the whole collection stays fairly constant. If this is the case and if we add 7000 more volumes in the next 3 years, the expected circulation in those 3 years, if the whole collection could be kept in the mezzanine, would be

$$1.1\,(30{,}300 + 32{,}600 + 35{,}000) \simeq 107{,}700$$

where $30{,}300 = 28{,}000 + 2300$ is the total number next year, 32,600 the total number the year after that, and so on.

If we retire 7000 oldest books to the basement, we will remove 5200 borrowings from this, for the 3 years. Thus we would expect that the 21,000 books left in the mezzanine, plus the 2300 accessions made each year, would circulate about 102,500 times in the 3 years, an average of about 140 borrowings per day (if we assume 250 "working days" per year). The retirement of 7000 old books would mean that about 7 persons a day, for the 3 years, would either have to go to the basement to get the book they wanted or else would give up borrowing the book.

How much this inconvenience should mean to the library is difficult to estimate, unless we knew what the additional delay would be to the borrower, to go to the basement, and what fraction of the expected borrowers would not borrow the retired book at all. But this calculation would be academic, because there is not room in the mezzanine for all the books and some have to be retired, even if it does involve discommoding some users. What is more important is to see whether any other scheme of retirement will discommode *fewer* users.

Suppose we use our model to estimate the users inconvenienced when the 7000 books retired are the oldest books *that have not circulated in the past year*. According to Table 6.2, two-thirds of the whole collection $(1.00 - 0.34 = 0.66)$ or 18,500 books did not circulate in 1962; we can choose the 7000 (about 0.38 of the 18,500) oldest of these. A glance at Table 5.11 shows that most of the 7000 retired under this plan would be more than 8 years old; probably the majority would be more than 12 years old, and we could again use $\alpha = 0.12$ for them. The expected circulation of this group would be less than the 5200 expected with the other plan, because the initial circulation of this group is zero, not 0.25. We have chosen the noncirculators of the old books, and these will circulate less often than the rest of the old books.

According to Eq. 5.7, for a group of books that did not circulate last year, $R(1) = 0$, their mean circulation after t years would be

$$R(t + 1) = \alpha[(1 - \beta^t)/(1 - \beta)]$$

and the total circulation added up for all of the t years would be $R(2) + R(3) + \cdots + R(t + 1)$ which would equal

$$R_r t[1 - \Delta(t)] \quad \text{where} \quad \Delta(t) = \frac{\beta}{t}\frac{1 - \beta^t}{1 - \beta} \tag{8.12}$$

and where R_r is given by Eq. 8.11. In other words, by choosing the noncirculating ones, among the oldest ones, to retire, we have reduced the circulation of the retired books by the factor $1 - \Delta(t)$ below that expected for retirement regardless of circulation.

Factor $\Delta(t)$ is plotted in Fig. 8.6 for different values of β and t. For the case under consideration, $\beta = 0.5$ and $t = 3$, this factor $\Delta(t)$ is about 0.3. In other words, by retiring only noncirculators, we have reduced the inconvenienced borrowers from 5200 to 5200 $(1 - 0.3) = 3600$ or about 5 a day rather than 7. Whether this reduction of user inconvenience would be worth the additional effort of picking out the noncirculators would depend on the amount of this additional effort. Undoubtedly the effort would be too great if the circulation records were not computerized.

Because randomness is inherent in book circulation, we can expect that a few books will regain popularity after they have been retired. Suppose we decide to bring back any retired book that circulates 4 or more times a year; how many of the retired books will have to be returned to the mezzanine in the 3-year period? For the first plan, to retire the 7000 oldest books, we can use the steady state circulation distribution (see Fig. 8.3) for $\alpha = 0.12$ and $\beta = 0.5$ and ask for the fraction of the retired books that circulates 4 or more times a year. Reference to the tabulation shows that this fraction is about 0.0023; about 7000 × 0.0023 = 16 books a year would have to be "resurrected," about 50 in the 3-year period. We note that, if our Markov model is correct, these

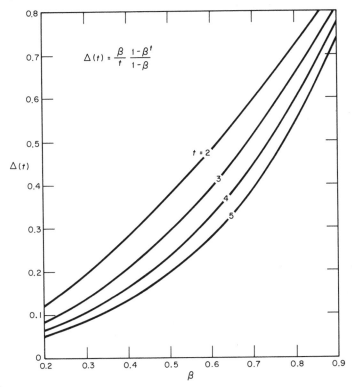

$$\Delta(t) = \frac{\beta}{t} \frac{1 - \beta^t}{1 - \beta}$$

Fig. 8.6. Function $\Delta(t)$ to estimate cumulative circulation for next t years for retired and nonretired books.

resurrected books would not revert to low circulation right away; if their mean circulation was 5 the year they were brought back, it would be 2.6 the next year, 1.4 the next, and so on, dropping below an average of 0.5 only after the fourth year.

For the second plan we have to use the full transition matrix $(T^t)_{0n}$ for the probability of circulation n times ($n = 4$ or 5 or 6 or $\cdots$) t years after the book had no circulation. These values, for $t = 1, 2, 3$ (and adding the T for $n = 4, 5, 6, \cdots$) for $\alpha = 0.12$ and $\beta = 0.5$ give the expected fraction of these retired books $F_t'(\geq 4)$, originally noncirculating, which, t years later, circulate 4 or more times; $N_t(\geq 4) =$

$7000 \times F_t'(\geq 4)$ is the number of such books that would appear in the tth year. See Table 8.2, which is to be compared with the 50 needing

Table 8.2   Estimates of Books to Be Resurrected from Retirement

$t =$	1	2	3	Sum
$F_t'(\geq 4)$	0.00002	0.00057	0.00107	0.00166
$N_t(\geq 4)$	—	4	8	12

resurrection with the first plan. Thus retiring the oldest noncirculators, instead of just the oldest, not only reduces the number of inconvenienced borrowers but also considerably reduces, for the first few years, the number of books that might have to be resurrected. After about 5 years, of course, the second-plan collection would have reached steady state and would be indistinguishable from the first-plan retired group; $F_t'(\geq 4)$ would reach the steady-state value 0.0023.

Future Problems

Now let us look ahead about 10 years, when about as many books would be in the basement as would be in the mezzanine, and it *may be* the practice to retire a tenth of the mezzanine collection each year. Suppose things have settled down so that 30,000 books are in the mezzanine and 30,000 in the basement and each year 3000 books are bought and 3000 retired to the basement. We assume that books and users have not changed appreciably, so that the parameters we have worked out still have the same values. With the average age of retirement 10 years (30,000 volumes in the mezzanine, 3000 retired a year) the value of α for the collection in the basement would be not more than 0.125 (with a steady-state circulation of 0.25 per book) and the average α for the whole collection would be about 0.23 (see Eq. 8.11), and thus a mean value of α for the mezzanine books would be 0.33, so that the average of 0.33 and 0.125 is 0.23.

With this larger number of old books in the total collection, the average circulation per book $\overline{R}$ would have diminished somewhat from the 1962 value of 1.1. The mean circulation per book of the 30,000 books in the mezzanine would have correspondingly increased somewhat, because the mezzanine books would be somewhat younger, on the average, than they were in 1962; 10 years of the retirement operation would have culled nearly all the books over 10 years of age. We would expect that the per-book circulation from the mezzanine would have reached a more or less steady-state value $\bar{R}_m$. Thus the circulation from the mezzanine in year 0 would be $30{,}000\bar{R}_m$, as would be the circulation from the mezzanine in year 1. But, during the year, 3000 old books would be retired, the circulation rate of the remaining 27,000 would have reduced to $(\alpha + \beta\bar{R}) = \frac{1}{3} + \frac{1}{2}\bar{R}_m$, and 3000 accessions would have been added, with a mean circulation of 4.4 per book (if purchasing choices are as good as they were in 1962). Thus

$$30{,}000\bar{R}_m \simeq 27{,}000\left(\frac{1}{3} + \frac{1}{2}\,\bar{R}_m\right) + 13{,}200$$

or

$$16{,}500\bar{R} \simeq 22{,}200$$

or

$$\bar{R}_m \simeq 1.35 \tag{8.13}$$

which is somewhat larger than the 1962 value of 1.10.

Thus for Plan A (retire 3000 of the oldest books each year, regardless of their circulation) the circulation in year 0 would be $1.35 \times 30{,}000 = 40{,}500$ (162 per day) from the mezzanine and $0.25 \times 30{,}000 = 7500$ persons (30 per day) would have to go to the basement or forgo borrowing the older book. In year 1, there would be 33,000 books in the basement, and the number thus inconvenienced would have risen to 8250 or 33 per day, with the steady-state mezzanine of 30,000 books circulating 40,500 per year as in year zero.

For Plan B, when we would retire the 3000 oldest books that did not circulate the previous year, the circulation from the basement would consequently be reduced, as we noted in Eq. 8.12. Assuming an α of about 0.2 for the books being retired, their mean circulation the first year of retirement would be $\alpha + m\beta = \alpha$, since m is 0 for this group; during the second year of retirement their expected circulation would be $\alpha + \alpha\beta = \frac{3}{2}\alpha$ for $\beta = \frac{1}{2}$; during the third year it would be $(7/4)\alpha$, and so on. The mean circulation would rise asymptotically to the steady-state value 2α (for $\beta = \frac{1}{2}$). In Plan A the circulation rate of the retired books would be the steady-state value 2α from the first year of retirement (α, of course, would diminish with increased age of the book, from 0.2 down toward 0.1). Thus the difference between Plans A and B is that in Plan B the circulation of the retired books is α, instead of 2α in the first year, $\frac{3}{2}\alpha$ instead of 2α in the second year of retirement, and so on, corresponding to a net reduction of circulation from the basement of 1 year's worth of retired books. (Really it would be somewhat more than a year's worth, since these deficiencies are taken from the youngest of the retired books; a more detailed calculation indicates that the deficiency is about 1.5 year's circulation of the average book in the basement.)

Thus for Plan B, the circulation from the basement would be not 30,000 (10 × 3000) times 0.25 but 25,500 (8.5 × 3000) times 0.25, which is about 6400. Since the total circulation must be the same for both plans (since we are just rearranging the location of the books, the circulation from the mezzanine must be 48,000 (40,500 + 7500 from Plan A) minus 6400, or 41,600, about 166 per day. The comparison is shown in Table 8.3. Thus Plan B still has an advantage, in reducing the expected number of users who have to go to the basement to get their book, by about 1130 persons a year (about 5 a day).

A calculation, similar to that related to Table 8.2, could be carried out to estimate the number of books, per year, that might need to be brought back to the mezzanine. As before, Plan B would involve fewer resurrections than would Plan A.

As pointed out several times before, the difference in inconvenience to the library user is but half of the balance sheet the librarian must study before choosing between alternative plans. The other half is the difference in cost, in purchases or in staff time, between the two policies. In the present case, the more discriminating retirement Plan B would cost more in staff time to find, relocate, and recatalogue individual books than would the more wholesale retirement method of Plan A (and still more than the retirement of a whole class of books, regardless of age). This balancing of gains against costs is the essence of the operations research method; it will be discussed again in Chapter 9.

To reach a balance, we will have to compare staff time spent to users' time lost, a problem similar to the one discussed at the end of Chapter 4 and one gone into in Chapter 9. In addition to user time spent getting the less accessible book, recently collected data indicate that the circulation parameters α and β of a book collection are altered by a change of location of the collection. (This was to be expected, but to measure the effect it was necessary to wait several years after some collections had been moved to the basement to amass the needed records.) Thus retirement acts like circulation interference, increasing the number of persons who do not read the book and who would have read it if it had been on the open shelf (the reduction in circulation is about 30 percent in the example discussed here); this recently found effect has not been included in Table 8.3.

This increase in unsatisfied customers should be added to the users' time lost, when they do go to the basement, before balancing it against increased staff time in deciding on a retirement policy. Equating lost

Table 8.3 Comparison of Expected Circulations for the Two Retirement Policies

		Plan A				Plan B			
		Circulation from Basement		Circulation from Mezzanine		Circulation from Basement		Circulation from Mezzanine	
Number in Basement	Number in Mezzanine	Per Year	Per Day	Per Year	Per Day	Per Year	Per Day	Per Year	Per Day
Year 0	30,000	30,000	7500	30	40,500	162	6370	25	41,600	167
Year 1	33,000	30,000	8250	33	40,500	162	7120	28	41,600	167

circulation to staff time is not easy, but it is done implicitly, many times a year, by most librarians. The point of this book is that it is better done explicitly, even though very approximately. As will be shown in Chapter 9, the average book in the Science Library at M.I.T. has circulated about 10 times in its total lifetime there. Therefore, it has been decided already that 10 circulations are worth the cost of the book plus the cost of cataloguing and shelving it. In this way we can reach a rough dollar price to place on a single circulation; if we can express staff time in dollars, we can begin to compare policies quantitatively, as suggested on pages 79 and 80.

9 Recapitulation

We have gone into considerable detail on questions of circulation, in an effort to squeeze the most understanding out of fragmentary data, and have worked out a number of examples of how this understanding can help the librarian to set operating policy; let us back away from details in this last chapter. In Chapter 1 we listed 9 general questions that most librarians have to answer, occasionally or often, directly or by default. Let us re-examine these questions to see whether we can answer them for the particular library we have analyzed or, if not, what additional data would be needed to answer them (or to assist in answering them).

Book Retirement and Book Duplication

We have just been examining Questions 2 and 6, concerned with retirement of surplus books to less accessible locations. We have seen how circulation data can enable us to estimate how many people would be inconvenienced by this retirement and how these estimates differ with the choice of books to retire. To see which of the various policies is desirable, we would have to find out how inconvenient it is for the user to get a retired book (see the last three paragraphs of Chapter 8). Perhaps we could relate hours of delay with hours of staff work. For example, for the steady-state situation represented by Table 8.3, we saw that about 1000 more users a year would have to go to the less-accessible stacks for Plan A than for Plan B. Suppose it would take about 3 man months (1000 man-hours) of additional work to carry out Plan B, instead of Plan A, for book retirement. Then, if it took only 15 minutes more for the user to get the retired book than to get a book from the open shelves on the mezzanine, the total user time lost per year would only be about 250 hours, quite a bit less than the 1000 hours of additional staff work. On the other hand, if the retired books were in some central repository, where it would take a day (8 hours) longer to retrieve the book, then the additional 8000-odd hours lost by users if Plan A were in effect might make it worth spending the 1000 additional staff hours to implement Plan B.

We also have spent some time answering part of Questions 1 and 2, particularly the portions related to the purchase of duplicate copies of popular books. In the end, in Eq. 8.5, we argued that, since the average book in the collection circulates about 3.3 times in 3 years, we should buy a duplicate if, by doing so, we can expect to have 10 more persons borrow the book, in 3 years, than could have done so without the duplicate. If we can afford to buy the average book, we should be justified in buying a duplicate if it will get 3 times the average use, at least for its first 3 years.

However, this criterion must be examined by the librarian, in the light of his budget and with the realization that the duplicate will drop off in use more rapidly than the single copy. The average book in the Science Library has circulated about 11 times in the roughly 10 years this average book has been on the shelves, about 8 times in its first 3 years of shelf life, 3 times in the other 7 years. A duplicate of a high-use book, of the sort specified in Eq. 8.5, would circulate about 10 times in its first 3 years and perhaps only once from then on. However, whether or not the criterion of Eq. 8.5 is the appropriate one for a library, some such criterion should be chosen and applied as consistently and expeditiously as the adequacy of circulation records will allow.

Circulation Restriction and Reserve Shelves

Next we should turn to Question 3, the difficult problem as to whether a high-use book should be restricted to in-library use. Central to the problem is the question of the relative value, to the user, of taking the book home for 2 weeks versus studying it for a shorter time in the library. The survey summarized in Table 2.2 indicates that, on the average, books in the Science Library were used in the library 4 times as often as they were borrowed. But of the books consulted in the library, half of them were tables, general references, and books on reserve; therefore, of the books in the mezzanine, which could be borrowed, on the average they were used twice in the library for every time they were borrowed.

This ratio, of course, varied greatly from book to book and from book class to book class; for example, ratio of in-library use to withdrawals of chemistry books was 8 to 1 instead of 4 to 1. The difference undoubtedly reflects a difference in the way different classes of books are used.

Rather than entering the labyrinth of arguments regarding the subjective value of having a book at home for days at a time versus that of scanning it in a crowded library, we might just estimate the mean length of time a user has the book, open, in front of him. No exhaustive survey has been made of the length of time a user of the Science Library spends with a borrowed book at home or with a borrowable book in the reading room, but there are some fragmentary data that can illustrate how better data could help answer Question 3.

The data plotted in Figs. 2.5 and 2.6 indicate that the persons who used the facilities of the Science Library stayed, on the average, about 100 minutes. Since, during that time, they performed an average of 3 tasks, including withdrawing some books, reading some books as well as periodicals in the library, and consulting the card catalogue, we can estimate that the mean time taken for any one task is about 30 minutes. Since reading a book or periodical takes longer than using the catalogue or borrowing books, we can estimate that, on the average, a user of the Science Library spends about an hour on a book used in the library. Results of a questionnaire survey,[11] indeed, indicated a mean time of an hour spent on a book, about 40 minutes on a bound journal volume, and about 15 minutes on an abstract journal volume.

There are no surveys of time spent at home on a book borrowed from the Science Library, but some measures of the writer's habits plus some sporadic questioning of colleagues indicate that 10 hours, on the average, is not a gross error in estimate. Certainly 30 hours for an average value would be too great and 3 hours, on a technical book that had been borrowed for 2 weeks, would probably be too small. We thus estimate, with various degrees of uncertainty, that, on the average, for every time a book is borrowed, it is used by the borrower for about 10 hours, but also it is used in the library by two other readers for about an hour each sometime during the year.

Now let us consider a fairly recent book that happens to have circulated 7 times in the past year but is average in its use pattern otherwise. If our estimates of time spent are correct, this book has been used for about 70 hours during the year by borrowers and for about 14 hours by readers in the library. In addition, since it is an average book with return rate $\mu = 14$ (see Table 6.3), the 7 borrowers had the book out just about half of the year. Since would-be borrowers come at random, we estimate that another 7 persons came by, while the book was out, who would have borrowed it if it had been in and another 14 would have used it in the library. Thus the 7 borrowers kept the book from being used for another 70 hours by other borrowers and another 14 hours by users in the library.

To alleviate the circulation interference, the library may buy a duplicate, or it may put the book it has on reserve, eliminating the borrowing, or it may shorten the borrowing period (or, of course, it may do nothing). According to Fig. 4.4, the 2 copies would be borrowed by 11 of the 14 would-be borrowers, indicating that both books would be out of the library simultaneously only 1/5 of the time. Therefore 4/5 of the potential use time of 168 hours per year would be consummated and the 2 copies would be used for an estimated 134 hours, with only 34 potential use hours not satisfied; roughly 11 persons of the potential 14 would borrow one of the books, and 23 of the potential 28 in-library readers would be able to use one.

On the other hand if the library put the book on the reserve shelf, none of the would-be borrowers could take it out. At best they could read it in the library, consequently we could add these 14 to the 28 persons who used the book in the library anyway. There is such a thing as in-library interference (which we shall take up later), but an in-library use of 42 persons a year is too small to expect appreciable interference. Thus, if the book is on the reserve shelf, it will be used (to the extent that one can in 1 hour) an expected 42 hours during the year; the single book, if it could be borrowed, would be used about 84 hours during the year and would not satisfy another potential 84 use hours. Putting it on reserve would allow all 42 persons to get their hands on it in the library but would approximately halve the expected number of hours the book would be actively used during the year and would increase the unconsummated use by a factor of 1.5, from 84 hours to 126 hours. On the other hand a duplicate copy would reduce the unsatisfied use time from 84 hours to 34 hours, a reduction by a factor of 0.4. Even if our estimates of average use hours are out by a factor of 2, the conclusions would be the same.

Of course this analysis, with its implications, holds only for the average book in the borrowing part of the library. There are a number of books that are not usually read clear through but are consulted for just one portion, such as books of tables or formulas, bound periodicals, abstract journals, and the like.[11] (One might here include books referred to chapter by chapter by some teacher but not books the instructor expects the students to read through in one sitting.) These volumes may be restricted to in-library use, without cutting off a lot of potential out-of-library use, for at least two reasons. In the first place, the volume would be used for much less than 10 hours, even if it were borrowed for 2 weeks. If the volume were a bound periodical, for example, in most cases only one article is of interest at the time, and the article can perhaps be read in less than an hour. In fact[11] the mean time of use of a bound periodical in the library is about 40 minutes. In such cases it is manifestly unfair to other users for a person to take the book from the library for 2 weeks just to use it for an hour or less, when he could just as well use it in the library. In the second place, in the relatively rare cases when a person does want to spend more than an hour studying the article (or a few pages of a set of tables), he can now get a photocopy made of the few needed pages at a reasonable cost.

Thus the decision whether to restrict a book's circulation or to buy a duplicate should depend on how the book is used. In some cases this will be easy to decide (in the case of periodicals, tables, etc.). In other cases the decision may have to depend on the relative number of times the book is borrowed and is used in the library (if the library has means of measuring this ratio). If the book is consulted in the library 10 or more times for every time it is borrowed, then in-library use is evidently efficient and, anyway, cutting off circulation will not frustrate many users.

Two other comments may be of interest. First, some books on reserve shelves may be taken out overnight, which would add to the use a reserve book may get. This would add complication to the analysis but would involve no new principles. If the average number of overnight borrowings per book per week were known for the reserve collection as a whole, and if some estimate of time the overnight book were used (perhaps 3 hours per time would be a good value), and also if the mean time the book is returned in the morning is determined (so one can estimate the interference factor of overnight use), then the additional use time per week or per year for overnight borrowing can be added before the comparison is made. It is unlikely that this would change our conclusions for the Science Library.

In the second place, we have not commented on the effect of reducing the borrowing time from 2 weeks to 1 week. University libraries seem loath to do this, though it is a usual policy for public libraries. Increasing the return rate μ from about 15 to 40 or 50 per year definitely reduces the number of unsatisfied customers (U_1 in Fig. 4.4) by more than a factor of 2. Even if the use time spent on a 1-week book were somewhat less than that spent on a 2-week book (6 hours instead of 10, for example), making a 7-circulations-a-year book a 1-week book would increase the usage hours per year, by reducing circulation interference, more than the drop from 10 to 6 hours per borrowing would reduce it. Thus, if it could be enforced, 1-week borrowing time for moderately high-use books would seem to be preferable to putting the book on the reserve shelf. Once the popularity of a book, measured in circulations per year or by in-library use per week, is known, the tables and graphs of Chapter 4 (supplemented with the discussion of Chapter 7) will make it possible to compare the expected results of the various alternative actions possible.

Book Reshelving

Further light on the questions discussed in the last section may be shed by an analysis of the use pattern[11] of the 1600-odd books on reserve in the Science Library in 1962. The mean use rate was $\overline{R} = 0.85$ in-library uses per week per reserve book, and as mentioned earlier, the mean length of time of each individual use was about an hour. This corresponds to about 1360 hours of reserve book study per week, corresponding to about 50 minutes of use per book per week, on the average. But this does not mean that each book is accessible, for another user to take off the shelf and use during all the other 2350 minutes of a 5-day, 8-hour week.

Another study[12] analyzed the rapidity with which a book, once used in the library, got back on the shelves, so someone else could find and use it. In the Science Library in 1962, this time was more nearly 4 hours, on the average. This was checked in several ways. In the first place about a third of the books, used in the library, were reshelved by the user, and thus were off the shelf, on the average, only about an hour. The other two-thirds, returned by the library personnel, took much longer, between 4 and 8 hours. An independent check of the average time off the shelf was obtained by noting that the average number of books off the shelves (on the tables, in use or not, and in the reshelvers carts) during the day was about half the number of books used per day in the library, indicating again that it took about half a day on the average to get a book back on the shelf.

Thus, for books and periodicals used in the library, the mean return rate μ, the parameter to be used to determine use interference (see

Fig. 4.4), is about 10 per week. Thus, to return to the discussion of Fig. 4.4, any book used in the library more than about 5 times a week will suffer a noticeable limitation in use because of user interference, not because each user uses the book an inordinate length of time but because it takes so long, on the average, for the book to get back on the shelf so another user can find it.

Use distribution was also measured[11] by tagging a random number of reserve books and recording the number of times they were removed from the shelves. The use varied as widely as did the circulation of books. In fact the distribution was approximately geometric, with a long "tail" of high-use books. If we assume that the distribution is purely geometric with a factor $\gamma = [\overline{R}/(1 + \overline{R})] \simeq 0.46$ then the number $N(\geq m)$ of the reserve books that are used m or more times a week is as follows (see Eq. 2.20):

$$
\begin{array}{lccccccc}
m = & 0 & 1 & 2 & 3 & 4 & 5 & 6 \\
N(\geq m) = & 1600 & 740 & 340 & 155 & 72 & 33 & 15
\end{array}
\tag{9.1}
$$

For the 33 reserve books that are used in the library 5 or more times a week, Fig. 4.4 shows that another 5 or more persons per week were potential users but did not find the book on the reserve shelf when they looked for it. In fact use of the geometric distribution $N(m) = N(\geq m) - N(\geq m + 1) = 860\gamma^m$ of the number of reserve books that circulated exactly m times a week times U_1, the number of unsatisfied users for $R_1 = m$ (obtained from Fig. 4.4), indicates that

$$
185(0.4) + 83(1.3) + 39(2.8)
$$
$$
+ 18(5) + 8(9) + 4(18) + 2(25) = 580 \tag{9.2}
$$

persons a week lost the use of a reserve book because it was not on the shelf when they looked for it. They might not all have been looking for it, but the statistics indicate that if the book had been on the shelf they would have used it; also some who missed finding the book the first time may come back for it later, but it remains that they were frustrated the first time. This is to be compared with the $1600 \times 0.85 = 1360$ successful users per week. Thus, even when a book is withheld from circulation, a fair number of potential users are not able to use a popular book in the library.

If the reshelving could have been speeded up so the mean time off the shelf was 2 hours instead of 4 (so that μ was 20 instead of 10 per week), the number of unsatisfied users could be reduced sharply. Recalculation indicates that, if reshelving could be speeded up so that $\mu = 20$, the number of unsatisfied users could be reduced from 580 to 130 per week. If all users reshelved all the books they used, so that mean time

off the shelf was 1 hour, on the average, and μ was 40 per week, this number of unsatisfied users would be cut to about 60.

In-Library Use of Periodicals

Data concerning use of bound periodicals, which are restricted to in-library use in the Science Library, are again quite fragmentary. Two surveys[4,11] indicated that the mean length of time a person used a bound periodical volume was about 40 minutes (but, of course, it did not get put back on the shelf sooner than about 4 hours, on the average). A restricted number of high-use periodicals were tagged to get use data, and a number of the tagged volumes were used 2, 3, and 5 times a week, the average being somewhat less than 1 time per week per volume. But this was not typical of the whole collection.

In 1962 there were about 24,000 bound periodical volumes in the Science Library. A rough estimate of a mean use rate for them all can be made by the following indirect method. We know, from Table 2.2 that, on the average, 7 periodicals were consulted in the library for every book borrowed. Since there were $1.1 \times 28,000 \simeq 31,000$ book withdrawals in 1962, periodicals must have been used about 220,000 times in the same year. Since there were 24,000 periodical volumes, each volume must have been used, on the average, about 9 times a year, or about 0.2 time per week per volume.

Thus there are many volumes of periodicals that are not consulted for years on end, and there are probably a few that are used several times a week. These high-use volumes would be subject to the same interference effect as that discussed for reserve books. If and when in-library use distribution for bound periodicals has been measured, the mathematical models developed in Chapters 4 and 7 can be applied and decisions regarding duplicate subscriptions can be made on the basis of quantitative knowledge of use behavior and estimates of unsatisfied demand.

Lost Books

Some data are available to assist in answering Question 5. The 1600 reserve books were inventoried[13] once a week for several months to check on losses. About 2 volumes a week, or about 100 a year, disappeared without record from this collection, but not all of these stayed lost. By the end of about a month, 4 out of 5 of the "lost" books reappeared on the reserve shelves, having been gone, on the average, about 2 weeks. The other 1 out of 5 never turned up again.

In other words, in 1962 about 80 books out of the 1600 reserve

volumes disappeared for an average of about 2 weeks apiece, and about 20 volumes disappeared permanently. Since the reserve books on the average are used by 0.85 person a week, the number per year of potential, in-library users who did not get a chance to use the missing books was

$$0.85[20(50) + 80(2)] \simeq 1000$$

In still other words, about 1000 hours of book use per year were not consummated because of book loss.

Data on loss from the 28,000 borrowable books in the mezzanine or from the 24,000 periodical volumes are not as complete. The inventory taken in the summer of 1962 found[10] that somewhat more than 10 per cent of the volumes, supposed to be on the shelves, were missing. About a quarter of these were found in the library, misshelved. Since this inventory was the only one taken in the history of the Library, it is not possible to tell exactly when these books disappeared.

There is some indication that, of the books that disappear from their appointed places on the library shelves, two-thirds of them eventually return (or are found misshelved somewhere else in the library) with a mean time lost of about a year; the other third never come back. If these figures are correct, if a fraction f of the collection is lost per year, after T years $\frac{1}{3}fT$ of the collection will be permanently gone and the last year's $\frac{2}{3}f$ would still be missing but would eventually return. Since the mean age of the books in the Science Library is about $10 = T$ years, and since $\frac{1}{3}f(T + 2)$ is about 0.12, we estimate that a fraction $f = 0.03$, 1 book in 30, or about 840 books a year disappeared from the Science Library in 1962. The fraction disappearing per year from the reserve shelves was 100 out of 1600 or 0.06, about twice the loss factor f for the whole collection. One would expect a larger loss rate from the highly used books on the reserve shelfs, so the two numbers, arrived at from independent data, seem to corroborate each other.

Of the 840 books per year disappearing from the mezzanine collection, 560 will come back a year or so later, but meantime even these "temporarily lost" volumes are adding their total to the number of potential users whose needs were left unsatisfied. To estimate the magnitude of this loss to library users, we first assume that, after about 4 years, on the average, a "permanently lost" book is found to be lost and will either be replaced or its card will be removed from the catalogue. (This is a shorter "realization time" than held in the Science Library in 1962, but we may assume that by more frequent inventories or by other computerized means the process of discovery of the loss of a book can be somewhat accelerated.) Thus, in any year there would be about 4 years' crop of permanently lost books (and 0.01 of the collection is permanently lost per year) plus 0.02 of the collection that will have been out of circulation (misshelved or "temporarily stolen") for about a year before they turn up again, making up about 0.06 of the collection in all, or $28,000 \times 0.06 = 1680$ books missing from the 1962 mezzanine collection, if our latest assumptions hold.

Since an average book circulates 1.1 times a year and is used in the library 2.2 times a year, each of these books, if they had not been lost, would have been used $(1.1) \, 10 + (2.2) \, 1 \simeq 13$ hours during the year (One could argue that the more popular books are more likely to be. "lost" and thus that this figure should be more nearly 15 or 20 hours, but let us be quite conservative.) Therefore the 1680 missing books represent about 22,000 lost user hours, which the library would have made available to its clientele if these books had not been lost.

The books lost from the reserve shelves numbered about 100 per year, as we mentioned. Presumably the reserve shelves are examined each year and restocked, so that none of these 100 have been missing more than a year. As noted earlier, each reserve book was used about $0.85 \times 50 = 42$ times a year, roughly an hour per use, adding up to another 4200 lost hours of use.

The 24,000 periodical volumes were each used about 9 times a year, on the average, and each use averaged about 40 minutes, corresponding to about 6 hours a year per bound volume. As with the books on the mezzanine, about 0.06 of them are missing each year, so that $0.06 \times 24,000 \simeq 1400$ periodicals are missing, each representing a loss of 6 hours, adding up to another 8400 lost hours per year. The total number of user hours lost per year, because of lost books, is thus $22,000 + 4200 + 8400 \simeq 35,000$ hours, to be compared with the

$$28,000 \times 1.1 \times 12 + 1360 \times 50 + 220,000 \times 0.67 \simeq 600,000$$

hours of use the remainder of the collection supplied to the clientele.

Though the lost hours are only about 6 per cent of the hours of actual use, they may be compared to the hours a library guard might spend if the guard could reduce the number of books "lost" per year. The guard would not prevent the misshelving of books, nor could he prevent all the losses from persons who, thoughtlessly or not, take books out without signing for them. But if 2500 hours a year of guard time could reduce the losses by a third, it would cut the lost user hours by 10,000 per year, which might be considered a justification for hiring the guard. Put another way, there were about $54,000 \times 0.06 = 3240$

books, periodicals and reserve books missing in 1962. If a guard could cut this loss by 1000 books of average cost to the library of about $10,000, the guard might be worth hiring.

Browsing

Questions 4, 7, and 8 of Chapter 1 remain to be discussed. Since the data at present amassed are insufficient to answer either, there is little to be said. The question of central versus branch libraries depends on the degree of *cross use* of books. If chemists read only chemistry books and few nonchemists use chemistry books, then it doesn't matter whether the chemistry collection is in a central library or is placed more conveniently to the chemists, at least as far as other users are concerned. But if the chemistry books are used by nonchemists half the time and if, at the same time, chemists often read physics books and periodicals, then neither chemists nor physicists will like having the two collections separated. Of course, if the library has no budget restrictions (a rather rare occurrence!), the chemistry library could be supplied with those physics books that the chemists might need once or twice a year, and the physics library could be supplied with the chemistry books used at least as often as the average physics book was used. With adequate data on the cross-disciplinary use of books, the number of such additional books that would have to be bought could be estimated, and their cost balanced against the advantages of departmental libraries. In addition, of course, must be added the difference in operation and construction costs between a number of branch libraries and one central library.

By browsing the author means the action of the library user in wandering through the open shelves, picking off the shelf a book that looks interesting, examining it, replacing it, and going on to another, or else deciding to study it further, taking it to the reading area, or signing it out to take home. Browsing, as a method of finding the book or periodical desired, is at least as popular as the use of the card catalogue, as is suggested by the fact (see Table 2.2) that the catalogue was used on only about half the visits to the Science Library, whereas a library book was either read in the library or was borrowed on every visit, on the average.

It is likely that browsing is an effective method of widening one's field of knowledge or of breaking into an area that is not one's area of specialty (though it probably also is useful, even in one's area of specialty, for keeping up-to-date). A carefully thought out factual (not opinion) survey of browsing habits, as contrasted to catalogue use (relative frequency of use of the two methods, how long each took to find a book of interest, what kinds of books resulted, etc.) might help clarify the problem. A check should also be made to see how much the use of books decreases when they are transferred from open shelves to closed stacks, where browsing is difficult or forbidden (see the comments at the end of Chapter 9).

It is possible that there is an optimum size of open-shelf library for the browser. If it is too large, the average person may not be able to cover enough ground in the half-hour or so he has available; if it is too small, there may not be enough from which to choose. If one could demonstrate such an optimality, it would be of considerable assistance in planning the balance between space for open shelves and space for storing the less used books.

The Future

Books are still the most convenient packages of information, but this may no longer be true in the future, when electronic means of storing, sorting, and reproducing information become simple to operate, dependable, and relatively inexpensive. When this comes about, the stored information will be in different packages; but it is likely that the general models we have been discussing in this book will still apply. The popularity of various packages will diminish with time in a more or less random manner, and the Markov model probably will still be useful to predict use factors, which will be needed to utilize available hierarchies of memory as effectively as possible. Queuing theory will still be useful in designing the search system to reduce interference between users, though the time scale may be in seconds instead of weeks or years. This is another reason for studying the adequacy and applicability of the methods of analysis outlined in these pages.

Appendix

Tables of the Markov-Poisson Process

The Markov-Poisson process is a discrete Markov chain, defined by saying that, if the system is in state m at time t, the transition probability that it will be in state n at time $t + 1$ is for $\alpha, \beta < 1$

$$T_{mn} = \frac{(\alpha + \beta m)^n}{n!} \exp(-\alpha - \beta m) \qquad (A1)$$

Tables are given, in succeeding pages, of values of the matrix elements T_{mn}, for different values of m and n. Transition probabilities over longer periods of time, the probabilities that the system will be in state n at time t, if it is in state m at time $t = 0$, are given by powers of T,

$$T_{mn}^2 = \sum_k T_{mk} T_{kn}$$
$$T_{mn}^{t+1} = \sum_k T_{mk}^t T_{kn} \qquad (A2)$$

Values of the matrices T^2 and T^4 also are tabulated. In the limit of $t \to \infty$ the matrix T_{mn}^t reduces to its steady-state form, in which all rows are equal, as $t \to \infty$

$$T_{mn}^t \to P_n^\infty \qquad (A3)$$

These steady-state probabilities also are tabulated.

We should note that if the system starts, at $t = 0$, in state m, then the mean value of n at time t is as $t \to \infty$

$$\bar{n}_m(t) = \sum_n nT_{mn}^t = \alpha \frac{1 - \beta^t}{1 - \beta} + m\beta^t \to \frac{\alpha}{1 - \beta} \qquad (A4)$$

and the variance of n then is

$$\sigma_{mn}^2(t) = \sum_n n^2 T_{mn}^t - [\bar{n}_m(t)]^2$$

$$= \alpha \frac{(1 - \beta^t)(1 - \beta^{t+1})}{(1 - \beta)(1 - \beta^2)} + m\beta^t \frac{1 - \beta^t}{1 - \beta} \to \frac{\alpha}{(1 - \beta)(1 - \beta^2)} \qquad (A5)$$

If, at $t = 0$, the system is distributed among the states according to the probability distribution $P_m(0)$, with mean value M of m and variance σ^2, the distribution, the mean value of n and its variance, at time t, are

$$P_n(t) = \sum_m P_m(0)T_{mn}^t$$

$$\bar{n}(t) = \bar{n}(\infty) + [M - \bar{n}(\infty)]\beta^t \qquad \bar{n}(\infty) = \frac{\alpha}{1 - \beta} \qquad (A6)$$

$$\sigma_n^2(t) = \alpha \frac{(1 - \beta^t)(1 - \beta^{t+1})}{(1 - \beta)(1 - \beta^2)} + M\beta^t \frac{1 - \beta^t}{1 - \beta} + \sigma^2\beta^t$$

The matrices T^t are infinite in extent, of course. What is tabulated are finite square matrices of extent such that the last columns of T^t for large t have no element of order as large as 0.001. Terms in last columns of lower powers of T include the rest of each row, so that each row sums to 1.000. Thus matrix T, as tabulated, is a finite Markov matrix. The original tables, from which these were taken, were 30 by 30 matrices, computed to 5 decimal places on an IBM-7094.

$$\beta = 0.3 \; ; \; \alpha = 0.2$$

T_{mn}

n =	0	1	2	3	4	5	6	7+
m								
0	.819	.164	.016	.001	–			
1	.606	.303	.076	.013	.002	–		
2	.449	.300	.144	.038	.008	.001	–	
3	.333	.366	.201	.074	.020	.005	.001	–
4	.247	.345	.242	.113	.039	.011	.002	.001
5	.183	.310	.264	.149	.064	.022	.006	.002
6	.135	.271	.271	.180	.090	.036	.012	.005
7	.100	.231	.265	.203	.117	.054	.021	.009

T^2_{mn}

n =	0	1	2	3	4	5	6	7+
0	.777	.190	.028	.004	.001	–		
1	.719	.224	.047	.009	.001	–		
2	.665	.251	.065	.015	.003	.001	–	
3	.616	.274	.083	.021	.005	.001	–	
4	.570	.291	.101	.029	.007	.002	–	
5	.527	.304	.118	.037	.010	.003	.001	–
6	.487	.314	.134	.046	.014	.004	.001	–
7	.451	.321	.149	.055	.018	.005	.001	–

T^4_{mn}

n =	0	1	2	3	4	5	6	7+
0	.762	.199	.033	.005	.001	–		
1	.758	.201	.035	.005	.001	–		
2	.752	.204	.037	.006	.001	–		
3	.747	.207	.038	.007	.001	–		
4	.742	.210	.040	.007	.001	–		
5	.738	.212	.041	.008	.001	–		
6	.733	.215	.043	.008	.001	–		
7	.728	.217	.045	.008	.002	–		

Steady state, P^{∞}_n

	0	1	2	3	4	5
all m	.761	.199	.034	.005	.001	–

$$\beta = 0.3 \; ; \; \alpha = 0.4$$

n = 0	1	2	3	4	5	6	7+

m T_{mn}

m	0	1	2	3	4	5	6	7+
0	.670	.268	.054	.007	.001	-		
1	.496	.348	.122	.028	.005	.001	-	
2	.368	.368	.184	.061	.015	.003	.001	-
3	.273	.354	.230	.100	.032	.008	.002	.001
4	.202	.323	.258	.138	.055	.018	.005	.001
5	.150	.284	.270	.171	.081	.031	.010	.003
6	.111	.244	.268	.197	.108	.048	.017	.007
7	.082	.205	.256	.214	.134	.067	.028	.014

T_{mn}^2

m	0	1	2	3	4	5	6	7+
0	.604	.295	.080	.017	.003	.001	-	
1	.559	.311	.099	.025	.005	.001	-	
2	.517	.322	.118	.033	.008	.002	-	
3	.479	.330	.134	.042	.011	.003	.001	-
4	.443	.335	.150	.052	.015	.004	.001	-
5	.410	.337	.164	.062	.020	.006	.001	-
6	.379	.337	.178	.072	.024	.007	.002	.001
7	.351	.335	.189	.082	.030	.009	.003	.001

T_{mn}^4

m	0	1	2	3	4	5	6	7+
0	.581	.303	.090	.021	.004	.001	-	
1	.577	.304	.092	.022	.004	.001	-	
2	.574	.305	.093	.022	.005	.001	-	
3	.570	.306	.095	.023	.005	.001	-	
4	.566	.307	.097	.024	.005	.001	-	
5	.562	.308	.098	.025	.006	.001	-	
6	.559	.309	.100	.025	.006	.001	-	
7	.555	.310	.102	.026	.006	.001	-	

Steady state, P_n^∞

all m	.579	.303	.091	.021	.005	.001	-

$$\beta = 0.3 \; ; \; \alpha = 0.6$$

n = 0	1	2	3	4	5	6	7	8+

m T_{mn}

m	0	1	2	3	4	5	6	7	8+
0	.549	.329	.099	.020	.003	–			
1	.407	.366	.165	.049	.011	.002	–		
2	.301	.362	.217	.087	.026	.006	.001	–	
3	.223	.335	.251	.125	.047	.014	.004	.001	–
4	.165	.297	.268	.161	.072	.026	.008	.002	.001
5	.122	.257	.270	.189	.099	.042	.015	.004	.002
6	.091	.218	.261	.209	.126	.060	.024	.008	.003
7	.067	.181	.245	.221	.149	.080	.036	.014	.007
8	.050	.149	.224	.224	.168	.101	.050	.022	.012

T_{mn}^2

m	0	1	2	3	4	5	6	7	8+
0	.470	.344	.136	.039	.009	.002	–		
1	.434	.348	.152	.049	.013	.003	.001	–	
2	.402	.349	.167	.059	.017	.005	.001	–	
3	.372	.347	.181	.070	.022	.006	.002	–	
4	.344	.344	.193	.080	.028	.008	.002	.001	–
5	.318	.340	.204	.090	.033	.011	.003	.001	–
6	.295	.334	.213	.101	.039	.013	.004	.001	–
7	.273	.327	.221	.110	.045	.016	.005	.002	.001
8	.252	.320	.228	.120	.052	.019	.006	.002	.001

T_{mn}^4

m	0	1	2	3	4	5	6	7	8+
0	.443	.346	.148	.047	.012	.003	.001	–	
1	.440	.346	.149	.048	.013	.003	.001	–	
2	.437	.346	.151	.049	.013	.003	.001	–	
3	.435	.347	.152	.049	.013	.003	.001	–	
4	.432	.347	.153	.050	.014	.003	.001	–	
5	.429	.347	.154	.051	.014	.004	.001	–	
6	.425	.347	.156	.052	.015	.004	.001	–	
7	.423	.347	.157	.053	.015	.004	.001	–	
8	.420	.347	.158	.054	.016	.004	.001	–	

Steady state, P_n^∞

all m	0	1	2	3	4	5	6
	.441	.346	.149	.047	.013	.003	.001	–

$$\beta = 0.5 \; ; \; \alpha = 0.2$$

T_{mn}

m \ n	0	1	2	3	4	5	6	7	8	9	10+
0	.819	.164	.016	.001	–						
1	.496	.348	.122	.028	.005	.001	–				
2	.302	.361	.217	.087	.026	.006	.001	–			
3	.182	.311	.264	.150	.064	.022	.006	.001	–		
4	.111	.244	.268	.197	.108	.048	.017	.005	.002	–	
5	.067	.182	.245	.221	.149	.080	.036	.014	.005	.001	–
6	.041	.130	.209	.223	.178	.114	.061	.028	.011	.004	.001
7	.025	.091	.169	.209	.193	.143	.088	.047	.022	.009	.004
8	.015	.063	.132	.185	.194	.163	.114	.069	.036	.017	.012
9	.009	.043	.100	.157	.185	.174	.136	.091	.054	.028	.023
10	.006	.029	.075	.129	.168	.175	.151	.113	.073	.042	.039

T_{mn}^2

m \ n	0	1	2	3	4	5	6	7	8	9	10+
0	.758	.197	.037	.007	.001	–					
1	.623	.256	.086	.026	.007	.002	–				
2	.511	.288	.128	.049	.017	.005	.002	–			
3	.420	.300	.161	.073	.030	.011	.004	.001	–		
4	.344	.299	.187	.097	.044	.018	.007	.003	.001	–	
5	.283	.288	.205	.119	.060	.027	.011	.004	.002	.001	–
6	.232	.272	.216	.138	.076	.038	.017	.007	.003	.001	–
7	.191	.252	.220	.153	.092	.049	.024	.011	.005	.002	.001
8	.157	.231	.220	.166	.106	.061	.032	.015	.007	.003	.002
9	.129	.209	.216	.174	.120	.073	.040	.021	.010	.005	.003
10	.106	.188	.209	.180	.131	.085	.050	.027	.014	.006	.004

T_{mn}^4

m \ n	0	1	2	3	4	5	6	7	8	9	10+
0	.719	.213	.051	.013	.003	.001	–				
1	.689	.224	.062	.018	.005	.002	–				
2	.659	.233	.073	.024	.008	.002	.001	–			
3	.633	.241	.083	.029	.010	.003	.001	–			
4	.604	.249	.092	.035	.013	.004	.002	.001	–		
5	.580	.255	.101	.040	.015	.006	.002	.001	–		
6	.555	.260	.110	.046	.018	.007	.003	.001	–		
7	.534	.264	.118	.051	.021	.008	.003	.001	–		
8	.510	.268	.126	.056	.024	.010	.004	.001	.001	–	
9	.489	.270	.133	.062	.027	.011	.005	.002	.001	–	
10	.470	.272	.140	.067	.030	.013	.005	.002	.001	–	

Steady state, P_n^{∞}

all m	0	1	2	3	4	5	6
	.706	.217	.056	.015	.005	.001	–

$$\beta = 0.5 \; ; \; \alpha = 0.4$$

T_{mn}

m \ n	0	1	2	3	4	5	6	7	8	9	10+
0	.670	.268	.054	.007	.001	–					
1	.407	.366	.165	.049	.011	.002	–				
2	.247	.345	.241	.113	.039	.011	.003	.001	–		
3	.149	.284	.270	.171	.081	.031	.010	.003	.001	–	
4	.091	.218	.261	.209	.125	.060	.024	.008	.003	.001	–
5	.055	.160	.231	.224	.162	.094	.045	.019	.007	.002	.001
6	.033	.113	.193	.219	.186	.126	.072	.035	.015	.006	.002
7	.020	.079	.154	.200	.195	.152	.099	.055	.027	.012	.007
8	.012	.054	.119	.174	.192	.169	.124	.078	.043	.021	.014
9	.007	.036	.089	.146	.179	.175	.143	.100	.061	.033	.031
10	.005	.024	.066	.119	.160	.173	.156	.120	.081	.049	.047

T_{mn}^2

m \ n	0	1	2	3	4	5	6	7	8	9	10+
0	.573	.299	.095	.025	.006	.002	–				
1	.470	.317	.139	.051	.017	.005	.001	–			
2	.386	.319	.172	.077	.030	.011	.004	.001	–		
3	.317	.310	.197	.101	.046	.018	.007	.003	.001	–	
4	.260	.294	.213	.124	.062	.028	.012	.004	.002	.001	–
5	.214	.274	.222	.143	.079	.039	.018	.007	.003	.001	–
6	.176	.252	.225	.158	.095	.050	.025	.011	.005	.002	.001
7	.144	.229	.224	.170	.110	.063	.033	.016	.007	.003	.001
8	.119	.206	.218	.178	.123	.075	.042	.021	.010	.005	.003
9	.097	.184	.210	.183	.135	.087	.051	.027	.014	.007	.005
10	.080	.163	.199	.185	.144	.098	.061	.034	.018	.009	.009

T_{mn}^4

m \ n	0	1	2	3	4	5	6	7	8	9	10+
0	.515	.306	.119	.041	.013	.004	.001	.001	–		
1	.494	.307	.128	.047	.016	.005	.002	.001	–		
2	.473	.308	.136	.053	.020	.007	.002	.001	–		
3	.454	.308	.143	.059	.023	.009	.003	.001	–		
4	.434	.308	.150	.065	.027	.010	.004	.001	.001	–	
5	.416	.306	.157	.071	.030	.012	.005	.002	.001	–	
6	.399	.305	.162	.077	.033	.014	.006	.002	.001	–	
7	.382	.303	.169	.082	.037	.016	.007	.003	.001	–	
8	.366	.301	.173	.088	.041	.018	.008	.003	.001	.001	–
9	.351	.298	.178	.093	.045	.020	.009	.004	.001	.001	–
10	.336	.295	.182	.098	.049	.023	.010	.004	.002	.001	–

Steady state, P_n^∞

	0	1	2	3	4	5	6	7	8	9	10+
all m	.498	.306	.125	.045	.016	.005	.002	.001	–		

$$\beta = 0.5 \; ; \; \alpha = 0.6$$

T_{mn}

m \ n	0	1	2	3	4	5	6	7	8	9	10+
0	.549	.329	.099	.020	.003	–					
1	.333	.366	.201	.074	.020	.005	.001	–			
2	.202	.323	.258	.138	.055	.018	.005	.001	–		
3	.123	.257	.270	.189	.099	.042	.015	.004	.001	–	
4	.074	.193	.251	.218	.141	.074	.032	.012	.004	.001	–
5	.045	.140	.216	.224	.173	.107	.056	.025	.010	.003	.001
6	.027	.098	.177	.212	.191	.138	.083	.042	.019	.008	.005
7	.017	.068	.139	.190	.195	.160	.109	.064	.033	.015	.010
8	.010	.046	.106	.163	.188	.173	.132	.087	.050	.026	.020
9	.006	.031	.079	.135	.172	.175	.149	.109	.069	.039	.036
10	.004	.021	.058	.108	.152	.170	.158	.127	.089	.055	.058

T^2_{mn}

m \ n	0	1	2	3	4	5	6	7	8	9	10+
0	.434	.339	.152	.053	.016	.005	.001	–			
1	.356	.332	.185	.081	.031	.011	.003	.001	–		
2	.292	.317	.208	.107	.047	.019	.007	.002	.001	–	
3	.240	.297	.222	.129	.064	.029	.012	.004	.002	.001	–
4	.197	.274	.229	.149	.082	.040	.018	.007	.003	.001	–
5	.162	.250	.230	.164	.098	.052	.025	.011	.005	.002	.001
6	.133	.225	.227	.175	.113	.065	.034	.016	.007	.003	.002
7	.109	.202	.220	.182	.127	.077	.043	.022	.010	.005	.003
8	.090	.179	.210	.187	.138	.090	.052	.028	.014	.007	.005
9	.074	.158	.199	.188	.147	.101	.062	.035	.019	.009	.008
10	.061	.139	.186	.186	.154	.111	.072	.043	.024	.012	.012

T^4_{mn}

m \ n	0	1	2	3	4	5	6	7	8	9	10+
0	.370	.330	.177	.077	.030	.011	.004	.001	–		
1	.354	.326	.182	.083	.034	.013	.005	.002	.001	–	
2	.340	.322	.187	.089	.038	.015	.006	.002	.001	–	
3	.325	.318	.192	.095	.042	.017	.007	.003	.001	–	
4	.312	.313	.196	.100	.046	.020	.008	.003	.001	.001	–
5	.299	.309	.199	.105	.050	.022	.009	.004	.002	.001	–
6	.286	.304	.202	.111	.054	.025	.011	.004	.002	.001	–
7	.275	.299	.205	.116	.058	.027	.012	.005	.002	.001	–
8	.263	.294	.207	.120	.062	.030	.014	.006	.003	.001	–
9	.252	.289	.209	.125	.066	.032	.015	.007	.003	.001	.001
10	.241	.284	.211	.129	.070	.035	.017	.008	.003	.001	.001

Steady state, P_n^{∞}

all m	0	1	2	3	4	5	6	7	8	9	10+
	.352	.325	.183	.084	.035	.013	.005	.002	.001	–	

$$\beta = 0.6 \; ; \; \alpha = 0.3$$

T_{mn}

m \ n	0	1	2	3	4	5	6	7	8	9	10	11+
0	.742	.222	.033	.003	–							
1	.407	.366	.165	.049	.011	.002	–					
2	.222	.335	.251	.126	.047	.014	.004	.001	–			
3	.123	.257	.270	.189	.099	.042	.015	.004	.001	–		
4	.068	.182	.245	.220	.149	.080	.036	.014	.005	.001	–	
5	.037	.122	.201	.221	.182	.120	.066	.031	.013	.005	.002	–
6	.020	.079	.154	.200	.195	.152	.099	.055	.027	.012	.005	.002
7	.011	.050	.112	.169	.190	.171	.128	.082	.046	.023	.010	.008
8	.006	.031	.079	.135	.172	.175	.149	.109	.069	.039	.020	.016
9	.003	.019	.054	.103	.147	.168	.159	.130	.092	.059	.033	.033
10	.002	.012	.036	.077	.121	.152	.159	.144	.113	.079	.050	.055
11	.001	.007	.024	.055	.095	.131	.151	.149	.128	.098	.068	.093

T_{mn}^{2}

m \ n	0	1	2	3	4	5	6	7	8	9	10	11+
0	.647	.258	.071	.018	.005	.001	–					
1	.494	.294	.132	.052	.019	.006	.002	.001	–			
2	.377	.299	.174	.087	.038	.016	.006	.002	.001	–		
3	.287	.285	.201	.118	.061	.028	.012	.005	.002	.001	–	
4	.219	.260	.213	.143	.083	.044	.021	.010	.004	.002	.001	–
5	.167	.232	.215	.161	.104	.060	.032	.016	.008	.003	.001	.001
6	.127	.202	.209	.172	.122	.077	.044	.024	.012	.006	.003	.002
7	.097	.173	.198	.177	.136	.092	.057	.033	.018	.009	.005	.005
8	.074	.147	.183	.177	.146	.106	.070	.043	.025	.014	.007	.008
9	.057	.123	.166	.173	.152	.118	.083	.054	.033	.019	.010	.012
10	.043	.102	.149	.166	.155	.127	.095	.065	.042	.025	.015	.016
11	.033	.085	.131	.156	.154	.133	.105	.076	.051	.032	.019	.025

T_{mn}^{4}

m \ n	0	1	2	3	4	5	6	7	8	9	10	11+
0	.580	.271	.097	.035	.012	.004	.001	–				
1	.536	.275	.113	.046	.019	.007	.003	.001	–			
2	.494	.277	.127	.058	.025	.011	.005	.002	.001	–		
3	.455	.278	.140	.068	.032	.015	.007	.003	.001	.001	–	
4	.422	.276	.150	.078	.039	.019	.009	.004	.002	.001	–	
5	.390	.273	.159	.088	.046	.023	.012	.005	.002	.001	.001	–
6	.359	.269	.167	.097	.053	.028	.014	.007	.003	.002	.001	–
7	.332	.265	.173	.105	.060	.032	.017	.009	.004	.002	.001	–
8	.307	.259	.178	.113	.066	.037	.020	.010	.005	.003	.001	.001
9	.283	.252	.182	.119	.073	.042	.023	.013	.007	.003	.002	.001
10	.261	.245	.185	.125	.079	.047	.027	.015	.008	.004	.002	.002
11	.241	.238	.187	.131	.085	.052	.030	.017	.009	.005	.003	.002

Steady state, P_{n}^{∞}

	0	1	2	3	4	5	6	7	8
all m	.548	.273	.108	.043	.017	.007	.003	.001	–

$$\beta = 0.6 \; ; \; \alpha = 0.5$$

n =	0	1	2	3	4	5	6	7	8	9	10	11+
m						T_{mn}						
0	.606	.303	.076	.013	.002	–						
1	.333	.366	.201	.074	.020	.005	.001	–				
2	.182	.311	.264	.150	.064	.022	.006	.001	–			
3	.100	.231	.265	.203	.117	.054	.021	.007	.002	–		
4	.055	.160	.231	.224	.162	.094	.045	.019	.007	.002	.001	–
5	.030	.106	.185	.216	.189	.132	.077	.038	.017	.007	.002	.001
6	.017	.068	.139	.190	.195	.160	.109	.064	.033	.015	.006	.004
7	.009	.043	.100	.157	.185	.174	.136	.091	.054	.028	.013	.010
8	.005	.026	.070	.124	.164	.174	.154	.116	.077	.045	.024	.021
9	.003	.016	.048	.094	.138	.163	.160	.135	.100	.065	.039	.039
10	.002	.010	.032	.069	.112	.145	.157	.146	.119	.086	.056	.066
11	.001	.006	.021	.049	.087	.124	.147	.149	.132	.104	.074	.106

n =	0	1	2	3	4	5	6	7	8	9	10	11+
m						T_{mn}^2						
0	.484	.322	.131	.044	.014	.004	.001	–				
1	.369	.318	.177	.082	.034	.013	.004	.002	.001	–		
2	.282	.299	.205	.115	.057	.025	.010	.004	.002	.001	–	
3	.215	.270	.219	.142	.080	.041	.019	.008	.004	.001	.001	–
4	.164	.238	.220	.162	.102	.058	.030	.014	.007	.003	.001	.001
5	.125	.207	.214	.174	.121	.075	.042	.022	.011	.005	.002	.002
6	.095	.177	.202	.180	.136	.091	.056	.031	.016	.008	.004	.003
7	.073	.149	.186	.180	.147	.106	.069	.042	.024	.013	.006	.005
8	.056	.125	.169	.176	.154	.118	.082	.053	.032	.018	.010	.008
9	.042	.103	.151	.168	.156	.128	.094	.064	.040	.024	.014	.016
10	.032	.085	.133	.158	.156	.135	.105	.075	.050	.031	.018	.022
11	.025	.070	.116	.146	.153	.139	.113	.085	.059	.039	.024	.031

n =	0	1	2	3	4	5	6	7	8	9	10	11+
m						T_{mn}^4						
0	.402	.314	.161	.072	.031	.012	.005	.002	.001	–		
1	.372	.307	.171	.084	.038	.017	.007	.003	.001	–		
2	.343	.300	.178	.094	.046	.022	.010	.004	.002	.001	–	
3	.317	.291	.185	.103	.054	.026	.012	.006	.003	.001	.001	–
4	.292	.283	.190	.112	.061	.031	.016	.008	.004	.002	.001	–
5	.270	.274	.193	.120	.068	.037	.019	.010	.005	.002	.001	.001
6	.250	.265	.196	.126	.075	.042	.023	.012	.006	.003	.001	.001
7	.230	.256	.198	.133	.082	.047	.026	.014	.007	.004	.002	.001
8	.213	.246	.198	.138	.088	.053	.030	.016	.009	.005	.002	.002
9	.197	.236	.198	.143	.094	.058	.034	.019	.010	.005	.003	.003
10	.182	.227	.197	.147	.100	.063	.038	.022	.012	.006	.003	.003
11	.168	.217	.196	.150	.105	.068	.042	.024	.014	.008	.004	.004

Steady state P_n^∞

	0	1	2	3	4	5	6	7	8	9	10	11+
all m	.366	.305	.171	.085	.040	.018	.008	.004	.002	.001	–	

$$\beta = 0.7 \; ; \; \alpha = 0.2$$

T_{mn}

n = m	0	1	2	3	4	5	6	7	8	9	10	11	12+
0	.819	.164	.016	.001	-								
1	.407	.366	.165	.049	.011	.002	-						
2	.202	.323	.258	.138	.055	.018	.005	.001	-				
3	.100	.231	.265	.203	.117	.054	.021	.007	.002	-			
4	.050	.149	.224	.224	.168	.101	.050	.022	.008	.003	.001	-	
5	.025	.091	.169	.209	.193	.143	.088	.047	.022	.009	.003	.001	-
6	.012	.054	.119	.174	.192	.169	.124	.078	.043	.021	.009	.004	.001
7	.006	.031	.079	.135	.172	.175	.149	.109	.069	.039	.020	.009	.007
8	.003	.018	.051	.098	.143	.166	.160	.133	.096	.062	.036	.019	.013
9	.002	.010	.032	.069	.112	.145	.157	.146	.119	.086	.056	.033	.033
10	.001	.005	.019	.046	.084	.120	.144	.149	.134	.107	.077	.050	.064
11	-	.003	.012	.030	.060	.095	.125	.141	.140	.122	.097	.069	.106
12	-	.002	.007	.020	.042	.072	.103	.127	.137	.131	.112	.088	.159

T^2_{mn}

n = m	0	1	2	3	4	5	6	7	8	9	10	11	12+
0	.740	.200	.045	.011	.003	.001	-						
1	.521	.267	.125	.054	.021	.008	.003	.001	-				
2	.365	.277	.176	.097	.048	.022	.009	.004	.001	.001	-		
3	.257	.257	.201	.132	.076	.041	.020	.009	.004	.002	.001	-	
4	.181	.225	.206	.155	.103	.062	.034	.018	.009	.004	.002	.001	-
5	.127	.189	.198	.168	.124	.083	.051	.029	.016	.008	.004	.002	.001
6	.089	.155	.181	.171	.139	.101	.068	.042	.025	.014	.007	.004	.004
7	.063	.124	.161	.166	.147	.116	.084	.056	.035	.021	.012	.007	.008
8	.044	.098	.140	.156	.149	.127	.098	.070	.047	.030	.018	.011	.012
9	.031	.076	.119	.143	.146	.133	.109	.083	.059	.040	.025	.016	.020
10	.022	.059	.099	.128	.140	.134	.117	.094	.071	.050	.034	.022	.030
11	.015	.045	.081	.112	.130	.132	.122	.103	.081	.060	.043	.029	.047
12	.011	.034	.066	.097	.119	.127	.123	.109	.090	.070	.052	.036	.066

T^4_{mn}

n = m	0	1	2	3	4	5	6	7	8	9	10	11	12+
0	.672	.217	.069	.026	.010	.004	.001	.001	-				
1	.590	.231	.096	.045	.021	.010	.004	.002	.001	-			
2	.517	.237	.118	.063	.033	.017	.008	.004	.002	.001	-		
3	.454	.239	.135	.078	.044	.024	.013	.007	.003	.002	.001	-	
4	.398	.237	.148	.092	.055	.032	.018	.010	.005	.003	.001	.001	-
5	.349	.231	.157	.104	.066	.040	.023	.014	.008	.004	.002	.001	.001
6	.305	.224	.164	.114	.075	.048	.029	.018	.010	.006	.003	.002	.002
7	.268	.214	.167	.122	.084	.056	.035	.022	.013	.008	.005	.003	.003
8	.235	.204	.168	.129	.092	.063	.042	.027	.016	.010	.006	.004	.004
9	.206	.193	.168	.134	.099	.070	.048	.031	.020	.012	.008	.005	.006
10	.181	.181	.166	.137	.106	.077	.054	.036	.024	.015	.010	.006	.007
11	.159	.170	.162	.139	.111	.083	.060	.041	.028	.018	.012	.007	.010
12	.139	.158	.158	.140	.115	.089	.065	.046	.032	.021	.014	.009	.014

Steady state P^{∞}_n

	0	1	2	3	4	5	6	7	8	9
all m	.622	.223	.085	.038	.017	.008	.004	.002	.001	-

$$\beta = 0.7 \; ; \; \alpha = 0.4$$

T_{mn}

n = 0	1	2	3	4	5	6	7	8	9	10	11	12+
m												
.670	.268	.054	.007	.001	-							
.333	.366	.201	.074	.020	.005	.001	-					
.165	.298	.268	.161	.072	.026	.008	.002	-				
.082	.205	.256	.214	.134	.067	.028	.010	.003	.001	-		
.041	.130	.209	.223	.178	.114	.061	.028	.011	.004	.001	-	
.020	.079	.154	.200	.195	.152	.099	.055	.027	.012	.004	.002	.001
.010	.046	.106	.163	.188	.172	.132	.087	.050	.026	.012	.005	.004
.005	.026	.070	.124	.164	.174	.154	.116	.077	.045	.024	.012	.009
.002	.015	.045	.089	.134	.161	.161	.138	.103	.069	.041	.023	.019
.001	.008	.028	.062	.103	.138	.155	.148	.124	.092	.062	.038	.041
.001	.005	.017	.041	.076	.113	.139	.147	.136	.112	.083	.056	.074
-	.002	.010	.027	.054	.088	.119	.138	.140	.126	.102	.075	.119
-	.001	.006	.017	.038	.066	.097	.122	.134	.131	.116	.098	.179

where the m column runs 0, 1, 2, 3, 4, 5, 6, 7, 8, 9, 10, 11, 12.

T^2_{mn}

m	0	1	2	3	4	5	6	7	8	9	10	11	12+
0	.548	.296	.106	.035	.011	.003	.001	-					
1	.386	.301	.169	.083	.037	.015	.006	.002	.001	-			
2	.271	.278	.202	.123	.067	.033	.015	.007	.003	.001	-		
3	.190	.242	.211	.152	.096	.054	.029	.014	.007	.003	.001	.001	-
4	.134	.203	.205	.168	.120	.076	.045	.025	.013	.006	.003	.001	.001
5	.094	.165	.190	.174	.137	.096	.062	.038	.021	.011	.006	.003	.003
6	.066	.132	.169	.171	.147	.113	.079	.052	.032	.018	.010	.005	.006
7	.047	.104	.147	.162	.151	.125	.094	.066	.043	.027	.016	.009	.009
8	.033	.081	.125	.149	.149	.132	.107	.079	.055	.036	.023	.014	.017
9	.023	.063	.104	.133	.143	.135	.116	.091	.067	.047	.031	.019	.028
10	.016	.048	.086	.117	.134	.135	.121	.101	.078	.057	.040	.026	.041
11	.011	.037	.070	.102	.123	.130	.124	.108	.088	.067	.049	.034	.057
12	.008	.028	.056	.087	.111	.123	.123	.113	.096	.077	.058	.042	.078

T^4_{mn}

m	0	1	2	3	4	5	6	7	8	9	10	11	12+
0	.452	.292	.140	.065	.029	.013	.006	.002	.001	-			
1	.396	.283	.156	.082	.042	.021	.011	.005	.002	.001	.001	-	
2	.347	.272	.167	.097	.055	.030	.016	.008	.004	.002	.001	.001	-
3	.305	.259	.174	.110	.067	.039	.022	.012	.006	.003	.002	.001	-
4	.268	.245	.178	.121	.077	.047	.028	.016	.009	.005	.003	.002	.001
5	.234	.231	.180	.129	.087	.056	.035	.021	.012	.007	.004	.002	.002
6	.205	.216	.180	.136	.096	.064	.041	.026	.016	.009	.005	.003	.003
7	.180	.202	.177	.140	.103	.072	.048	.031	.019	.012	.007	.004	.005
8	.158	.188	.174	.143	.109	.079	.054	.036	.023	.015	.009	.005	.007
9	.138	.174	.169	.145	.115	.085	.060	.041	.027	.018	.011	.007	.010
10	.121	.161	.163	.145	.119	.091	.066	.046	.032	.021	.013	.009	.013
11	.106	.148	.157	.145	.122	.096	.072	.052	.036	.024	.016	.010	.016
12	.093	.137	.150	.143	.124	.100	.077	.057	.040	.028	.019	.012	.020

Steady state P^∞_n

all m	0	1	2	3	4	5	6	7	8	9	10	11	12+
	.387	.277	.155	.085	.045	.024	.013	.007	.003	.002	.001	.001	-

$$\beta = 0.7 \; ; \; \alpha = 0.6$$

T_{mn}

m \ n	0	1	2	3	4	5	6	7	8	9	10	11	12+
0	.549	.329	.099	.020	.003	-							
1	.273	.354	.230	.100	.033	.008	.002	-					
2	.135	.271	.271	.181	.090	.036	.012	.003	.001	-			
3	.067	.182	.245	.221	.149	.080	.036	.014	.005	.001	-		
4	.033	.113	.193	.219	.186	.126	.072	.035	.015	.005	.002	.001	-
5	.017	.068	.139	.191	.195	.160	.109	.064	.033	.015	.006	.002	.001
6	.008	.039	.095	.152	.183	.175	.140	.096	.058	.031	.015	.006	.003
7	.004	.022	.062	.113	.156	.171	.157	.124	.085	.052	.029	.014	.011
8	.002	.013	.039	.081	.125	.155	.160	.142	.110	.076	.047	.026	.024
9	.001	.007	.024	.055	.095	.131	.151	.149	.128	.098	.068	.043	.050
10	.001	.004	.014	.037	.070	.106	.134	.145	.138	.117	.089	.061	.084
11	-	.002	.009	.024	.049	.082	.113	.134	.139	.128	.106	.080	.134
12	-	.001	.005	.015	.034	.061	.091	.117	.132	.132	.119	.097	.196

T_{mn}^{2}

m \ n	0	1	2	3	4	5	6	7	8	9	10	11	12+
0	.406	.328	.162	.067	.025	.008	.003	.001	-				
1	.285	.300	.203	.113	.056	.025	.011	.004	.002	.001	-		
2	.200	.260	.217	.147	.087	.047	.023	.011	.005	.002	.001	-	
3	.141	.217	.213	.168	.114	.070	.039	.020	.010	.005	.002	.001	-
4	.099	.177	.198	.176	.134	.091	.057	.033	.018	.009	.005	.002	.001
5	.070	.141	.177	.175	.147	.109	.074	.047	.028	.016	.008	.004	.004
6	.049	.111	.155	.167	.152	.123	.090	.061	.039	.024	.014	.007	.008
7	.034	.086	.132	.154	.152	.132	.104	.075	.051	.033	.120	.012	.015
8	.024	.067	.110	.139	.147	.136	.114	.088	.064	.043	.028	.017	.023
9	.017	.051	.091	.123	.138	.136	.121	.099	.075	.054	.037	.024	.034
10	.012	.039	.074	.106	.127	.133	.124	.107	.086	.064	.046	.031	.051
11	.008	.021	.060	.091	.115	.126	.124	.112	.094	.074	.055	.039	.073
12	.006	.022	.048	.077	.102	.118	.122	.115	.101	.083	.064	.048	.094

T_{mn}^{4}

m \ n	0	1	2	3	4	5	6	7	8	9	10	11	12+
0	.304	.294	.189	.106	.055	.028	.013	.006	.003	.001	.001	-	
1	.267	.276	.194	.119	.068	.037	.020	.010	.005	.002	.001	.001	-
2	.233	.258	.195	.129	.080	.047	.027	.015	.008	.004	.002	.001	.001
3	.205	.240	.194	.138	.090	.056	.033	.019	.011	.006	.003	.002	.001
4	.179	.223	.192	.144	.099	.065	.041	.025	.014	.008	.005	.003	.002
5	.157	.206	.187	.148	.107	.073	.048	.030	.018	.011	.006	.004	.005
6	.138	.190	.182	.150	.114	.081	.054	.035	.022	.014	.008	.005	.007
7	.121	.175	.176	.151	.119	.087	.061	.041	.027	.017	.010	.006	.009
8	.106	.161	.168	.151	.123	.093	.067	.047	.031	.020	.013	.008	.012
9	.093	.147	.161	.150	.126	.099	.073	.052	.035	.024	.015	.010	.015
10	.082	.135	.153	.147	.128	.103	.079	.057	.040	.027	.018	.012	.019
11	.071	.123	.145	.144	.129	.107	.083	.062	.045	.031	.021	.014	.025
12	.063	.112	.137	.140	.129	.110	.088	.067	.049	.035	.024	.016	.030

Steady state P_n^{∞}

	0	1	2	3	4	5	6	7	8	9	10	11	12+
all m	.240	.259	.191	.125	.077	.046	.027	.015	.009	.005	.003	.002	.001

Glossary of Symbols

Symbols used in several chapters are listed below, together with reference to equation or table number where they are first defined.

C cost, Eq. 4.11

$C_m(t)$ fraction of books having circulation m during their tth year, Eq. 5.16

D expected demand, Eq. 7.4

$E(x)$ expected value of x, Eq. 2.1

e $= 2.718$, base of natural logarithms, Eq. 2.32

$F(\geq m)$ fraction having m or more, Eq. 6.1

F_k or $F(k)$ fraction having exactly k, Eq. 2.19

J mean number of books on loan, Eq. 6.2

K expected value of k, Eq. 2.24

k, l integers, number of tasks, etc., Eq. 2.20

L mean number waiting, Eq. 4.2

$M(m)$ number of books with circulation m, Tables 5.5 and 5.9

m, n integers, number of circulations, etc., Eq. 5.1

$N(m)$ mean circulation this year of those books that circulated m times in the previous year, Eq. 5.3

$n!$ $= 1 \cdot 2 \cdot 3 \ldots (n - 1) \times n$, called n factorial, Eq. 3.5

$P(a \mid b)$ conditional probability of a, given the occurrence of b, Eqs. 2.6 and 7.2

$P(\geq m)$	probability of m or greater, Eq. 7.6
P_n	probability of n occurring, Eqs. 2.1 and 3.5
Q	circulation parameter, Eq. 7.6
R	mean circulation rate, Eqs. 4.4 and 6.1
S	total rate of leaving, Eq. 2.34
T	mean wait in queuing process, Eq. 4.2
T_{mn}	transition probability in Markov process, Eq. 5.9
t	time in minutes, days, or years, Eqs. 2.31 and 5.10
U	unsatisfied demand, Eqs. 4.4 and 7.8
W	mean number of reserve cards on hand per book, Eqs. 4.10 and 7.16
X_t	probability that a book has not circulated for t years, Eq. 5.14
α, β	Markov circulation parameters, Eqs. 5.3 and 8.1
γ	parameter in the geometric distribution, Eqs. 2.20 and 8.7
$\Delta(t)$	special function, Eq. 8.12
δ	fraction of potential borrowers who leave a reserve card, Eqs. 4.10 and 7.15
η	mean discouragement rate, Eq. 4.9
λ	arrival rate, Eq. 4.1, or demand rate, Eq. 7.2
μ	service rate, Eq. 4.1, or return rate, Eqs. 6.2 and 7.2
π	$= 3.1416$ ratio circumference to diameter of circle, Eq. 3.9
ρ	utilization factor $= \lambda/\mu$, Eq. 4.1
σ	standard deviation, Eq. 2.13
τ	mean time, Eq. 2.32
$\equiv$	by definition equal to
$\simeq$	approximately equal to

References

On library statistics, see the material and the bibliographies in

Library Statistics, by the staff of the Statistics Coordinating Project, Joel Williams, ed., American Library Association, Chicago, Ill., 1966.
Patterns in the Use of Books in Large Research Libraries, by H. H. Fussler and J. L. Simon, University of Chicago Library, Chicago, Ill., 1961.

and also current articles in library journals, such as *American Documentation*, *Library Trends*, and *College and Research Libraries*.

On systems analysis, operations research, see the material and the bibliographies in

Systems Engineering Handbook, by Robert E. Machol, ed., McGraw-Hill Book Co., Inc., New York, 1965.
Introduction to the Theory of Operational Research, by B. van der Veen, Springer-Verlag, New York, 1967.
Queues, Inventories and Maintenance, by P. M. Morse, John Wiley & Sons, Inc., New York, 1958.

Specific references, referred to by number in the text are

1. D. J. de Solla Price, "Networks of Scientific Papers," *Science*, Vol. 149, July 30, 1965, p. 510.
2. G. C. Bush, H. P. Galliher, and P. M. Morse, "Attendance and Use in the Science Library at M.I.T.," *American Documentation*, Vol. VII, p. 87, 1956.
3. P. M. Morse, *Queues, Inventories and Maintenance*, John Wiley & Sons, Inc., New York, 1958. See also T. L. Saaty, *Elements of Queuing Theory with Applications*, McGraw-Hill Book Co., Inc., New York, 1961.
4. Carolyn R. Elston, "Survey of In-Library Use of the M.I.T. Science Library,"

Operations Research Course 8.75 Term Report, M.I.T. Libraries, Cambridge, Mass., Dec. 1966.

5. Edward A. Silver, "Quantitative Appraisal of the M.I.T. Science Library Mezzanine Books, with an Application to the Problem of Limited Shelf Space," Operations Research Course 8.75 Term Report, M.I.T. Libraries, Cambridge, Mass., Jan. 1962.

6. C. S. Dawson, E. E. Aldrin, and E. P. Gould, "Increasing the Effectiveness of the M.I.T. Science Library by the Use of Circulation Statistics," Operations Research Course 8.75 Term Report, M.I.T. Libraries, Cambridge, Mass., Jan. 1962.

7. H. H. Fussler and J. L. Simon, *Patterns in the Use of Books in Large Research Libraries*, University of Chicago Library, Chicago, Ill., 1961, pp. 126–128. See also F. G. Kilgour, "Recorded Use of Books in the Yale Medical Library," *American Documentation*, Oct. 1961, p. 268.

8. R. W. Trueswell, "Determining the Optimum Number of Volumes for a Library's Core Collection," *Libri*, Vol. 16, 1966, p. 54.

9. Michael Rothkopf, "The Future Circulation Rate of a Book, and An Application of Queuing Theory to Library Problems," Operations Research Course 8.75 Term Report, M.I.T. Libraries, Cambridge, Mass., Jan. 1962.

10. Jean-Louis Pourny, "Missing Books," Operations Research Course 8.75 Term Report, M.I.T. Libraries, Cambridge, Mass., Jan. 1962.

11. K. P. Scott, P. Sonnenblick, and P. F. Uller, "An Analysis of the In-Room Use of the M.I.T. Science Library," Operations Research Course 8.75 Term Report, M.I.T. Libraries, Cambridge, Mass., Jan. 1962.

12. A. J. Rolfe, J. Terninko, and C. T. Whitehead, "In-Room Use of Library Books," Operations Research Course 8.75 Term Report, M.I.T. Libraries, Cambridge, Mass., Jan. 1962.

13. H. F. Ayres, R. C. Norris, and R. S. Robinson, "An Investigation of Missing Books in the M.I.T. Science Library," Operations Research Course 8.75 Term Report, M.I.T. Libraries, Cambridge, Mass., Jan. 1962.

Those desiring to purchase copies of reports listed "M.I.T. Libraries" should communicate with the Librarian, M.I.T., Cambridge, Mass. 02139.

Index